Conversations with Rita Dove

DATE DUE FOR RETURN

Litera

Peggy
Genera

This book may be recalled before the above date.

Photo credit: Lynda Koolish

Conversations with Rita Dove

Edited by
Earl G. Ingersoll

University Press of Mississippi
Jackson

www.upress.state.ms.us

The University Press of Mississippi is a member of the Association of American University Presses.

Copyright © 2003 by University Press of Mississippi
All rights reserved
Manufactured in the United States of America

11 10 09 08 07 06 05 04 03 4 3 2 1

♾

Library of Congress Cataloging-in-Publication

Dove, Rita.
    Conversations with Rita Dove / edited by Earl G. Ingersoll.
        p.   cm. — (Literary conversations series)
    Include index.
    ISBN 1-57806-549-6 (alk. paper) — ISBN 1-57806-550-X (pbk. :
alk. paper)
        1. Dove, Rita—Interviews.   2. Poets, American—20th
century—Interviews.   3. African American women poets—Interviews.
4. Poetry—Authorship.   I. Ingersoll, Earl G., 1938–   II. Title.
III. Series.
PS3554 .O884 Z467   2003
811'.54—dc21   2002013840

British Library Cataloging-in-Publication Data available

Books by Rita Dove

The Yellow House on the Corner. Pittsburgh: Carnegie-Mellon University Press, 1980.

Museum. Pittsburgh: Carnegie-Mellon University Press, 1983; London: Feffer and Simons, 1983.

Fifth Sunday. Lexington: University of Kentucky Press, 1985.

Thomas and Beulah. Pittsburgh: Carnegie-Mellon University Press, 1986.

Grace Notes. New York: Norton, 1989.

Through the Ivory Gate. New York: Pantheon, 1992.

Selected Poems. New York: Random House, 1993.

The Darker Face of the Earth: A Verse Play in Fourteen Scenes. Brownsville, Oreg.: Story Line Press, 1994; revised edition. Ashland, Oreg.: Story Line Press, 2000.

Mother Love. New York: Norton, 1995.

The Poet's World. Washington: Library of Congress, 1995.

On the Bus with Rosa Parks. New York: Norton, 1999.

Contents

Introduction

The number and the length of her interviews testify to Rita Dove's accessibility and commitment to the interview as a contemporary literary genre. She has been willing to be interviewed in part because she herself enjoys reading and listening to interviews with other writers. Although, as she asserts, it's the time that she minds and occasionally, she says, she wants to tell her interviewer, "I would rather write a poem!" she continues to be a cooperative and generous interviewee. As she sees it, she is in part "paying back" for the insights which other writers have shared in their interviews.

One writer whose interviews had a major impact on Rita Dove's development as a writer was Toni Morrison. In an interview conducted recently she confirms comments made earlier that when she was starting out as a writer "it *mattered*" to know what Morrison had to say about her craft; she adds that in interviews "it matters more to hear that voice directly than to read, say, an essay by the same author on craft." Interviews such as Morrison's are helpful, she argues, because "sometimes the inspiration one garners as a young writer comes in the pauses, the offhand remark." One example that she offers is Morrison's remark that when she writes in the morning she often waits for the sunlight to reach the blank page. This impulse to wait patiently to begin writing revealed a great deal to Dove about the readiness to begin composing. She generalizes that a response such as this one to an interviewer's question "can make all the difference in the world" to a beginning writer learning the craft of writing. The interviews to follow demonstrate just how generously Rita Dove has been willing to "pay back" for the help offered by the interviews of Morrison and other writers.

Conversations with Rita Dove begins with her first major literary interview, conducted by Judith Kitchen and Stan Sanvel Rubin during a Brockport Writers Forum visit in March 1985. (The term "literary interview" offers a useful means of designating a conversation between a writer and other writers or academics familiar with the interviewee's work, in contrast to the "celebrity interview" which can occasionally open with the interviewer's admission, "I haven't read any of your work, but I'd like to ask you about. . . .") Poets Rubin and Kitchen ask Dove about her fascination with the intersection of language and atrocity in the major early poem, "Parsley," and go on to explore with her other poems in her second collection, *Museum* (1983). (The first collection of poems, *The Yellow House on the Corner*, appeared in 1980.) Dove explains how the poem "Dusting," which "came out of nowhere," generated the poems of her maternal grandparents in *Thomas and Beulah*. Dove shared with her interviewers the imminent appearance of her collection of short fiction, *Fifth Sunday*, in the Callaloo Fiction Series, in 1985.

Later in March 1985 Gretchen Johnsen and Richard Peabody interviewed Rita Dove by telephone for *Gargoyle*. In their interview Johnsen and Peabody explore Dove's early life, as a student at the University of Tübingen on a Fulbright after graduating summa cum laude from Miami University of Ohio and at the University of Iowa Writer's Workshop where she met her German husband, Fred Viebahn, and received her Master of Fine Arts degree. She explains that following the completion of her training she began writing short fiction, in part because she found it difficult for a time to break out of the conventions of the writer's workshop poem. In this conversation Dove begins to speak of her struggles as a young African American poet to identify herself first as a poet and second as an African American or a woman. She points to Zora Neale Hurston as a model of a writer struggling to preserve her artistic independence against the attempts of various groups to enlist her energies as their spokesperson. In addition, she describes the joys and challenges of motherhood, following the birth of her daughter, Aviva Chantal Tamu Dove-Viebahn, in 1983.

While working on her doctoral dissertation Susan Shibe Davis interviewed Rita Dove in 1986 at Arizona State University where she taught from 1981 to 1988. Dove speaks more extensively about her beginnings as a writer than in the other interviews, offering one of her favorite childhood memories: writing a chapter a week on a novel called "Chaos," using her second-grade spelling works. As she indicates in later interviews, she was already finding pleasure in the challenging strictures of form, forcing herself to use the spelling words in the order of their appearance on the weekly list. She tells the story of being invited by her high school English teacher, Margaret Oechsner, to a writer's conference in her hometown, Akron, where she heard poet and critic John Ciardi talk. For the first time in her life she encountered "real live people who wrote!" In addition, Dove explains her composition process: her need for absolute privacy and quiet, as well as the ritualistic elements of writing. She composes prose using a word processor, but poems have to be hand-drafted, for example. The size of the lined tablet is an important starting point, and she insists on a fountain pen for an activity she herself admits "nearly amounts to fetishism."

In 1989 Rita Dove participated in two major interviews following the publication that year of her third collection of poems, *Grace Notes*. In her conversation with Susan Swartwout, Dove continues the discussion of *Thomas and Beulah*, the book which in 1987 brought her national recognition as the first African American woman to win the Pulitzer Prize for Poetry since Gwendolyn Brooks in 1950. In response to Swartwout's question about her self-consciousness as a writer during the composing process, Dove talks about her efforts to reduce the potentially debilitating impact of such "self-consciousness" on her creativity and reaffirms her struggle, especially after receiving the Pulitzer, to continue writing poetry according to her own artistic principles. Steven Schneider, a poet-classmate at Iowa, further explores the background of *Thomas and Beulah* and what it meant for Dove to win the Pulitzer Prize. She indicates that she may not be entirely comfortable serving as a "role model," but she adds, "when I was growing up it would have meant a lot to me to know that a Black person had been recognized for his or her writing."

The next three interviews in the collection took place during the period of 1989–93, a period of great productivity and increased recognition of Dove's accomplishments. In 1989 her third book of poems, *Grace Notes*, appeared, and in 1993 Norton published her *Selected Poems*. In 1992 her novel, *Through the Ivory Gate*, appeared. In 1993 Dove's many awards and other recognitions were capped with her appointment as the youngest and the first female African American Poet Laureate, a post she held for two years.

Mohamed B. Taleb-Khyar's conversation with Dove delves more extensively than earlier interviews into her early life and her sense of herself as an African American, as well as her relationship with Africa and her preoccupation with history. Asked to speak about her background, Dove takes her interviewer back to Akron, where she was born, and where her father worked for Goodyear Tire and Rubber Company. He became the company's first Black chemist and, as she speculates, perhaps the first Black chemist in the entire rubber industry. As she does elsewhere, especially in speaking of *Thomas and Beulah*, Dove supports the contemporary focus on those who have been omitted from the history books because of their gender or ethnicity, or because of their class. History, she reminds us, also encompasses the lives of ordinary people. She speaks once again to the issues of representing her gender and ethnicity, especially in relation to questions of her "politics" as a writer. She argues that her efforts to see women or African Americans as individuals, and not simply as representatives of their gender or ethnicity, may be itself a more important political goal than being a "spokespoet." "Insisting upon that individuality," she maintains, "is ultimately a political act."

As a writer of fiction, Wayne Ude is especially enthusiastic about beginning the examination of Dove's novel *Through the Ivory Gate* in these conversations. She explains that the novel was a long time in the making and confirms her early readers' speculation that some of the novel is autobiographical. In this conversation Dove also begins a continuing discussion of ending, or closure, in fiction as well as in her poems, expressing her sense of anticipating the moment in the composition process when the disparate elements of the poem or story coalesce in a moment of epiphany for the writer, and later presumably for the reader as well.

Steven Ratiner completes this triad of important conversations with an extensive re-examination of Dove's concern with history, and with the history of African Americans, in particular, her own family. Ratiner focuses Dove's attention on the autobiographical poem "Crab Boil," which grew out of an early encounter with racism on a visit to Florida. Looking back, Dove recalls how relatives in Florida saw no need to protect her and her siblings from the reality of segregation, as her parents had in Akron. She indicates, for example, that she was a young adult before her father shared with her the stories of his encounters with discrimination in the armed forces during World War II and at Goodyear where he began by operating a elevator and experienced the painful irony of conveying white classmates up to jobs as chemists for which he was better qualified than they were. Ratiner focuses on the poem "Flash Cards" in which the father passes down the law his daughter will learn: "What you don't understand, master." When asked about the absence of "anger" from her poetry, Dove indicates that she herself is not lacking in anger; however, anger can impede thinking, and it is through thought that one can do something about that anger.

The conversation with fellow-poet Steven Bellin offers in many ways a classic example of the literary interview, beginning with questions about her formative years, leading into others concerning her refusal to be pigeonholed as a writer in a single genre, to the inevitable question about her responses to the Poet Laureateship. Some of this territory has obviously been covered before; at the same time, this interview vindicates the policy of Mississippi's Conversations Series mandating that each text be reprinted intact. Here, for example, Dove offers amplification of her background not found elsewhere. The Bellin conversation is also valuable as the first appearance of Aviva, Dove's daughter, in her awareness of her craft. In 1995, along with a collection of essays, *The Poet's World*, Dove would publish a new collection of poems, *Mother Love*, many drawing on her experience as Aviva's mother.

Similarly, the Grace Cavalieri interview covers familiar territory but offers up fresh insights as well. Here Dove talks more extensively about her grandparents and the complex relationship between biography and poetry. As she will indicate in the last interview, Dove becomes aware of the slippage between the two and, after the publication of the poems, the difficulty of ascertaining what she imagined and what was "real." That's why she inscribes her copy of the poems to her mother: "To Mom, the only one who knows which stories are true."

Of all the interviews in the collection, Malin Pereira's is without question the most comprehensive. Pereira elicits long and insightful responses concerning major issues, such as the unfolding statements in *The Darker Face of the Earth,* as Dove continued to revise her play: her connection of national history and the "personal present" of her later poems, her ongoing interest in writing in all the major genres, the way in which everything seems to come back to a concern with language. Pereira also extensively explores Dove's sense of identity as a Black woman, in part in relation to the Black Arts Movement of a generation ago, and focuses Dove's attention on the theme of incest in her play as well as in the "Aunt Carrie" figure in the *Fifth Sunday* story and in the novel *Through the Ivory Gate*.

The last two interviews in the collection have varying focuses. Robert McDowell, the publisher of the most recent, revised version of *The Darker Face of the Earth*, poses a number of questions concerning the play to enhance its usefulness in the classroom. And the last conversation in the collection offers Dove the opportunity to "talk back" to earlier interviewers about the experience of being an interviewed writer. When asked what questions she would like to answer but is not asked, Dove surprisingly responds that she misses being asked questions about her personal life, arguing that most readers seem to forget that avocations such as concert singing and ballroom dancing, for example, have an impact on her writing. At the same time, she indicates an awareness of the difficulty of living with her fame: "I'm frustrated by the fact that my life is not my own, that there's this 'Rita Dove,' whose life is a playing field for people." Dove also talks about her most recent collection of poetry *On the Bus with Rosa Parks* (1999), whose title

was inadvertently given to her by daughter Aviva when they attended a conference at which Rosa Parks was an invited guest and the conferees were
transported by bus from one location to another. Aviva whispered to her
mother: "We're on the bus with Rosa Parks." Dove speaks at length about
perhaps the most important figure in her early life—her father—and how she
sees her own personality in relation to his.

What the reader discovers in these frank and revealing conversations is a
portrait of the artist with an exceptional commitment to her art, an absolute
insistence on maintaining her artistic integrity. The reader sees it first in her
devotion to the craft of writing. There seems to have been very little, except
concerns for her family, which has been allowed to intrude on the time and
concentration needed to practice her craft as a writer. Even as a new mother,
Dove was concerned with working out a rigorous daily schedule with her
novelist-husband so that each could share the responsibilities of parenting
and yet also have time to write. She indicates that she has had to unlearn the
training of her Midwest culture which taught her that letters *had* to be answered and adds that the answering machine has made her time for writing
more inviolable.

Dove is well aware of the temptations to invest her energies in various
worthy causes and movements which might like to stake claims to her talents
because of her gender and race. She tells one interviewer, for example, "I've
been fighting with this kind of image thing all my life. The idea that people
would look at me and think, "Black," or "Woman," and have certain preconceptions. . . . I just want to keep writing. They can figure it out later" (Johnsen
interview). She was willing to become Poet Laureate, she says, in part because she decided she had complained too long about the nation's lack of
regard for poetry and that she had to be part of the solution, instead of the
problem, by being poetry's champion, even though she knew the price she
would pay in loss of privacy.

On several occasions Dove speaks of an incident early in her writing career
which might be likened to a rite of passage in the establishment of her artistic
identity. Her poem "Nigger-Song. An Odyssey" had been included in an
anthology for whose appearance the publisher had arranged a public reading
to which Alice Walker was invited. Walker made a point of publicly refusing
to participate because Dove had included the n-word in her poem. In retro-
spect Dove indicates that she can understand why Walker and others might
have been concerned that a word liberally used in the Black community, at
the same time it was used by whites as a racial slur, might be misunderstood

as authorizing racism. What Dove saw as an attempt to reclaim a word forced her to defend artistic freedom. As she says, she decided: "OK, this is it; this is my moment where I'm going to have to fight this one."

If a single aspect of Rita Dove's artistic identity dominates these conversations, that aspect is integrity. The root of the word for this dominant aspect denotes oneness, or wholeness, as the cognate *integer* reminds us. Her comments about composing poems reveal a reverence for the creative principle positioning the poet as the servant of artistic imagination, helping the poem come into being. Rita Dove takes that responsibility toward writing more seriously than some writers. It is a responsibility bordering on a religious awe before the sanctity and permanence of art—not art as poems, as artifacts, but art as human creativity moving through her and other poets in the making of poems. To give the interviewee her right to the last word, it is appropriate to close with her own perception of self, given in response to a question by Taleb-Khyar: "Well, politically I consider myself a feminist, but when I walk into my room to write, I don't think of myself in political terms. I approach that piece of paper or the computer screen to search for—I know it sounds corny—truth and beauty through language."

A project as complex as this collection of *Conversations with Rita Dove* generates a list of debts. First, I need to thank graduate students Earl Yarington III and Janice McKay at State University of New York, College of Brockport, who helped to prepare the manuscript for my editing with the generous support of the college's Scholarly Incentive Award program. As in earlier projects, I want to thank Robert Gilliam for his efforts in obtaining materials for this book as interlibrary loan specialist for the college's Drake Memorial Library. And a special thanks to my wife, Mary, for her patience during the completion of the project. Elsewhere, many have made major contributions, especially the interviewers who did so much of the work in preparing and asking the questions which made the collection possible. The largest debt is owed to Rita herself, who supported the project and generously offered hours and hours of her time to her interviewers, most recently to me.

EGI
2002

Chronology

1952	Rita Dove is born in Akron, Ohio, on 28 August, daughter of Elvira Hord Dove and Ray Dove.
1970	RD is named a Presidential Scholar, one of 100 top high-school seniors, one of two from Ohio, and begins her undergraduate degree at Miami of Ohio as a National Achievement Student, graduating summa cum laude in 1973.
1973–74	RD studies modern European literature at the University of Tübingen as a Fulbright fellow.
1975–77	RD begins studies at the University of Iowa Writers Workshop, earning an MFA in 1977.
1978	RD receives a fellowship from the National Endowment for the Arts.
1979	RD marries Fred Viebahn, German novelist.
1980	*The Yellow House on the Corner*, poetry, appears.
1981	RD joins the faculty of Arizona State University.
1982	RD serves as writer-in-residence at the Tuskegee Institute.
1983	*Museum*, poetry, appears. Aviva Chantal Tamu Dove-Viebahn is born. RD is named a Guggenheim fellow.
1985	*Fifth Sunday*, short fiction, appears in the Callaloo Fiction Series.
1986	*Thomas and Beulah*, poetry, appears. RD receives the Lavan Younger Poets Award.
1986–87	RD serves as the president of the Associated Writing Programs.
1987	RD receives the Pulitzer Prize for Poetry for *Thomas and Beulah*. RD receives the General Electric Foundation Award for Younger Writers.
1988	RD joins the faculty of the University of Virginia. RD receives

        the Ohio Governor's Award, a Rockefeller Foundation residency
        in Bellagio, Italy, and an honorary doctorate from Miami of Ohio.

1988–89 RD is named a Mellon fellow at the National Humanities Center,
         North Carolina, and receives an honorary doctorate from Knox
         College.

1989   *Grace Notes*, poetry, appears. RD receives a fellowship from the
         National Endowment for the Arts.

1991   RD receives the Charles Frankel/National Humanities Medal, the
         Ohioana Award for *Grace Notes*, the Harvard University Phi Beta
         Kappa poetry award, and the Literary Lion citation from the New
         York Public Libraries.

1992   *Through the Ivory Gate*, novel, appears.

1993   *Selected Poems*, poetry, appears. RD is named Commonwealth
         Professor of English at the University of Virginia. RD receives
         the NAACP Great American Artist Award and a Woman of the
         Year Award from *Glamour Magazine*.

1993–95 RD serves as Poet Laureate of the United States.

1994   *The Darker Face of the Earth*, play, appears. RD receives the
         Distinguished Achievement medal from the Miami University
         Alumni Association, the Renaissance Forum Award for leadership
         in the literary arts from the Folger Library, the Carl Sandburg
         Award from the International Platform Association, and honorary
         doctorates from the Tuskegee Institute, the University of Miami,
         Washington University in St. Louis, Case Western Reserve Uni-
         versity, and the University of Akron.

1995   *Mother Love*, poetry, and *The Poet's World*, essays, appear. RD
         receives honorary doctorates from Arizona State University, Bos-
         ton College, and Dartmouth College.

1996   *The Darker Face of the Earth*, revised, 2nd edition of play, ap-
         pears. RD receives the Heinz Award in the Arts and Humanities,
         the Charles Frankel Prize/National Medal in the Humanities, and
         honorary doctorates from Spelman College and the University of
         Pennsylvania.

1997   RD receives the Sara Lee Frontrunner Award, the Barnes & Noble
         Writers Award, and honorary doctorates from Notre Dame, North-
         eastern University, and the University of North Carolina.

1998   *Seven for Luck*, a song cycle for soprano and orchestra with music
            by John Williams is premiered by the Boston Symphony Orches-
            tra at Tanglewood. RD receives the Levinson Prize from *Poetry*
            Magazine.

1999   *On the Bus with Rosa Parks*, poetry, appears. RD is reappointed
            Special Consultant in poetry for the Library of Congress for
            1999–2000. RD receives the John Frederick Nims Translation
            Award from *Poetry* Magazine and an honorary doctorate from the
            State University of New York at Brockport.

2001   RD receives the Duke Ellington Lifetime Achievement Award.

Conversations with Rita Dove

Riding That Current as Far as It'll Take You

Stan Sanvel Rubin and Judith Kitchen / 1985

The following conversation took place 7 March 1985 during Dove's visit to the State University of New York College at Brockport. She spoke with Judith Kitchen, poet and editor/publisher of State Street Press, and Stan Sanvel Rubin, current director of the Writers Forum. Reprinted by permission of the Brockport Writers Forum and Videotape Library.

Rubin: I'd like to begin by talking about that long, powerful poem "Parsley," which you just read. The poem is based on a real incident concerning the Dominican dictator Trujillo, isn't it?

Dove: Yes, that's right. In 1957, Trujillo ordered 20,000 Black Haitians killed because they couldn't roll their R's. And he chose the Spanish word for "parsley" in order to test this. It was an act of arbitrary cruelty. But it fascinated me, not only for its political implications but for the way language enters into history at that point—that there's a word that determines whether you live or die.

Rubin: You say they died for the sake of a "single, beautiful word." Do you really believe the word creates history in that kind of tragic sweep?

Dove: Well, in a certain sense. In this case certainly the word, or the Haitians' ability to pronounce it, was something that created history. But also history is the way we perceive it, and we do perceive it through words in a way that it's presented to us in books. And language does shape our perceptions. So I wouldn't go so far as to say that history is language or anything like that, but the way we perceive things is, of course, circumscribed by our ability to express those things.

Rubin: There's a lot of things in the poem that are expressive of your work generally, and one of them is the trade-off between fact and imagination. It's based on this historical incident, but you get as imaginative as a novelist, if I might say so. You have Trujillo's mother die baking "skull-shaped candies" on the Day of the Dead. Is this, in fact, a product of research?

3

Dove: No, it isn't. In fact, the only thing in that poem which is a product of research is the actual fact that Trujillo made this happen and that the Haitians worked in the cane fields. And then the fact that when someone cannot roll an R, it usually comes out as an L; hence, you get *Katalina*, instead of *Katarina*. But the rest of it—what goes through Trujillo's mind as he tries to find a way to kill someone—is my own invention. It fascinated me that this man would think of such an imaginative way to kill someone, to kill lots of people; that, in fact he must have gotten some kind of perverse joy out of finding a way to do it so that people would speak their own death sentences.

Rubin: It's fascinating, the way you created him as a character, through flashbacks, to his mother's death, his memories of the battlefield, and the knot in his own throat before battle. It becomes totally alive, even with the sense of psychopathology, going back to the mother for the reasons that he did this. It's a fascinating way of working. Do you find your imagination compelled by historical events, by fact, very frequently?

Dove: I do, especially in *Museum*. When I started *Museum*, I was in Europe, and I had a way of looking back on America and distancing myself from my experience. I could look at history, at the world, in a different way because I had another mind set. I found historical events fascinating for looking underneath—not for what we always see or what's always said about a historical event, but for the things that can't be related in a dry, historical sense.

Kitchen: Let's look at the way in which the poem unfolds. Could you comment on the lyric moments of the poem and the formal aspects of the poem, the repetitions?

Dove: That poem took a long time to write! I started out with the facts, and that in a certain way almost inhibited me: The very action, the fact that he thought up this word, was already so amazing that I had a hard time trying to figure out how to deal with it. So when I wrote the poem I tried it in many different ways. I tried a sestina, particularly in the second part, "The Palace," simply because the obsessiveness of the sestina, the repeated words, was something I wanted to get—that driven quality—in the poem. I gave up the sestina very early. It was too playful for the poem. A lot of the words stayed—the key words like *parrot* and *spring* and, of course, *parsley*. The first part was a villanelle. I thought I was going to do the entire poem from the Haitians' point of view. And that wasn't enough. I had this villanelle, but it wasn't enough. And there was a lot more that I hadn't said, so I tried the sestina and gave that up. I think part of that driven quality remains in that second part.

Kitchen: Well, it doesn't seem accidental to me. Every line seems to have two or three words with an R prominent in the English language. It seems that "parody / of greenery" is a good example of something you seem to be playing with throughout the poem. Was it to call our attention?

Dove: I didn't think of it consciously, but I was very conscious of sound in the poem. And I didn't think consciously, I'm going to get American and Spanish R's in it. But the R has a kind of a growl to it even in English, a subdued growl I suppose in American English, that was essential to the sound cage of the poem. It's all there.

Rubin: You're very aware of sound power as you write. The word *parrot* in the opening has that R movement Judy was talking about. So in a sense, when you keep repeating the parrot, it's always an acoustic image as much as it's a visual image, and a kind of symbol. Very interesting.

Are you worried at all that you create a Trujillo so fully that even though he's a monster he's not beyond us, but in fact becomes human on some level, with thoughts and memories?

Dove: No, I'm not really afraid. I'm not quite sure what you mean by *afraid*—afraid of bringing that out in me, or afraid of making him too human? But either way, I believe all of us have inside us the capacity for violence and cruelty. You see it even in children, and it's something we have to deal with. If you ignore it, it's far too easy to be seduced into it later. And I frankly don't believe anyone who says that they've never felt any evil, that they cannot understand the process of evil. It was important to me to try to understand that arbitrary quality of his cruelty. And I'm not afraid that I'm making him too human. I don't believe anyone's going to like him after reading my poem. Getting into his head may shock us all into seeing what the human being is capable of, and what in fact we're capable of, because if we can go that far into his head, we're halfway there ourselves.

Kitchen: That's the final poem of this second book *Museum*, and it seems to encapsulate some of the other aspects of the book. The book as a whole seems to deal with the same aspect of looking back, looking into something either historical or artistic. It becomes a museum. Could you talk about that a little bit?

Dove: Sure. *Museum* was very carefully thought out in terms of a book, and the impression it would make. I suppose what I was trying to do in *Museum* was to deal with certain artifacts that we have in life, not the ordinary artifacts, the ones that you'd expect to find in a museum, but anything that becomes frozen by memory, or by circumstance or by history. There are some things which in fact are ideal museum objects—the fish in the stone, for instance, the fossil that we observe; but there are also people who become frozen or lifted out and set on a pedestal, a mental pedestal—like poems about Boccaccio's idealized love Fiammetta, who becomes an object of admiration. There's a whole section on my father; in a way that's the memory, childhood focusing on a father, what he seemed like to me then.

The other thing was to get the underside of the story, not to tell the big historical events, but in fact to talk about things which no one will remember but which are just as important in shaping our concepts of ourselves and the world we live in as the biggies, so to speak. So, that's why the dedication to the book is "for nobody who made us possible," and it's really for the Haitians and it's for Fiammetta, who isn't anybody really because she's not treated as real.

Kitchen: Were you able to write this because, having at that point moved to another country, you had that slight sense of displacement which seems to be underneath each of these poems? Do you think that had a bearing?

Dove: I think it really had a lot of bearing. When I went to Europe the first time—that was in '74, way before I had thought of this book—it was mind-boggling to see how blind I'd been in my own little world of America. It had never dawned on me that there was a world out there. It was really quite shocking to see that there was another way of looking at things. And when I went back in '80–'81 to spend a lot of time, I got a different angle on the way things are, the way things happen in the world and the importance they take. Also as a *person* going to Europe I was treated differently because I was American. I was Black, but they treated me differently than people treat me here because I'm Black. And in fact, I often felt a little like Fiammetta; I became an object. I was a Black American and therefore I became a representative for all of that. And I sometimes felt like a ghost. I mean, people would ask me questions, but I had a feeling that they weren't seeing *me*, but a shell. So there was that sense of being there and not being there, you know. Then because you are there you can see things a little clearer sometimes. That certainly was something, I think, that informed the spirit of *Museum*.

Rubin: Because the book is, as you both said, so carefully structured, I wonder if I could just go back through it for the subtitles for its sections, and just have you say something about each of them. The first is "The Hill Has Something to Say."

Dove: That comes from the title of one of the poems in the first section. A narrow way of looking at that title would be simply that every hill contains things which make it a hill, speaking specifically of Europe where practically every hill has ruins underneath it. So it has its history, if we would just listen, if we could look at what is very obvious—a hill—and imagine the layers of time. There's an archaeological sense and a magic that I was trying to get at in that title. But also I was trying to get at the inability of that hill to say anything. It's an inarticulate object. We have to dig into it, which is why at the end of that section, there are lots of characters, individuals from history who can't speak to us anymore, like the two saints Catherine of Alexandria and Catherine of Siena, and Boccaccio's Fiammetta, or Tou Wan, the Chinese. They unearthed Tou Wan and Liu Sheng's bodies and all of the artifacts, but they can't speak to us anymore. We have to go through what they've left behind and fashion it.

Rubin: Your second is "In the Bulrush."

Dove: "In the Bulrush." God, I never really thought about this one. That, too, comes from a poem, "In the Bulrush," and it has obvious religious connotations of Moses, but also the idea about becoming a chosen one from the weeds, an unlikely place to be lifted out of and to make an impact. The first poem is called "November for Beginners," and it talks about waiting for rain or that horrible weather in November to change. But that has more to do with the reedy quality of bulrushes than it does with being discovered. But then there are several people in that section who become objects for consideration, like Champion Jack Dupree, the blues singer, who seems out of place on the stage, put on the spot, made a hero. Or Banneker, who was a Black from Maryland who made the first almanac and helped to survey the grounds for Washington, D.C. So, there are those kinds of things happening in that section.

Also I hate to give people what they expect, so often I try to play off on those titles. They would reflect back on the section before. I didn't want "In the Bulrush" to be the title of the first section because there were some poems in it that dealt with saints and religion. I didn't want the *obvious* connection, right? So that's why it also became the title for the second section.

Rubin: What about "My Father's Telescope," the third part of the book?

Dove: The title? The entire third section deals with my father. And it's also taken from a poem in that section. There are obviously sexual connotations in that title, too. But I was trying to look forward into the fourth section with the telescope so that it becomes much more; it becomes the technological age, the scientific age, the nuclear age, that I'm looking forward to. But also my father is someone that I've had a hard time understanding. And so sometimes he seemed almost like a planet, very far away. And to draw him closer was also part of the sense of that title.

Rubin: You have a poem called "Anti-Father."

Dove: Yes, a lot of those poems were written right at the time when the satellites were reporting all those wonderful photos of Saturn and Jupiter back, and that was just incredible to see these pictures being painted, you know, line by line. So that also informed that whole section, and "Anti-Father" came right about that time.

Rubin: And finally you have the "Primer for the Nuclear Age," which extends the theme, as you said, to everything.

Dove: Yes, looking outward again after going to the father. I also didn't want the father poems to appear too early in the book. Again, I'm trying to keep people from thinking that they know what's coming. But after two sections where there's nothing personal at all, I wanted to go into the father poems and then to explode out of them into the nuclear age. And I do believe that the kinds of events which are formed by the cruelty of Trujillo or the carelessness of nuclear escalation nowadays start at very personal levels. If you're careless with your thoughts and if you're careless with your relationships to other people, you're going to be careless on a larger level. Hence, that move from the father all the way to the nuclear age.

Rubin: Ending with Trujillo is kind of ending with the ultimate nasty father, or evil father. Was it hard to write those poems about your father? Did they come naturally?

Dove: They were *hard*. They were very hard to write. But in a sense they were the most satisfying to write, because I was helping myself, too. And I felt closer to him afterwards. The poems helped me to understand him a little better.

Rubin: Has he read them?

Dove: I don't know! My father told me at one point—he's a chemist and he said that he didn't understand poetry—"Don't be upset if I don't read your poems." That was when I informed him I was going to be a poet instead of a lawyer, which is what he wanted me to be. But I don't know if he's read them. My parents have my books, and I've seen one in their bedroom. I don't know.

Kitchen: There's one part of *Museum* that we've left out, and I think there's a reason for that. It happens to be my favorite poem of yours, "Dusting." I'd like you to talk about why it's here, why it's placed where it is, and where it leads to.

Dove: I wrote "Dusting" in the middle of writing *Museum*; it came out of nowhere. And I didn't realize at that point that it was going to become part of a longer sequence. It's part of *Thomas and Beulah*, the next book. At that time I had been working on some of the poems from *Thomas and Beulah*, but mainly the poems were from Thomas's point of view. Maybe I should say something about the whole structure of that before I go any further.

Thomas and Beulah is based very loosely on my grandparents' lives. My grandmother had told me a story that had happened to my grandfather when he was young, coming up on a river boat to Akron, Ohio, my hometown. But that was all I had basically. And the story so fascinated me that I tried to write about it. I started off writing stories about my grandfather, and soon, because I ran out of real facts, in order to keep going, I made up facts for this character, Thomas. I was writing some of those while I was doing *Museum*.

Then this poem "Dusting" appeared, really out of nowhere. I didn't realize that this was Thomas's wife saying, "I want to talk. And you can't do his side without doing my side." So when I had finished *Museum*, this poem really didn't fit into the whole concept, or into any of the sections, but it did fit into the idea of *Museum*; that is, dusting, wiping away layers of unclarity and things like that. And that's why it's there as a first poem, and also because it's a poem that deals with people. That was the way to enter *Museum*, to deal with the dusting and the memory which is a museum in itself, and then to go from that to the artifacts, which is what the first section is about— the hills, the archaeology of things. Dusting is a kind of archaeology. That's why I put it ahead of all the other poems, as a prologue.

But after I finished *Museum* and started to finish up Thomas's poems, I became aware that she's got to say her part, too. So *Thomas and Beulah* became actually two sides of the same story—the story of a Black couple growing up in the industrial Midwest from about 1900 to 1969. And, the first part is Thomas's point of view; the second part is his wife's point of view.

Kitchen: You used the word *underside* before. You see these as being undersides of each other in some sense?

Dove: I'm always fascinated with seeing a story from different angles. But also in the two sequences I'm not interested in the *big* moments. Obviously some *big* things happened in those years. I wasn't interested in portraying them, those moments. I was interested in the thoughts, the things which were concerning these small people, these nobodies in the course of history. For instance, there's a reference in one of the last poems of Beulah's to the March on Washington, but it's a very oblique reference. She's much more concerned about the picnic she's at. I've added a chronology to the end of this book. I never thought I'd do this in my life, but I did a chronology from 1900 to 1960. It's a very eccentric chronology, but you can see what was happening in the social structure of Midwest America at the time this couple was growing up.

Kitchen: Does this remind you of Lowell's *Notebook*—where you play off the smaller against the larger forces of history?

Dove: Yes, it does. I didn't think of that while I was doing it, of course. I try not to think of anything else except the poem.

Kitchen: Talk about trying not to think about . . .

Dove: I think the worst thing that can happen to a poet is to be self-conscious, to think, I'm writing a poem, the moment that you're writing a poem. When you get that moment where things begin to click in a poem and you begin to go off in a direction that you didn't know you were going in, you'd better just ride that current as far as it'll take you. That's such a tenuous connection for me that any self-consciousness is going to kill it right away. I try not to know what I'm doing. That may sound facetious, but I try not to clutter my head up with literary theories and critiques and stuff like that. I don't really want to know where I've been. I only follow what I need. I needed at that point, especially after *Museum*, to get back to family and more personal things. But I wanted to do it on a third-person level. I didn't know that I needed that. It was something I wanted, and that's one reason why, I'm sure, it took me so long to figure out that this was going to be a long sequence. Probably anyone else looking at it from the outside would have seen it a long time beforehand. Each poem is a new field to enter. I wanted each one to be an epiphany, and so I had to enter each poem almost blind. I had the background of all the other poems and all that stuff behind me, but I tried to let it bubble up, rather than trying to just impose it onto the page.

Rubin: You really do combine what someone might call a novelist's kind of imagination of character and even interior monologue with the really intense lyric poet's love of language, of the individual word, of the moment of epiphany, as you said. Would you expand on this, on your feelings for language?

Dove: Language is everything. As Mallarmé said, "A poem is made of words." It's by language that I enter the poem, and that also leads me forward. That doesn't exclude perceptions and experience and emotions or anything like that. But emotion is useless if there's no way to express it. Language is just the clay we use to make our poems. It's something that a lot of people who are *not* writers take for granted. It would never dawn on someone who doesn't sculpt that they could simply walk up to a block of marble and just hack away; they know they have to acquire skills. Because all of us use language, we assume, Well, anyone can do that. I talk everyday. But it's a different use of language; it is the sounds of the language, the way of telling something, that makes a poem for me. There's nothing new under the sun, but it's the way you *see* it. For me as a poet, language becomes an integral part of that perception, the *way* one sees it.

Rubin: Pursue that in your own working methods a little further. Do you say your poems aloud as you're creating them? Do you revise much?

Dove: I revise incessantly. Usually when I'm starting to work on a poem, I don't read it aloud—not until it gets to a certain point. You can lull yourself with your own voice; but I hear it in my head. At a certain point I do read a poem aloud to myself, because it's also got to work for me as music. I never want to lose that part of a poem. Also when I write a poem, as you probably can tell by now, I don't start out with a notion of how this is going to proceed. Often I will enter a poem through a word or phrase that compels me. I think in "Dusting" it was the word *Maurice*. It really started with *Maurice*. I thought that this was a wonderful, romantic name, and I had it down in my notebook, but I didn't know what I was going to do with it. So I entered the poem through the last word in a way.

Rubin: You do keep a writer's notebook?

Dove: I keep a notebook, but I don't work from beginning to end. I can start in the middle. I keep everything in my notebook, though. I keep grocery lists in there. I try not to make it sacred, because I could get uptight, you know, if I thought, Oh, this is *my notebook*! You know, as if it only contains gems or something. Of course, it contains a lot of junk, too. But I keep a notebook because sometimes it is a word that attracts me, and I don't want to feel compelled to explain why it attracts me. So if I have a notebook, I just put it in there. I don't think about it anymore. If I overhear a conversation and there's something really wonderful about it, I put it in. I don't ask any questions; I just put it in. That way when I sit down to write, I'll leaf through my notebook and wait for something to hit me and say, "Oh, that's neat," without thinking about what I'm going to do with it. If I think it's nice, I'll start with it and see where it leads me. Of course, with "Parsley," I had the incident beforehand.

Rubin: Do you think of audience at some point?
Dove: No.

Rubin: Can you say briefly what got you started as a poet? What has been most helpful to you in finding your own language? That's a topic for another whole interview.

Dove: Yes, well, I'm trying to think what got me started. I hate to say I've always written. I think everybody's always written, but most people stop at a certain point and others just go on. I loved to write as a child. Talking about language and entering into language, something that happened to me in third grade, is probably indicative of that tendency to go toward language, rather than content. We did spelling lessons in class, you know, those horrible spelling books. We had to memorize twenty words each week. And we had to do those—to me it seemed fairly idiotic—spelling lessons using the words in a sentence. I got finished early in class, and so I started writing a little novel using the words. Each week I'd write a chapter, and I made rules for myself: the words in the order they appeared; I couldn't change them by making them plural or using a different verb tense. It was really fun to have a whole world open up that I hadn't predetermined. But from an early point it was that language that intrigued me.

Kitchen: I understand that you have a collection of short fiction, *Fifth Sunday*, that will be appearing in the Callaloo Fiction Series. Could you tell us something about these tales?

Dove: *Fifth Sunday* is a collection of eight stories. Most of the protagonists are women, though one story, "Damon and Vandalia," uses alternating first-person narrators and another, "The Spray Paint King," is the story of an adolescent male, a "brown baby" growing up in Cologne, West Germany.

Rubin: Was "The Spray Paint King" inspired by your own trips to Europe?

Dove: Oh, definitely. Cologne is really one of the most magnificent river cities in Europe, as well as an important center for art—and a few summers ago spray paintings had mysteriously appeared on the pristine walls of several public buildings. The outcry was pretty amazing—none of pictures were obscene, and several were artistically exciting; but the uptightness of the German mind set, the insistence on neatness and order—all this was at stake. It was this friction between individual artistic protest and social regulations that prompted that story.

Rubin: Does language play as important a role in your fiction as it does in your poetry?

Dove: That's a hard one. I'd say that it does, but it's not so flamboyant. Fiction requires that sometimes the language be nearly transparent— traditional fiction, that is. Metafiction's another kettle of fish altogether. While writing stories I welcome that possibility to let the reins slacken a bit. But there are other difficulties that aren't present in poetry: character development, passage of time, dialogue. In *Fifth Sunday*, though, I do explore the possibilities of prose language. Several pieces are fairly traditional, à la Joyce's *Dubliners*. "Zabriah" is a rhapsody or an aria; the major part of "Aunt Carrie" consists of a dramatic monologue.

Kitchen: Why did you call it *Fifth Sunday*?

Dove: "Fifth Sunday" is also the title of the lead story and refers to those occasional months where there are five Sundays. In the church I attended when I was growing up, fifth Sunday was youth Sunday, and the entire service—all except the sermon—was conducted with the church youth. Using that title for the book was an intuitive decision, one I can't really articulate. I suppose there is the sense of a fifth Sunday as something special— "once in a blue moon"—as well as the idea of being in control only occasionally, and in strict accordance with the social rules.

Rubin: Would you say that this theme—privilege enjoyed and withdrawn—is the dominant one in your book?

Dove: I'd hate to narrow it down that far. As I said, the title was chosen intuitively, and I would like to think that my subconscious was operating on many levels. Let's say "Fifth Sunday" was the most expansive title, the most effective umbrella for the book. All the stories, however, feature individuals who are trying to be recognized as human beings in a world that loves to pigeonhole and forget. Aunt Carrie is the old-maid aunt, but she has a story to tell, she has had a life. Damon and Vandalia's attempts at communicating with each other keep missing, because social stereotyping has scarred both of them too deeply. Not all the tales are sad, though. "The Zulus" is an upbeat piece, I think.

Rubin: Do you plan to write more fiction, or was this a sidestep?

Dove: Oh, I hope to write more stories, even a novel. And plays. Just as it's tragic to pigeonhole individuals according to stereotypes, there's no reason to subscribe authors to particular genres, either. I'm a writer, and I write in the form that most suits what I want to say. When an idea occurs to me, I usually know if it will be a poem or a story—even before I know the first line. Now, whether it will be a good story or good poem—*that* I can't tell. I just keep working at it, and hoping.

A Cage of Sound

Gretchen Johnsen and Richard Peabody / 1985

On 24 March 1985 Gretchen Johnsen and Richard Peabody interviewed Rita Dove by telephone from the Harriman Estate in George-
town, while Dove was teaching at Arizona State University. The
interview first appeared in *Gargoyle* #27 (Washington, D.C., 1985).
Reprinted with permission of *Gargoyle*.

Interviewers: What drew a woman from Ohio to study in Tübingen?

Dove: It was pure chance. It happened actually because I was studying
German. In junior high I had a choice between languages. And I didn't
choose French, because everybody else was choosing French.

Interviewers: A real maverick . . .

Dove: Yes, always a maverick. That left Spanish and German, and so I
chose German, mainly because they had told us that Spanish wasn't a good
language to go to college with. Those were the kinds of biases . . .

Interviewers: At that time.

Dove: And also because of my father . . . there were some German books
around the house because my father had studied German when he was a
soldier, so he could know the language of the enemy. I remember when I was
a child not being able to read them, so I was intrigued by them. I think that
too helped make my choice. So I learned German, and went through college,
kept taking it, because I was fascinated with the fact that there could be
another language which had its own rules and which shaped thought in a
different way. Right before I got out of college, I applied for a Fulbright,
actually because I wanted to see Europe and I didn't know any other way of
getting there, except through a grant.

That's how it happened, and I ended up in Tübingen; I wanted to go to
Berlin, but they thought, I think, that these American college kids would be
kind of freaked out by Berlin. They didn't send anyone right out of college
to Berlin that year [1974]. I got sent to a picturesque college town.

Interviewers: So was that before or after Iowa?

Dove: That was before Iowa. And I'm glad it was before Iowa, because I
think it gave me a different perspective on Iowa when I came back. Had I not

15

gone to Tübingen I might have been intimidated by Iowa. Or at least its reputation. By going to Europe first, where no one knew me, where I had to get along in a different language, I developed much more self-confidence than I had before. So when I came to Iowa I had already realized that there was a world out there, you know, besides the Midwest, besides America. Before that I had never been out of the Midwest. And that that world had a different perspective on events, on politics, that just made me realize there was a whole lot out there, and therefore Iowa certainly wasn't the world. It gave me a healthy attitude.

Iowa was both a good and a very bad experience. It was a good experience in that I *met* lots of people. I was incredibly naive when I went there. I had been writing and I really didn't know very much. I mean, I hadn't read very much, put it that way. It gave me a short-cut reading list. I'd hear names and just start picking it up, saying to myself, Gosh, I've never heard of these poets before, better read them. Then someone would *not* like a certain poet, and that would make me read him or her, too. Iowa was bad in the sense that I think what everybody says is true about that place: there is an Iowa Writer's Workshop poem, there is a poem that sounds like it comes from Iowa, and you can find yourself slipping into that stuff very easily. It's simply that old idea of positive reinforcement. If people in the workshop like your poem you try to do something like that the next time. Though I did learn some things technique-wise in Iowa, particularly in my first year there, which was very good, I also found myself starting to write these kinds of safe poems that don't take risks, and as a consequence, after Iowa, for over a year I really didn't write any poems. Instead, I wrote fiction. Let's say I didn't finish any poems, because whenever I tried to write one, it didn't sound like me. It sounded like a poem from some composite person.

Interviewers: From everything you'd read and heard at the workshops.

Dove: Well, not everything that I read and heard, but there's a certain style and I just knew more often than not that I didn't like it, and so I kept writing, but I wrote something very different. I wrote in a different form so that I wouldn't be influenced, I guess. Iowa was very high-powered, and the first year was a very good and very generous year. The second year, I felt, was not particularly generous in terms of people; I mean, just in terms of students getting together and caring for one another. It became much more political shuffling. I simply withdrew from that, I just didn't like it, and so the second year I don't think very many people saw me. I said "Bye" after class and went to my apartment. But in a way the experience. . . . I don't think it really slowed me down any. The first year might have slowed me down in terms of poetry. That's part of learning, too.

Interviewers: Is there anyone that's particularly memorable for you, there?

Dove: Well, there were several people who were quite good. Stanley Plumly . . . Bill Matthews was simply a joy to listen to, and Louise Glück was very good on a one-to-one basis for me. Other people might have preferred her in a workshop, but for me it was really good to work with her privately, in a conference.

Interviewers: We met Paul Engle recently when we passed through.

Dove: That was one of the really positive things about Iowa, the fact that the International Writing Program was there. It was great because there were these writers, twenty, twenty-five professional writers from all different countries, writers who had paid their dues, so to speak, and had been working at it a long time. And they gave a seminar every week! A two-hour talk about their literature, the literature of their country. It was just all there. I remember trying to get a couple of the graduate students in the Writer's Workshop to come to some of the seminars, and they shied away; they seemed not to want to see and hear from writers other than a few select Americans, and I was rather disgusted by that. There were probably several reasons. Certainly fear of the unknown, and I think some, not all, but certainly some of these graduate students wanted to believe that they were the only writers in the world. That's the kind of arrogance I don't like.

Interviewers: Maybe that was part of the Iowa scene.

Dove: Yeah, I think it is. One of the worst things in Iowa—it's very strange, but it's just a way of life there—is that everything ran by clique. The fiction writers stuck together, the poets stuck together. The wrestlers had a bar, the visual artists had a bar. It was crazy. So I think part of the reluctance to meet foreign writers was the tendency to stick to your group. I remember the year I had gotten a teaching/writing fellowship; they gave me an office, and they asked me if it would be all right if I shared an office with a fiction writer. I said, "Is something wrong with him?" And they said, "No, we just wanted to check." And I said, "Sure, that would be wonderful." And that was just great, you know. That was funny. That was part of that.

Interviewers: You met Fred out there.

Dove: Yeah. He was part of the International Writing Program. In fact, I was to translate some of his work. I wanted to keep my German up, and so I had volunteered my services as a translator, even before the program had begun that year. "If there's a German writer," I said, "I'd be willing to help translate." So that's how we met.

Interviewers: You said you started writing fiction.

Dove: Actually, I started as a fiction writer. When I started to write as a kid, I preferred fiction to poetry, though I wrote poems, too. Whenever I thought of becoming a writer, I thought of writing in terms of fiction; I always dreamed of writing a novel. I guess everybody wants to write a novel. I really believe that I'm more of a poet than a fiction writer, that it seems to fit me better. Well, you've heard why I started writing fiction again, why I came back to it. I wrote a novel, which of course is in a drawer, but it was a learning process, because I had to teach myself, really, from reading and experiences I had had. I started writing short stories in earnest while I was in Germany for the second, bigger lengths of time. When was it? 1980, 1981. Fred and I lived most of the time in Berlin in a one-room apartment with a tile stove, which all sounds romantic unless you have to carry the coals three stories up for it. Still, it was fun, because we were living on limited funds, but we were completely free, and we were doing work for German radio stations whenever we needed money. I don't know . . . there were simply ideas that occurred to me, and I couldn't do them in poems; they did not work as poems . . . so I suddenly needed to write stories. Up to that point, I guess I thought only in terms of novels or poems. Short stories seemed so incredibly difficult. And they are. That's such a demanding form. It's hard to explain what I mean when I say that certain things just didn't work out as poems, but it was never that I tried to write a poem and then said, "Oh, no, this is a story." I knew from the beginning if it was a story or a poem.

Interviewers: So you really approached them differently, right from the start.

Dove: Completely differently. Even in terms of how they get written. I mean stories I type, poems I write.

Interviewers: You're just about the first person I've ever heard say that, that you really have a different method or technique of actually physically approaching it.

Dove: That's also why I have a very difficult time switching back and forth. I'm either writing poems for a while or I'm writing stories for a while.

"Today I feel like writing a story"; it doesn't work. I think I look at the world differently when I write stories. I work on stories when I'm compelled. I'm not now working on a short story collection. The short stories I've already written will soon be put together into a short story collection [*Fifth Sunday*, Callaloo Fiction Series]. But I'm not working on one now.

Interviewers: You haven't published very many.

Dove: No, I haven't. Only a couple, and another one's coming out in the *Southern Review* sometime in the summer. Whenever my new book of poems comes out, either late this year, or early next year, in it there are separate lyrics, fairly short poems, but all together they tell a story. And so a lot of energy that would have been directed toward writing stories got directed in an odd way, into mixing the two genres. I am interested in stretching genres as far as they go.

Interviewers: Sort of a poetry cycle, then?

Dove: Yeah, it's a cycle. They're narrative poems, but they're also very lyric poems. There's even a chronology at the end of the book. So it becomes a story in poems, but the poems themselves are short and lyric. When they're put together they make a story, but most of them can actually stand on their own. These are rules that I set up for myself. I just didn't want to write another long narrative poem.

Interviewers: What's the title?

Dove: It's called *Thomas and Beulah*, and it tells the story of a Black couple in Akron, Ohio, from about 1920 to the 1960s. There are two sections, one section is from Thomas's point of view, and one section is from Beulah's point of view. So it's working with that sort of shifting.

Interviewers: That reminds me of Dara Wier's book, *The 8-Step Grapevine*.

Dove: But it's different. When Dara's book came out I was working on this one already.

Interviewers: Was your story "Sambo, or The Last of the Gibson Girls," in *Story Quarterly* in fact autobiographical? Or am I totally wrong?

Dove: Yes and no. The incident with the doll happened, but the parents are different.

Interviewers: OK, so I'm all wrong on that.

Dove: My father wasn't even there. The mother in "Sambo" is nothing like my mother at all. In fact, my mother is a very sweet woman, and I haven't written very much about her simply because there's no friction. Do you know what I mean?

Interviewers: Yeah.

Dove: It's like what Tolstoy says at the beginning of *Anna Karenina*: "All happy families are alike." That's a broad paraphrase, but for me at least happiness can be potentially boring in literature.

Interviewers: It seems that way. Most of the poets I read write out of anger or pain.

Dove: I rarely write out of anger, but there is something to be said for the friction that you get between subjects which are unpleasant or sad, and then making the form itself pleasing and beautiful. That kind of ambivalence is what I think makes a lot of poems memorable, what makes them even human. I think it's incredibly difficult to write a happy poem.

Interviewers: And not be corny, yeah.

Dove: And not be corny. Also, when people are happy, they rarely feel like writing. You're too busy enjoying life.

Interviewers: And writing is fairly solitary, most of the time.

Dove: That's true, too. When you're sitting down to write and you're *alone*, you just don't bounce around and be happy. You become more pensive. I'm not trying to suggest that I think that poems or short stories have to be sad in order to be good. Maybe *sad* is the wrong word. Contemplative is more like it; and as with anything, when you start becoming contemplative, when you ponder something, it's not necessarily that you're unhappy, but happy is not the word that occurs.

Interviewers: OK.

Dove: Maybe *happy* is also the wrong word to be used as the other pole. *Content* is probably better. You are inquiring, intellectual. You are not content. That doesn't necessarily mean that you're not having a good time being discontent.

Interviewers: Ira Sadoff is a poet who admitted to me that he's been writing fiction much longer than he's been writing poetry. How difficult is it to keep an image of yourself as one thing when the world perceives you differently?

Dove: I've never really had a problem in terms of being a fiction writer or poet; you know, in terms of how people perceive me. I really don't care. I've been fighting with this kind of image thing all my life. The idea that people would look at me and think, "Black," or "Woman," and have certain preconceptions about that. This is the kind of thing I've been fighting all the time, and in a certain way the misconceptions people have often amuse me; in an ironical way it's rather amusing. I'm not really concerned about how they perceive me. I just want to keep writing. They can figure it out later.

Interviewers: I'm surprised that your work hasn't appeared in traditional Black literary markets like *Callaloo*, *Obsidian*, *Freedomways*, et al. Especially poems from Part III of *Yellow House* or the "Sambo" short story.

Dove: Well, it's a twofold thing. One reason has a lot to do with my history, how I grew up and where I went to school, and the fact that I went to Iowa and got to know different markets. The other reason, though, was a resistance. I guess I've always had a resistance to being typecast, and did not want to, from the beginning, be put in a category of "Black Poet." I remember, going to college in the beginning of the '70s, when there was still quite a lot of emphasis being placed on Black poetry, and the fact that it had to pertain to Black subjects, that it had to have lots of "Blackness" in it.

Interviewers: And the idea of Black English as an accepted alternative to standard English . . . the language itself . . .

Dove: Well, I wasn't really thinking of the language itself. That's a positive thing, that some kind of emphasis has been placed on the fact that there is a different kind of English spoken by a majority of Blacks, that has its own rules, its own grammar. It's not just a hodgepodge. But I'm really referring to, well, something every minority fights against, and that's falling into a cubbyhole, being classified as a Black writer, and then being assigned certain topics. I mean, the first thing that happens is that someone, a critic, will call you a Black writer. Then you fall into a category where you're only compared to other Black writers. How often have you seen blurbs like, "This is the greatest Black novel since *Invisible Man*." I'm so tired of hearing stuff like that. Given my middle-class background, there were many kinds of experiences that I had which could not *only* have been experienced by Blacks. The earliest poems of mine that appeared in *Yellow House* are the poems about adolescence. I therefore felt they were topics which were for everyone, and I submitted them to magazines with that in mind. The slave narratives came a little bit later.

Interviewers: How are you treated by Black critics and Black audiences? I'm just curious if they treat you any differently, or do they welcome the universal?

Dove: When I give a reading to a predominantly Black audience, often they don't expect quite to hear what they hear; I don't know what they expect, but they like what I offer. At least I have the feeling that they like it. For about a year now I've been an advisory editor to *Callaloo*, and that came about because they liked my work. Basically, you're asking why some of those poems hadn't appeared in Black magazines, and the reason why was as I was growing up and starting to write I consistently resisted being typecast. At this point now I think I've relaxed a bit, and I think also the whole literary market has relaxed a bit. After Toni Morrison and Alice Walker, it's possible for people to imagine that a Black writer doesn't have to write about ghettos.

Interviewers: You're looked on as an individual.

Dove: There's much more of a readiness for people to accept that on both sides, Black and white.

Interviewers: I think that's a recent change. I think we've gotten away from the '60s when people said you have to write what you know.

Dove: It was a time of, I think, necessary overkill, especially in terms of Black literature—a time when, in order to develop Black consciousness it was important to stress Blackness, to make sure the poems talked about being Black, because it had never really been talked about before. It wasn't predominant, except in the Harlem Renaissance, but then we had, in a certain way, forgotten about that. So I think it was necessary and the pendulum had to swing back.

Interviewers: I just read the new paperback edition of Zora Neale Hurston's biography, and her biographer attacks her (I thought it was an awful introduction to a book, especially coming from your biographer) for not being political. And then he mentioned that her last novel had been written about white characters: every character was white, there weren't any Blacks in the novel. I never heard of that before, I'd never heard that anyone had ever done something like that, made that kind of crossover. I was delighted, I'd love to see the book. I agree, things should be more universal, and not . . .

Dove: Things get so wrapped up into what someone is . . . I mean, in minority groups, whether they adhere to a genre. It's like the genre is making them, instead of them making literature. And Zora Neale Hurston is a good example of someone who's suffered because of that. That's why she got lost for so many years. She was uncompromising and did what she thought was right, and there were Black writers during the Harlem Renaissance who rejected her because they thought she was . . . well, you hear these strange things, like they said she was "too loud," which I don't understand. What does that mean? On the one hand, she was accused of playing up to whites; on the other hand, she did these wonderful anthropological studies of folk tales in her book *Mules and Men*. A lot of the misunderstanding about Zora Neale Hurston comes from the fact that people were trying to fit her into some existing pigeonhole. And she resisted that.

Interviewers: There are people who read *Fiction/82* and didn't know that you wrote poetry, who really loved your story "The Spray Paint King" and said, "You mean she writes poetry, too?" They were astonished. So you reached a different sort of audience.

Dove: That's great. That's the best compliment I've ever gotten. Because I always felt that my stories, in a certain way, were coming from this background of poetry, that they seemed a little bit . . . disjointed, that they were, in fact, "poet's stories." And that was something I always feared, that someone would read one of my stories and say, "Oh, yeah, this is the kind of story a poet would write." So it's just wonderful to think that people didn't know it and were really surprised. That's delightful. Anyway, about "The Spray Paint King," it's the same old thematic, the idea of not fitting in anywhere, and the artist trying to come out. The story was based on actual paintings, sprayings that I had seen around Cologne and other German cities. They caught the person finally; he was not at all a mulatto or anything like that. It was a Swiss guy who went through Europe spraying his paintings on public walls. But by that time I didn't care about that kind of verisimilitude anymore.

Interviewers: What writers' work do you teach? And are there any who've particularly influenced your own work?

Dove: Let's see. This is one of those questions where my mind goes blank. When I was a kid, I used to read everything I got my hands on, good or bad, and one of the books that I tried to read but didn't understand was the *Iliad*. I also tried to read the *Aeneid*. But it was because my father had subscribed to these "Great Books of the Western World," the kind of thing where you got 50 books and a little bookshelf for them, too. He had read a few of them, and there they were, all these classics, and I just made up my mind one summer that I was going to read through them systematically. I must have been about thirteen or so. I didn't understand what I was reading, but it was intriguing, and I still liked it. It stuck with me in an odd kind of way. In terms of people who influenced me: when I started writing poetry, let's see, I really go blank on this kind of thing. I'll have to think about it. I'm sorry, but it's one of those questions I deplore. I really think I go blank as a self-protection device, too.

Interviewers: That's interesting, I'd never heard it put that way.

Dove: Yeah. I don't want to know the influences.

Interviewers: To invite comparison . . .

Dove: Yeah, and also because I've always been concerned with writing like myself, trying to find the voice that's truest and the style that's truest to my own voice, to my own thoughts. And though I certainly have influences, they change so rapidly, more from poem-to-poem or story-to-story, rather than through a writer's oeuvre. So that makes it kind of difficult. Influence is such an amorphous thing: it changes all the time, and I'd rather not know, at a given point, what is impressing me at that moment. I think also part of my reluctance . . . after all, I've been asked this question often enough in my life that I could have put down some answers, but I'm always at a loss. I think another reason why this happens is because I feel somehow healthier about not knowing exactly where I'm going, you know what I mean? Groping in the dark. . . . After the fact, I could tell you, "Oh, this poem certainly has been influenced by so-and-so," or "This story certainly has influences." But it changes all the time, so saying that this or that person influenced me *per se* would be false. A definitive answer slants things.

Interviewers: Oh, no, I appreciate the honesty. It's hard to get someone to be that honest. Most people would toss out five names.

Dove: Right, toss out five biggies and then forget it. Actually, certain writers have influenced me, but I don't think my work sounds like them at all, and it's because I admire them so much and yet there's nothing in me that works the same way, like Nabokov, for instance, or Heinrich Heine, who I really love, even though I don't write those kind of satirical ballads. I love Bertolt Brecht, who I think is great, but you know . . .

Interviewers: That moves you into our next question. You're married to a German writer, and have spent some time over there yourself. What contemporary German writing most interests you? Poets, fiction writers, others. What about films and film makers? Fassbinder, Herzog, Wenders, others?

Dove: The contemporary German writing that most interests me is fiction. The poets have been mostly disappointing in recent years, for me. There are a couple of poets I can think of, but they aren't very well known in the States because they haven't been translated. One of them is a man by the name of Friedrich Christian Delius. There's Heidi Pataki in Vienna who writes absolutely wonderful poems, which are almost performance pieces. Then there's another poet who's probably, I think, the best contemporary German poet writing now. His name is Dieter Schlesak. He's actually Rumanian, from German-speaking Rumania. His poems are incredibly complex. I've been trying to translate some for years, and am completely stuck. But they're absolutely wonderful. But in general, I think German poetry is suffering from the same kind of malaise that American poetry is suffering, that is, a kind of cult of the personality that would make anything into a poem simply because the poet says so. The kind of poem where the poet goes down to the store and buys a cantaloupe, or something. That kind of stuff. Especially in West Germany: it's poetry like that or it's stridently political.

Interviewers: And nothing in between.

Dove: Nothing that deals with language, I mean. The language seems to be merely a vehicle. Now, as far as fiction writers go I think Günter Grass is simply wonderful. I love his novels. And Peter Handke, though he's Austrian. But I haven't read a lot of the younger novelists. Films and film makers? Let's see. Since I have a child now, I haven't seen many films in the last two years. I used to see films all the time. I'm really behind. It's crazy. I liked some of Fassbinder very much; he had a wonderful version of, oh, what's the English title, *Der Blaue Engel.*

Interviewers: *The Blue Angel*, yes. *Lola* was the film.

Dove: Right. That was just great. I don't like Herzog very much, but I'm not qualified to speak of him because I've only seen two of his older films, *Kaspar Hauser* and *Aguirre, The Wrath of God*. I don't know what it is. I go into the theater to see a Herzog film and I start to laugh. I don't know, I recognize absolutely gorgeous scenes. I know in *Aguirre* there are wonderful scenes, especially that scene where they chop off the man's head.

Interviewers: I like the beginning and the end.

Dove: The cinematography is gorgeous. Obviously, he rubs me the wrong way. I acknowledge his greatness, because some part of me looks at it and says, "This is gorgeous." But some other part says, "No." So I don't feel that it's fair for me even to say that I don't like him, you know? Because that implies that he's bad or something, and he certainly isn't.

Oh! I remember another German poet who's influenced my work—Hans Magnus Enzensberger. I particularly loved a book of his that came out about ten years ago called *Mausoleum*. I think it was translated into English as well. I'm sure that that book, in fact, had an influence on *Museum*, when I think about it. After all, a museum is a mausoleum too. Maybe he overdid it, but what he did was to take characters, people from real life who influenced history in some kind of way, often in a kind of ineffectual way or a negative way, and some who didn't. Chopin's in there, and at the same time Bakunin is in there, and other people, like the man who invented, oh, I don't know, steam engines, or something like that. But he wrote these poems about them, sometimes interspersing direct quotes from their notebooks, stuff like that. Each poem, though, has just their initials as the title, and in order to find out who they are you have to look into a very complicated index: you look up the initials and then it refers you to a last name, and then you look up that. You have to struggle to find the person's whole name, to find out who they were. Which means that you tend to read the poems for themselves and for a particular view of what those people have done for the world. And then you find out that you aren't blinded by the name. It's a kind of theater of a book.

Interviewers: We ran an excerpt in an early issue from a book that Enzenberger wrote on how to write poetry. He'd taken a lot from Poe, which was interesting.

Dove: It's true, there is something from Poe in *Mausoleum*, too. In the way he works the rhythms, yeah.

Interviewers: It was the evolution of one of his poems, how he'd gotten the first line, and grown from there. We ran an excerpt, we didn't run the whole piece. I think it's almost book length.

A recent issue of *Field*, a survey and anthology of East German poetry, emphasizes the different lines of development taken by East as opposed to West German poetry, and the East German trend, in the late '60s and '70s, toward a more personal lyricism, imagery, etc., as opposed to more consistently, overtly political themes and methodology in the work of West German writers. Has your reading made you conscious of the divergence? If so, do you have any comments as to the effects of organized, or undisguised, artistic and political repression on the work of the writers involved? Your own poems seem closer to those of the East Germans, in terms of style and perspective.

Dove: One of the reasons why the East German trend has been toward a more personal lyricism in imagery is obviously the political situation and that overtly political opinions other than party line are not allowed. So the East German writers have learned to write between the lines, and people have learned to read between them. There are several different kinds of poems and stories. You can get the overtly lyric, and the one which really has nothing to do with the political situation. But I think most of the ones which are literature, serious literature, are somewhere in between. There's always a concern for the language, the lyricism and the imagery, but there is also something in between the lines which is talking about oppression. And it's often a point, I think, to see how far you can get before they ban you. Since the late '70s, when many of the best East German poets, fiction writers, and dramatists were banned from the writers' union, and consequently driven into exile in West Germany, I think their writing is changing, and for the worse. One of the obvious cases for that is someone like Sara Kirsch, whose work I used to love, and whose latest poems seem very lax. If you separate someone from their roots and from their home you take away the juice; there's also nothing to strain against. One of the best ways to keep someone quiet, actually, is to agree with them. There's no real resistance, as they know it, in West Germany. You can do whatever you want to. People can just choose not to be affected by it. They can choose to ignore you. That's more effective than any kind of repression. That kind of acceptance, being taken into the Western capitalist culture, and even being touted as being a great Eastern dissident writer, can certainly take the wind out of someone's sails for several years.

Interviewers: "Shakespeare Say" brings it all together for you—an American blues man playing in a Munich club.

Dove: Yeah, I'm glad that you mentioned that, because it's true, that's where everything really does come together. It's the feeling of being displaced, of being someone on the edge. Or of being misperceived, that it's people seeing you in a different way and yet still going on about your art.

Interviewers: You translate Fred's poems into English. How do you approach the translator's task?

Dove: I translated a few of Fred's poems into English. I stopped translating his work, we stopped translating—he used to translate some of mine into German—we stopped doing it because we know each other too well.

Interviewers: It's *too* close.

Dove: It's just too close, and I think ideally the person who's being translated shouldn't even know the translator. I've gotten to that point. It's fine if the translator calls and asks what tone is right for a certain passage, but if you know someone too well you tend to demand too much. So I would say to Fred, "Gosh, you *know* there's this, you missed that," and get angry with him, and he would get angry at me because I couldn't get something into English. It was too much of a strain, so we stopped. Now, I do translate still; in fact, I mentioned the Schlesak poems; but I translate rarely now, and when I do I approach it as an impossible task. It's as hard as writing poems, with less reward, because you have a ball and chain. I think the thing that makes translation so absolutely impossible, though it has to be done, is that each language has its own cage of sound. The best writers work within that cage—I don't mean that in a negative sense—but work in that mesh of sounds, and kind of rub against the edges of it, and strain it, and make you therefore aware of the music of that language.

Interviewers: I know the idioms tie people up. We know Tom Whalen, one of the people who translates Robert Walser, a Swiss writer who wrote in German, and playing with idioms really drove everyone crazy.

Dove: A writer who really cares about language, of course, is straining to the hilt, playing with it. And how do you bring that to another language? It's not going to be a one-to-one correspondence. But translation has to be done. I admire translators so much because theirs is such a thankless task, and yet it's such an important one and it's so demanding, and most people tend to toss it off.

Interviewers: I've never seen a photo of Fred, but the resemblance in Christian Schad's cover painting to *Museum* is uncanny, where you're concerned.

Dove: Well, Fred doesn't look anything like the man on the cover.

Interviewers: Oh, I was joking.

Dove: I never saw any resemblance between me and the woman either, though Fred had. But also my daughter, who was one year old then, looked at the book for the first time and said, "Mama." She didn't do that with every Black woman she saw. She was really the unbiased judge in that case. So I had to acknowledge the resemblance. You know how it is: you never notice that someone looks like yourself.

Interviewers: Maybe that's the block.

Dove: Yeah. But finding the picture was interesting; what happened was that in Berlin Fred and I had gone to an art opening, a retrospective of Schad's work, because he'd been rediscovered at the age of eighty-five or whatever. And we saw the painting and it was really riveting, and bought the catalog which told a little bit about the two people. When I wrote the poem "Agosta the Winged Man and Rasha the Black Dove," I sent it to Christian Schad, just because I thought he should know. I didn't know if he knew English, but it turned out he did. Then I met him afterwards and talked to him, and he gave me permission to use the painting on the cover of the book. That was a year before he died.

Interviewers: I think that's wonderful, that you actually met the artist.

Dove: A lot of people didn't like the cover. Let's say they were uneasy. But I wanted them to be uneasy. Again, it was that kind of friction I was after. I wanted the book to be physically beautiful, but the picture is disturbing. So it's not something that you just look at and say, "Oh, this is gorgeous." I actually like those reactions—when people say, "Oh, this cover is really, ah, *interesting*."

Interviewers: We showed it to someone yesterday who kind of backed off when they looked real close.

Dove: People do back off from it, yeah. It's to Carnegie-Mellon's credit that they put it on. When I had talked to Jerry Costanzo, the editor, I said, "I have this great picture for the cover," and I was afraid that he was going to say, "This is not going to sell the book." But he was great. He just said, "I love the picture, and we're going to run it." I think that's really great. I could imagine with a larger publisher the marketing people would have screamed.

Interviewers: You wouldn't get that kind of control. The free artist.

Dove: No, and that's one of the things that I find so great about working with Carnegie-Mellon, that I'm allowed some kind of input, that Jerry listens. I wanted this baroque frame around the picture, and he said, "OK, sounds good to me."

Interviewers: Your work is nothing like the majority of work we see from the Southwest. Does that make it difficult to teach at Arizona State? How do you relate to that work? That vision?

Dove: My work, sure, it's not what people imagine as Southwestern. I came to Arizona in 1981; I had never been in the Southwest before except for going through on a camping trip. And when I got here I really felt like I was on the moon. I don't feel like that anymore now; I feel like it's my home. I enjoy it here. Let's just say that it doesn't make it difficult for me to teach at Arizona State. There are other people here whose vision is not particularly Southwestern. Norman Dubie, for example; he's not particularly Southwestern. Well, Alberto Rios's vision is Southwestern—he is from Arizona. But the common denominator is the language, and the students are not all from Arizona; there is quite a large contingent form Illinois and Michigan. I don't know why.

Interviewers: That's strange.

Dove: It's too cold up there. There are so many Michigan and Illinois license plates, it's crazy. But this phenomenon does raise something else, and that's the question of landscape. Landscape has always had a great importance in my life, but I've never written about a place while I'm living there. I had to leave home before I even wrote poems that dealt with my childhood. There are a lot of poems in *The Yellow House* which, at least for me, take place in my backyard.

Interviewers: You had to get the distance on it, yeah.

Dove: Most of the poems in *Museum* were written after I had left Europe. They were written actually when I first arrived in Arizona. I got the distance on it, but then it became an act of imagination to be sitting in 115 degree heat and writing about November in Europe. And the force it took to get myself back into it. That's one of the reasons it isn't difficult for me to live here. Gee, I don't know. See, I'm not even sure what Southwestern work or vision is. I think there are two kinds of things going on; you get the distinctly Hispanic vision, which also has to do with language, and being on the border so to speak, both sides of the Rio Grande. I like that kind of stuff, because that's where I come from, too . . . two different cultures. So there's the Indians and the Hispanics, and then of course the Anglos, who are sprinkling water all over the desert and filling up their swimming pools. It's the people who live on the border, who have the vision, and that's where I've always been: watching the rest of the people make fools of themselves. So, I feel really comfortable here. I just love the weather, too.

Interviewers: You've had a child recently. Are you managing to carry on your routine? You said you hadn't gone to a movie in two years. What are your future plans?

Dove: Gosh, it's killing me. That's one of the biggest changes in my cul-tural life, I guess, the fact that we haven't been able to see movies. And it makes quite a difference. I didn't realize how much I'd gotten from them. Of course, the other thing about having a child (and you've probably heard this a thousand times but it bears repeating) is that there is little concentrated time left. Time gets really broken up into snippets and it's extremely frustrating. How we managed to carry on a routine—well, luckily, shortly after Aviva was born I got a Guggenheim, so I got a year off from teaching when she was six months old. We did travel, but most of the time we stayed here, got an answering machine, and set up a schedule, because we realized that all we had been doing was staring at the baby. We were getting really disgusted with ourselves. So we set up a fairly elaborate schedule so that, for instance, on a given day we got up late (we're both night people). So, let's say from 11:00 in the morning until 3:00 I would take care of Aviva and then from 3:00 until 7:00 Fred would take care of her. Then we would have dinner—whoever took care of her through the 3:00 to 7:00 shift had to fix dinner as well—then we ate dinner for an hour, and then after that we would go onto the third shift, and the person who took care of her in the morning would also take care of her at night. The next day that would all switch around. So what happened was that every other day I would get two blocks of time to work, right? And the other days, one. Plus a few hours late at night.

That worked great for a while. At first it was rough, it was like living in boot camp, always looking at the clock. We did this five days a week and on the weekend we came out and saw other people. But we realized after a while that we weren't seeing each other. That in fact Aviva wasn't getting both of us together. So after the first couple of months we relaxed a bit. The first couple of months were important. We just needed to write again; we had to do it kind of hard core. And after the first couple of months we just relaxed and just did it twice a day. One of us would work from 11:00 to 3:00, and then for four hours in the middle of the day we would talk together, go shopping, have lunch and both of us would take care of her. And then in the evening the other person would work. We did that for most of that year.

Then I went back to teach, and I didn't write, there was no time. I don't know how people do it, I mean, there was just no time. Fred took care of Aviva at home; he wasn't writing either because he was taking care of Aviva. And we kept her at home until she was two. We think that's important for a child, and it was a great experience for us, also, if you forget about the writing; but as soon as she turned two she went into pre-school for half a day.

That's where we're at now. She goes to school for three-and-a-half hours in the morning, we've had to change our whole schedule to become morning people, and we write for those three-and-a-half hours. When she comes home she usually goes to bed and sleeps for another two hours. In fact, every time she sleeps or goes away we write.

Interviewers: You run to your desk.

Dove: We run to our desks, and we don't clean the house, and we don't make elaborate meals. All that stuff is not important. Because we have to write. Starting in September she'll be gone from 9:00 to 2:00. We'll have more time. We're coming out gradually. We don't plan to have any more children. We're extremely unorganized—both of us are unorganized. In the amount of time I waste getting things in order, other people would have written a chapter or poem already. It's part of our personalities. We just know that we couldn't handle two. But I'm *glad* that I have a child. She's great, and it is really wonderful. All that corny stuff that people say is true.

Interviewers: Oh, but I hear so many awful poets read awful poems about their baby's bellybutton glinting in the sun.

Dove: I know. I haven't written a single one about her, and I don't think I'll ever do it.

Interviewers: Good for you.

In the *Georgia Review* article on *Museum* Peter Stitt stated that you handled both narrative and circular poems in the book. Do you consciously try to write in different styles?

Dove: I do try to write in different styles, I try not to repeat myself. That would be boring. If I've noted that my poems are beginning to look all alike, then I will give myself actual tasks. Part of the new book arose out of taboos that I set up for myself. There were so many poems running around that used "I," and there were so many poems that used "you" in a false way. Was the "you" really an "I," but they were trying to kid you? I told myself, "No poems with 'you' in it, and no poems with 'I' in it." It was after *Yellow House on the Corner*, I was trying to move in a different direction, and that didn't leave very much. It left "we" and "he" and "she." But that's what started, in a way, this new book, *Thomas and Beulah*. Because even though the book is from two different points of view, the poems are all in "he" and "she," and there are no "I"s running around in there. So every once in a while I will set up tasks for myself. After I had finished *The Yellow House* *on the Corner*, I wanted to write longer poems, because I'd noticed I tended to stop after about fifteen lines. So I consciously tried to write longer ones. I consciously tried to write poems that were narrower, that were skinnier, just because I had written poems that were much more blocky. But, I guess I really didn't understand that whole narrative and circular stuff in Stitt's essay.

Interviewers: I thought he was really stretching.

Dove: I thought he was, too. But just to answer the second part of your question, I do try to write different styles.

Interviewers: Form means a lot to you, then? The actual shape of the poem on the page?

Dove: It does mean a lot to me. I think that the poem engages all of your senses, and the first thing that happens when you look at a poem is that you *see* it as a silhouette. And poems choose their silhouettes. I mean, they do choose their silhouettes at some point, and that makes a big difference.

Interviewers: I like your sense of humor. The Boris Karloff epigraph, and dedicating *Museum* to nobody.

Dove: Thank you. I was so happy when I found the epigraphs. I was watching the movie, you know, *The Raven*, when he said that, and it was wonderful. It's certainly humorous. It has its undercurrent, too, of—its more serious implications.

Interviewers: But you do balance one against the other—throughout.

Dove: Oh, thank you—I tried! You know, there's something to be said for that old blues lyric that goes, "You're laughing just to keep from crying." It's the healing laughter of the blues. That kind of irony can give you a much sharper vision, because it keeps you from being overwhelmed by the misery of the world. But I'm glad you saw the humor.

Interviewers: You've written a lot of poems about your father, while your mother gets short shrift.

Dove: You know, I've been thinking a lot about my mother, and the fact that I've never really ever put her in anything. Like I said, the mother in the "Sambo" story is not my mother at all. So I have a feeling something about my mother is going to come up very soon. And I have a feeling it's going to come out in stories and not in poems. I can't really say why I have that feeling, but that's the way it's been bubbling under the surface. I've written a lot of things about my father because he's so enigmatic to me. I'm trying to figure him out.

Interviewers: I find personally that it's difficult to write—again, I need that distance, and the one time I've written about my father he became very ill, as though the power of words had done that? So I stopped. I don't know if your mother and father are both alive or not.

Dove: They're both alive, and I don't know if they've read the poems or not. They have all my books, but they've never said anything about them. My father is a chemist. He told me when I first began writing poems, when I told him I wanted to be a poet instead of a lawyer (he wanted me to be a lawyer), to his credit, he said, "Well, I've never really understood poetry, so don't be upset if I don't read them. Just go ahead and do whatever you want to do, but I don't understand them." So I accepted that—at least I never really waited for his opinion. But I've also seen my books in their bedroom. So someone must be reading them.

Interviewers: Do you see a conflict between the academy (AWP, etc.) and the small press *per se*? I don't mean to introduce a can of worms . . . just wondered if you've noticed political squabbling. I know you were just on an NEA panel. Do you have any thoughts on that?

Dove: Well, the NEA panel—I have to say that that was one of the most positive experiences I've had in terms of literary *circles* and stuff like that. It was not at all what I—I don't know what I expected, but I remember being so pleasantly surprised. And I guess it was because, going through all those discussions and evaluations, in the end it really became the poem that counted. It sounds corny, but it was really poetry, and people getting carried away by poems. That was immensely positive. But, on the other hand, I also think there's certainly a conflict between the "academic establishment" and the small press. I think it's a conflict that's always going to be there, and it's a conflict simply by definition. In academia, there's a certain complacency that occurs in any establishment. Whoever has the power, *per se*—the money, power, the acceptance, the recognition, immediately—they become blinded in a way. It's similar to the president being briefed by all of his advisors. If you don't see it with your own eyes, you are blind, no matter how sensitive or well-meaning you are or want to be. Any establishment necessarily, I think, starts to feed on itself. That's not to say that there can't be great writers coming out who are accepted by the establishment, but I think just by definition establishments tend toward conservatism and opportunism. As far as the small press is concerned, there may be circles within circles. But not having the same kind of power and influence, first of all, eliminates the kind of people who do it for the fame. It eliminates those kind of people because there's not going to be enough of that. In the small press world, you get people who are truly, truly dedicated to the work. To literature. Whereas you're going to get a lot of dross in the establishment. People who have had promise at the beginning and kind of faded out, but they already have a foot in the door so they go on, you know.

Interviewers: They have tenure.

Dove: They have tenure, right. The small press is a lean operation. There's no room for fat. There's political squabbling everywhere, and I've seen it. I guess we've all seen it, but I try to stay out of it.

Interviewers: You seem to be a really independent person. You don't seem to be part of any clique or any sort of group or anything. Which interests me.

Dove: I am a bit of a hermit. The fact is that getting an answering machine was one of the greatest things in my life. I screen every call. All of my friends know that. It has nothing to do with them. They sometimes leave these wonderful messages. I guess acting the hermit has something to do with the fact that somewhere I know how easy it is to get drawn in and to be influenced. We all want to be liked. That's one of the serious problems of Americans *per se*. Americans *want* to be liked. We want the whole world to like us, and we're upset when they don't. Germans, on the other hand, don't expect to be liked. There's a sort of belligerence that goes along with that. It's interesting what that does to your consciousness. I'm like everyone else. I want to be liked, but I want to like myself, too. So I guess I don't trust myself to be strong enough. I try to stay away from it, then. Well, the NEA panel—I thought it was time to put a foot out and see what it was like. To see if I could still maintain a distance. Which I think I have. That's another one of the reasons why living abroad for over two years, first in Jerusalem and then in that little one-room apartment in Berlin, was so wonderful, because I was away from *everything* here. I didn't know what people were doing. I could read literary magazines, but then I'd have to go to the American Cultural Center, and they were old. I couldn't be influenced by my own culture, because it was so far away.

Interviewers: Your piece in *Porch* on the Frankfurt Book Fair was memorable. Everyone tells me that's the only fair that matters. I'm always surprised at just who has a reputation in Europe and who doesn't, and the flipside in America.

Dove: It has a lot to do of course with who's translated or not. In Germany I was amazed that the biggest American poet is Bukowski.

Interviewers: We found the Beats are about all that's read in England and in Germany.

Dove: It's true. In Germany I think it has a lot to do with the fact that there's a certain drive in the rhythm of many of the Beats that translates well into German. I also think the Beats, their lifestyle, the whole idea of it is immensely appealing to Germans, who are traditionally rather uptight.

Interviewers: Getting back to the cult of the personality?

Dove: No, not really. With the Beats, it becomes almost an Everyman kind of personality. When Ginsberg is going on in "The Wichita Vortex," I mean, that's in a way the most complete cult of the personality because it's been taken from exactly what he said as they were driving out of the country. "Turn left here," and all that stuff. But it becomes so transparent, that the personality disappears. I don't know if that makes any sense.

Interviewers: How do you feel about the way Europeans treat books as opposed to how we treat them here?

Dove: Well, we're Philistines.

Interviewers: Oh, well, that's quotable!

Dove: You know, number one, just in terms of distribution, because we all know how abysmal the distribution system is here. I still don't understand why it takes six weeks to get a book. Whereas the distribution system at least in Germany is so good that you can get any book within three days. I know we have a larger country, but we could have a better system.

Interviewers: It's partly because the bookstores here don't pay their bills.

Dove: Well, the whole system seems so unmanageable here. It's hopeless. Also, many Europeans are more at home with books, you know? And Americans are really afraid of them. I'm talking about Americans in general. That's why literature has retreated to the universities, which is the worst place for it, because it's so unreal. When I go to Europe, I see real people reading books. You know what I mean. "Normal" people. In Germany writers appear on TV, giving their opinions on national politics. In Italy they can fill stadiums with poetry readings.

Interviewers: At the Super Bowl two years ago, right before the L.A. Raiders stomped my Redskins, one of the Raiders, Todd Christensen, with a camera trained on him, recited a poem that he'd written. He probably had the largest single audience for a poem in the history of mankind, (I don't actually know how many million people watched the Super Bowl), but he was on TV with everyone getting ready to watch the game, like a minute before kickoff, and he recited a poem.

Dove: Great! Was it any good?

Interviewers: Not really! But it was sort of amazing that he would do it.

Dove: I love it. All we need now are great football or baseball players or boxers who can write good poems and who will recite them every time they get in front of TV cameras. Unfortunately, I never have these kind of people in my classes, and so I'm afraid we'll have to go on with the old ways: I mean, with their ignorance and our arrogance and so on.

Entering the World through Language

Susan Davis / 1986

Susan Shibe Davis interviewed Rita Dove at Arizona State University 26 April 1986. Printed by permission of Susan Shibe Davis.

Davis: I'd like to begin by talking about how long you've been composing.

Dove: When I grew up, my parents encouraged us to read. We were allowed only a certain number of hours of television a week, and our programs were closely monitored, which is a real blessing, I think, because that meant that we did have a lot of time to read. One place we could always go (assuming that it wasn't storming or sleeting) was the library. Of course, we could always abuse that privilege: "I'm going to the library," and then I'd make a little side trip, but we did go to the library because we had to bring books back. What I remember most about my childhood was curling up in a corner reading, reading, and reading. In summer that was the thing I did. That was the thing I did to fill those long, boring days, because you get too much free time in the summer. My first love was reading, and it took me to different worlds. I was very shy—I still am—but I was very shy then, so it was a way of dealing with the world.

I started to write as I think many kids do—just at school. They always make you write poems and stuff like that. Well, I loved it. This was the period that I loved the most. In terms of concrete writing that I did as a child that I can remember, or that I still have, the only was when I was in second grade. (It's a long story. Are you ready for this one?).

Remember those spelling books we used to have with words, twenty words on this side of the page, and then you had to do all these stupid exercises with them? Our second grade teacher made us do those exercises in class. I would get through with them early and just be sitting around. You had to be quiet, so what I started doing (I started with the third lesson into the third week of school) was trying to write a story, using those words, and it got to be so much fun—because the words were very strange—that every week I would finish my homework quickly so I could write the next lesson.

I never looked ahead to see what the next week's words were going to be,

38

so it was really an exercise in semi-automatic writing. It became a kind of forty-page (because there were forty lessons) thing called "Chaos." It was a little novel about robots taking over the earth because that's what I was into in the second grade. It was fun playing with the words, and watching the words develop their own world. I was entering the world through language when I look back on it.

I also wrote a little doggerel verse like a lot of children do. I have an older brother, who is two years older than I am. During the summer—every summer—we would start a magazine, or a newspaper, and every summer we would break it off because I wanted to be editor, and he was. Every time we would break it off I would start my own magazine called "Poet's Delight," but I never got further than the cover page. (I would draw this elaborate picture.)

I also wrote comic books. Our parents let us read comics. Their philosophy was that you could read anything. If you wanted to read it, you could read it. If we understood it, fine. If we didn't, well, we'd stop. I think that was wise because I loved comic books for awhile, but later I outgrew them. I really did grow up on Wonder Woman and Superman and all these super American heroes.

I stopped writing in junior high. I wrote in eighth grade. I was put into an accelerated class that was an experiment to take supposed top students and see if we could be pushed further ahead. One of the results of that class was that I never had grammar because they gave grammar in the seventh grade. I missed it completely! I couldn't diagram a sentence. I learned it later—out of fear.

In the eighth grade I had a teacher who made us write every Tuesday, the first hour of class. Without saying a word, we had to write. It was wonderful! To wake up, to go into school, to be half sleepy, or whatever, and to sit down and we didn't have to perform to anyone in a public sense. We could be private and sit down and write about anything we wanted to. It didn't have to be a story; it could be whatever. I think that was really instrumental in forming my sense of the real calm and salvation that composing gives me— this feeling of getting it together.

But then in ninth grade I had an English teacher who was wonderful in the sense that he pushed us. He made us read Eliot and Pound and all those people and showed us that we didn't have to be afraid of not understanding something: you just try to figure it out. On the other hand, he was not into writing at all. I remember that one day we asked him—and we worshiped this man—if we could write our own stuff, and he said, "I don't feel like reading a bunch of sing-songy poems." Well, that crushed us, and I believed in him so much that I thought he must be right. We're all writing a bunch of sing-songy poems. And I stopped writing. I didn't write again until twelfth grade. Finally it dawned on me that this was really stupid. Also, I had a twelfth grade teacher (I still correspond with her) who really encouraged me to read and to write. In fact, one Saturday, when I was in twelfth grade, she took me to a day-long writer's conference they had at a downtown hotel in Akron, Ohio. It was a small thing, only four high school students. Somehow she had found out that I liked to write. You see, I had never told anybody. Even when I started writing again, I never told anybody because I was ashamed. I don't know how she found out. I never asked her, but somehow she found that out and asked me if I would like to go to this, and I said, OK.

The authors were not very well known—that didn't mean anything to me. What mattered was here were real live people who wrote! Some of them made a living at it. There was a poet, there was a non-fiction writer, there was a fiction writer. These were grown people who weren't ashamed to say, "Yes, I write." So that made a difference; that was a turning point when I realized that writing wasn't anything to be ashamed of, but it was certainly something that I could say proudly that I was trying to do. That experience was the groundwork for writing for me.

Davis: You said that you compose because it's your salvation?

Dove: Yes, salvation in the sense that the sensation of composing, of writing, for me is one where I am first creating a new world through language. I'm working with this restrictive art form, and something happens when I write. The world gets larger. Things develop. In that sense, it is an exalting experience. That sounds very religious, but in that sense it is an opening, and salvation in a way because I think that in our society we move very fast. Everything is reductive. We channel our energies at things. People specialize. We are always getting smaller, restricted in most of the things we do in life. Composing is a moment when things open up from the inside, and I think that is in a certain way salvation, because you need that, too.

Davis: Do you require a special state or mood before you compose? Do you wait on this? What do you do to call up this state or mood? This is a fun question.

Dove: I do not require a special mood or state. Sometimes that happens, but I try to give myself specific times to write. That doesn't always work out

lately because of Aviva, but before (in the ideal world) I did, in fact, have
certain times, and I do write better at night. I'm a night person. My energies
are at a peak at night after 10:30 until four. It's always been this way. Before
I even wrote, my mother said as a baby I woke up at three at night and I
wanted to play and that was it. So that is just my biological makeup. My
energies are highest at that moment. On the other hand, there are times when
I don't feel like writing, or I feel like being lazy, like most of us do, and I
will make myself write.

I do not wait for that mood because I know that you can get yourself into
the mood. I also know that inertia usually wins out, and if you wait for a
mood, you'll be waiting all the time. Also, I really believe that writing is no
different from many other creative disciplines: you have to warm up; you
have to keep practicing your skills. In a way there is a kind of writing that is
like doing scales for a pianist. If I haven't been writing, or maybe writing
junk, or I haven't been trying to write, to put things down, or thinking about
it that way, when the mood comes, I'm rusty. It doesn't make any sense, so
I do write, and I try to write everyday. When I'm teaching, I try to write on
Thursdays, Fridays, and Saturdays. Those are the days when I can calm down.
By Sunday I'm thinking about school again. But I try to do concentrated
writing on those days. The other days I may be able to write for an hour or
two. Maybe if I can squeeze out the time. I keep a notebook so that there is
always that going on.

What do I do to call up this state or mood? Yes, I do have rituals for doing
this. It's all hocus-pocus, but it's a way of starting to gear myself to the
mood. I shut my door. I can't stand people to interrupt me. I put on music,
and I put on something which is not too intrusive. I usually play it over and
over again. Very often I will either put on early music— baroque music,
medieval music (the kind with viols and recorders) or jazz like Keith Jarrett
or someone like that. No words. I can't have words being spoken. I usually
have one light on, and it's dark in the rest of the room. All of this is just the
way I tend to do it. That's all.

I write by hand when I'm writing poems, and with prose I type directly
onto the page. I'll write by hand until I can't make sense of it anymore. Then
I'll go to the typewriter, and then go through more revisions. That's generally
how I do it.

Davis: Where do you get your material?
Dove: How much is external? How much is internal?

I get my material anywhere I can get it. And I don't believe there is anything that cannot be used. When I was in graduate school at Iowa, I made it a habit every two weeks to go the library. I would just walk into the stacks—someplace where I had never been before. I'd say, "Oh, let's try the third floor in this corner." Regardless of what books could be there—they could be on law, or they could be on geography, or on math—I would take out the titles that looked interesting to me. I would take down twenty books (which were as many as we could take out) and check them out. Then I'd go home, and I'd browse through these books. The librarian would always ask, "What is your major?" But what it was . . . it was fascinating, and I did get poems. I didn't do it to get poems, but I did it because there is so much I didn't know, and I couldn't ever learn everything, but I was curious. Poems did emerge from that. I've written a poem on geometry, and I've written a poem on road-building and things like that—some fascinating stuff.

I rebelled immediately in graduate school against the kind of poem that only uses literary allusions. It seemed to me so defeating, because, for me, when I first started reading, what fiction and poetry did was open up the world to me. It let me go places I couldn't go. I saw no reason to keep it then strictly literary. To me, to write is to open up the world again, so that everything that happens in the world should be used. That is something that . . . I still do that when I can.

I can't really answer how much is external and how much is internal because it's really a symbiotic kind of relationship. Also, an impression will be gotten from something external. I'll overhear something in a conversation or read something in a book that I think is interesting, or I'll clip out a want ad. I put these things in my notebook—anything that comes from the outside—in that kind of form. A word that I run across that I think is a beautiful word, I'll put it in, but then there are also some things which are internal like a line that floats up out of nowhere, whatever that means. Something floats up, or I suddenly remember something from my childhood, and I think that that is something I should write about. Probably it's 50–50. I've never gone to check.

Davis: Do you mean that almost anything can get you started?

Dove: Aha! Yes, I do begin with small things—almost always with very small things. It can be a small thing like a word. One poem I started with the name Mauricc. It turned out to be the last line of the poem. I didn't know where, what it was going to be, but it started out with that name, and it worked from there. Things can start with an image like E. I don't know. I can't think of one right now. The poem I perhaps should give you is called "Dusting." It might give you an idea if I can talk a little about how that poem came together. Just what happened.

This poem is two or three different things. First of all, the name Maurice. I met someone named Maurice and thought, Oh, yeah. I had heard of this name before, but what a nice name! It would really be a nice word to use, so I put it down in my book. I was in Berlin at the time. I met an actress, and we were talking. Berliners like their apartments very cold. They always open the windows in the morning to air them out. Well, her boyfriend told me this story: they had a goldfish, and he said that one morning they had opened up the windows, and they forgot to close them again when they went out. When they came back late in the evening after their performances (it was pretty late), it had snowed that day. There was snow on the floor, and the goldfish was frozen. This was a cold apartment. They can get that cold because these are those old buildings that have no central heating. The goldfish was frozen in the bowl. Well, he said they took the goldfish and put it on the stove, and just let it warm up slowly. He said the goldfish was alive again. You know, fish do this.

Now this was just a little story, but I thought it was great, so I wrote that down in my book. I had no idea what I was going to do with it. These things occurred far apart from one another, too. I'm not sure if there's more. Then, yes, I was doing something . . . I was into names then for some reason, and hit upon the name Beulah. When I was a child it was a name like Bertha, and you made jokes about Beulah, Big Beulah. I thought, Wouldn't it be nice to use the name Beulah and try to get it in a poem. So I looked up the derivation of Beulah because I knew it was a biblical name and played around with that. That was where the poem actually began. I was playing around with this idea of Beulah.

Then another thing came in. I was reading Gaston Bachelard's *Poetics of Space*, which is a wonderful book. In this book (he's a philosopher), he was talking about spaces like shelves and drawers and attics and how we relate to them in a phenomenological way. He talked about dusting in a very romantic way. There was someone dusting to restore something. It's almost like excavating. When you restore something, you discover the shine in it. So he was talking about that. That happened at the same time I was reading about Beulah, so I decided to make Beulah dust. That's how the poem started. She was dusting. I had no idea where it was going to go from there, but it started relatively small with a name, trying to figure out what the name meant. The name does mean "desert in peace." It has different derivations.

She is dusting in a very bright room, and there's a sense of dust and desert. It was all mixing up, but I had no idea where it was going to go. When I get stuck (and I often get stuck), I'll stop writing. Sometimes I stop writing because I don't know where it's going, and I'll pick it up another day. I looked through my notebook—which is one way I have of warming up—and I saw the story with the fish. I put it in there, and I started working with that. It was a memory that she had as she was dusting. And then I thought, Where did she get this fish? Then, going back from that, I thought, Where do people get goldfish? I thought about the fairs and how someone wins you a goldfish, this tradition or thing. So she remembers an old boyfriend whose name she can't remember (this came in later) who had won the fish for her. How the fish had frozen one day, how she warmed it up, and it could swim again. By the end of the poem (the poem is about memory), she's trying to remember his name because it was a long time ago. She can't remember his name. She thinks it's Michael, and then at the end it turns out to be Maurice.

Now that was the first poem in a long series which actually started *Thomas and Beulah*. The poem is also in my previous book because I didn't realize it was part of a series. I started developing a whole life around Beulah. One of the things that goes through the book (and this is another one of these small things that became a larger issue in the book) is this whole idea of being something bright and fragile, trapped in some way, so there are lots of canaries in the book. There are also references to (there's this French thing going through the book) her dreams of getting away. Her dream is France. Europe, or Paris is the romantic ideal, so that pops up in a lot of poems. It really started with this poem. Maurice then becomes this French name that is somehow a romantic name for her. That did start a whole section of this book when I think about it. But it all started with small things. I did not plan that from the larger thing down. So the book does transform or change independently of myself in a way.

Davis: Do you let the poem develop itself after you get to a certain point? For instance, Stephen [Davis] says he starts out with his paintings with very definite ideas, definite shapes. He may see a skyline before he starts. He says that when he gets about half-way through the picture, it just takes over itself.

Dove: Well, I think it does. It's not half and half with me. I think it's in thirds. Often in the beginning, when I'm starting to write, it's not under control in the sense that I may start out with something very small. I have no idea where it's going to go. I am working blind, and I'm floating. That's a very scary part, but one that I like a lot. Just that sitting down with the blank piece of paper, playing around, letting my mind just go where it wants to go. There's a certain point (about a third of the way through) where it starts to take shape, when I think I know what it's going to be about, or I have a sense of it. When I'm working toward that, I feel in control.

Then there is (it's not always like this), but there is this point two-thirds of the way through where I am stuck. I seem to be in control, but it's not going anywhere. That's the point where I have to—and again this is the hardest part for me—have to suffer that indecision and that kind of feeling of help-lessness and let the poem sit for awhile until I can get back to that first stage again, which is floating. This is another period where I let the poem go and let it decide what it wants to do. Then I come back again. But usually—it's like thirds, or it doesn't go—I don't start out with a definite idea. I can imagine that with a painter that visual sense which gives you more concrete things. Does that make sense?

Davis: Yes. Perhaps you begin with an idea or produce a piece that does not work.

Dove: Oh, yes!

Davis: Do you later find yourself using that idea and creating a piece that does work? If so, can you recall some of the differences between the two and perhaps some of the elements that made it work later?

Dove: For every poem that I've written there are at least five that didn't work—that either were abandoned or were finished but are very dull and just didn't work. I do use ideas and create a piece that does work sometimes. I never throw away anything, which makes my life a complete mess, but I never throw away drafts. I never throw away failed poems, and I do find myself going back to older poems and looking through them and lifting things that seem interesting, but didn't work on the whole.

I can tell you one; it's not the best example, but it will do. There's a poem (it's a longish poem) in *Museum* called "Parsley." It's in two parts. This poem started out differently. It was because I had the idea, and I knew the facts before I began. It was an historical event that had happened. It was an incident, and I wanted to try to make a cycle, a drama, and investigate evil from the interior of the main character's mind, the villain's mind. So in a way, I was encumbered by the fact that I knew where it had to end. I had everything in the middle, and it took about three years to write—on and off and off and on.

I decided to try it in strict forms. I decided to try the poem in a villanelle, and I did that pretty well. Then I tried to do it in a sestina. The villanelle seemed to work. I had finished that first, and I was trying to convince myself that that was the whole poem. I showed it to Fred, who sees everything, and he said, "Well, this is very nice, but it's not the whole poem." And I stomped away furiously. I knew it wasn't the whole poem. I was trying to kid myself. I had been working on a sestina, which is a real weird thing. It's these six-line stanzas and you have six words that are the end word on every line, six different words, and then there's a certain arrangement. They switch around. Each stanza has to end on those words—really a torture of a form—but I needed something very obsessive. I needed something to work this main character into the fury that he needed in order to kill 20,000 people.

I was working on that sestina, and it was just *awful*. It was *awful*, and I kept working at it. I was very frustrated, so I put it away. I said, This poem is dead. I'll never be able to finish this! But it haunted me. A couple of months later I took it out in a fury. I went to my room, and I said, This is it. I'm going to do it. I wrote it all in prose. I took this whole sestina. I just wrote, wrote, wrote. As I was writing it, I was forcing myself to write just as fast as I could. As I started to get into it, I started making lines. It started breaking into lines, so there was a breakthrough. In a way that duplicates that three-part thing I was telling you about before. In a way, it worked because I tried to put it in a form, and afterwards I bust out of it. Then I could come down to some medium ground. It took a lot of time in between.

I have taken ideas that did not work as poems and made them into stories.

Davis: I didn't realize you did short stories.

Dove: Yes, I have a little book [*Fifth Sunday*] that came out. It's interesting how it works because I don't think that the two composition processes are that similar. At least for me, they are not. They're different—very different. I can't even explain it. I wish I could.

Davis: Are you confined by form in poetry?

Dove: No. It has little to do with that. Usually I know if something is going to be a story or a poem. But there have been ideas which could have gone either way. I'll try it either as one or the other, but if I start out with a word or a line, I know if it's going to go into a poem or a short story. There are ideas that I've done in both forms, but I emphasize different things. For instance, a story that my grandmother told me about my grandfather coming north on the river boat. I ended up not emphasizing the main event of the story, which was the death of his friend by drowning in the river. I ended up talking much more about what happened to him afterwards in the short story. Whereas when I did it in the poem, that event of his friend drowning became the pivot. I can't explain why. I don't know.

Davis: If problems develop, are they usually related to you or your environment?

Dove: Well, there are two kinds of problems: one of them is just this "getting stuck" thing, and I don't consider that a problem really. I consider that part of the whole creative process. There are points where I feel that our minds are so adept at "protecting" us that you have to use a lot of tricks in order to fake it out. We repress a lot of things. When I'm writing, the hardest part is to get at things that have been tucked away, so I consider that problem—getting stuck—just a natural problem. That's just something that naturally comes out. You get exhausted; you've been writing for awhile; the energy goes, and everything shuts down. So you just have to do something else. Thomas Edison used to take a nap. That makes sense.

But problems—what I consider problems—are usually related to my environment, and that is simply not having the time to write. Not having the right kind of time—three hours I think is a minimum amount to start writing poetry. I can do prose in less. I mean, I can write a page of prose in less—or get prepared to write it. But with poetry, the first hour and a half is spent just clearing the junk away that's in the mind. Just trying to get started, just scribbling and doing stupid stuff like writing a letter form to get it out of the way, cleaning up my desk, maybe reading a little bit, maybe just listening to a little music, leafing through my notebook—all of this is just a kind of preparation for learning or getting quiet enough to listen.

Davis: OK, so while you're doing all of that, you're still trying to heed that inner force?

Dove: Yes, and I'm just decompressing a little bet. So problems for me are things which hinder that process, which means not enough time to do it. If I have an hour, it's *not enough time*. It's just frustrating. If I have the feeling that I'm going to be interrupted (I'm unfortunately one of these people if I get interrupted that's it), I'm frustrated, and I'm furious, whereas Fred can get interrupted, and it doesn't bother him. So if I know, for instance, that

Aviva is around the house playing (even if she isn't near me) it's very hard for me to write because she may come in any minute and ask me something.

The telephone was an awful problem until we got the answering machine. That's why I don't listen to it. The answering machine does all the work. That was a saving thing—to have an answering machine. Before that I could not let the telephone ring. It drove me crazy just to hear it ring, so that was a real problem.

Davis: Are the results sometimes unexpected?

Dove: Oh! I always have unexpected results. Always. I mean, everything is unexpected. Some are more unexpected than others, but, as I said, it's very rare that I know exactly where it's going to end.

Davis: In fact, that poem that you had problems with, "Parsley," didn't you say that it was because you had the ending in mind?

Dove: Yes. I *knew* the ending. It was terrible. I mean, I knew . . . I didn't know the words of the ending. I knew what was going to happen by the end. There are poems that start with the last line. I mean, I may have the last line. With that other poem "Dusting" I knew that fairly early in that composition process. But that's different from knowing the ending. OK? And I don't work from the beginning to end either. The poem may start in the middle. I may have a line that seems like the middle line. I don't know why.

Davis: Then after you've done it, you may realize it needs something.

Dove: Yes. I used to never start with titles. With my first book, I think that every poem was an agony deciding the title. I had a great problem, but with the second book, *Museum*, almost every poem started with the title. It was bizarre! I had a list of titles, and I don't know why. I had a list of titles and no poems for a long time. Then the poems came. I don't know why that happened. I have no idea. With this third book [*Thomas and Beulah*] it was half and half.

Davis: And when you had the titles, did they frequently come from images that you had or something pulled from your notebook?

Dove: There were often things pulled from notebooks. I didn't use all the titles. There were some where I tried to write a poem, and it didn't work. I was living in Germany at the time. That might have had something to do with it. Titles are different in German (that's a different subject altogether), but I would go to bookstores a lot. I love to look at the German books. I like the designs. They are very classy. I just looked at titles. There were some wonderful titles, and they were different from titles in America. I can't really explain that, but it might be that that just got me geared toward titles. It was the most bizarre thing I've ever had happen to me. I had a list of twenty-four titles. No poems.

Davis: What restraints are on you as you work? Do you work best under the pressure of a deadline?

Dove: When I think of the constraints that are on me from the outside, it is time, and now that's just everything—time. Am I going to do this?

I don't work best under pressure or a deadline. I fall apart. I'll get it done, but I do not like that. I think it really comes from growing up and being taught as I grew up that you do things, and you don't wait until the last minute. You do it early. This sounds terrible: I always had my papers done beforehand. It sounds so goody-goody, but it's just that I hate pressure. I really dislike pressure. I tend to worry a lot, and it's just bad for me, so I don't like pressure. One of the things that is hardest for me recently is that I've had pressure and deadlines where things did get done at the last minute simply because there wasn't enough time to do it when I wanted to do it. A lot of that has to do with having a child and having the day broken up so that I couldn't do it when I wanted to do it. (I'm under a deadline right now that's going to murder me.)

When I usually think "deadlines," that is non-creative work. I refuse to allow myself to be put under pressure for poems. One of the hardest things that's happened recently is to have people from magazines write to solicit work, to ask me if I could send them some poems. I want to do it, but the very fact that they just asked me stops me from writing. I mean, it's as if suddenly there is someone who wants this poem, so I have this person in the background. I much prefer writing without knowing that it's ever going to be published. You know, writing into the void. So the hardest thing is to know that if I finish this poem I'm going to send it to this magazine. God, I hate that! So I have to push all that away. I can't work like that! It drives me crazy.

Davis: And the audience. Do you gear your work for a specific audience?

Dove: No. I do not. I have no sense of what my audience is, and I do not gear it toward a specific audience—mainly because I think I can't even determine who that audience is. For me, I think it would be very limiting to think of a certain kind of audience. I think it would limit where the work could go and who it could reach.

Just recently I came back from a conference—a women writers' conference in Lexington, Kentucky. I did a reading/talk, talk/reading in the community. It turned out that I was in a Black community, a slum community, at a church. Most of the people who came were over sixty and obviously had not read very much in their lives. It was the first time that I was confronted so starkly with this kind of situation where this was not maybe who I imagined my audience to be necessarily. I talked about storytelling, and I read a story from my short story book, and it *worked*. Then I realized that if I had thought about who my audience was it might have limited me in a way.

I prefer thinking that the audience is whoever is out there who picks it up and is touched by it. I suppose I am enough of an optimist (though generally speaking, I am not an optimist) to imagine that if I feel something deeply and try to get it across in the best way I know how that there is someone out there who can also feel it.

Davis: Then what type of response do you hope to get from your audience?

Dove: I hope to get someone who can read something that I've written and feel that it rejuvenates—that it opens up something for them. The kind of response I would hope is the kind of response that I had as a child and even now when I read something—the "Yes, I know what you mean" that makes me stop and knocks me out of the race, so to speak. That's what I hope.

Davis: How much do you revise? How many times? How much later?

Dove: I revise *a lot—an awful lot*. Most of the time I never count, but I would say that most poems have at least twenty drafts. When I say drafts, I mean not from the notation in the notebook (if it's in the notebook), but from the point where I take it out of the notebook and try to make it into a specific poem, so I would say at least twenty drafts.

As I said, I write by hand and usually do about five or six drafts by hand. It may not be complete. It may be two-thirds of a poem or something. And that is the point where I *need* to see the line. I need to see the *shape* the poem has taken on the page. I'll start typing, and I'll type up a draft, take it out of the typewriter and immediately start marking it up. Now I have a computer, so I just print it out again.

Davis: So you do use a word processor?

Dove: I do use a word processor when I start to do the typing, but I don't like to revise on the word processor. I don't like to say, Oh, let's switch this line around and see. I don't know why. Maybe it's old-fashioned of me because I just started using it. I *need* the pen touching the paper—you know—at points, certain points during that composition process.

And even with prose. If I type, I can type prose directly into the word processor, and I do do that. But when I'm going to revise it, I don't read it on the screen and make revisions. I print it out, and then I take the pen and I mark it, and I have to have that. Otherwise, I feel like I'm not touching it. I have to touch it!

If there is a point where I will revise a poem much later, it's when it is about to go into a book. In one book I had I had two sets of galleys. There were so many changes made in the first set because I had revised a couple of poems. That's the latest that I have ever done it. I believe really that once it comes out in a book I should leave it alone and go do something new. I mean, I'm not like Yeats running around, saying, "Let's revise everything again."

Davis: Stephen was telling me the other day about Robert Motherwell who saw one of his paintings thirty years later and asked the gallery if he could take it home for the evening. Then he went home and added something to the painting. It wasn't finished.

Dove: Wow! That's a wonderful story. That hasn't happened yet, but it might happen. What's happened so far with me is that by the time the book comes out there's such a gap. It's sometimes a whole year. I'm in a different place, and to me it seems redundant unless something is unfinished inside of me—something to go back to. There must be a different way of approaching the problem. I would rather write a new poem.

Davis: When do you consider it finished?

Dove: It's finished when it's finished. I don't think there's a single poem that I've written that I think is finished.

Davis: Well, that's the reaction I get from most people.

Dove: It's like, OK, this is the best I can do. Here it is. There's always wrinkles.

Davis: Finally, is there anything you might want to add?

Dove: Well, the only thing (I don't know if this is something you want) I suppose is that because I do both poetry and fiction, maybe I should talk a little bit about the differences in the composition processes between the two. For me, they are very different. I mentioned this before. I can't really define it. (That helps you a lot!)

Part of the difference is the materials I use. For poetry I use a fountain pen or a medium ball point pen. I write by hand on lined paper, either yellow legal paper (8 1/2 x 11, not the legal length) or, when I can get it, white lined paper without holes. (I'm very particular. I suppose it nearly amounts to fetishism. I even have dreams about being in stationery stores with my choice of rag bond, tablets and notebooks, etc .) I *hate* flair pens and use pencil only when I'm feeling extremely insecure. I need the contact of the pen on paper; I like to hear the scratch and/or feel the ink gliding onto bond. The slowness of writing by hand seems ideally suited to composing poetry; and the unevenness of handwriting (e.g., one can't really *see* the relative lengths of lines) prevents me from forcing lines into pretty patterns; instead, I trust my inner ear, my breathing.

Prose is another matter entirely. I need the speed of the typewriter (nowadays, the word processor) to keep the story from falling apart. (Incidentally, I think more logically and clearly when I "think" on the typewriter. Logic is not a useful commodity when composing poetry.) I type single-spaced for a similar reason: to see the whole as a piece, a fluid bulk. When I get a first draft, I rarely revise on the screen. Instead, I make a print-out and scribble in corrections and additions, deletions, etc., by hand. Again, I feel the need for the physical contact with the paper.

There are also differences in mood. As I mentioned, I need large blocks of pure time in order to compose poetry; prose—or snippets of a story—can be accomplished in 1 1/2 hours or so. I've even managed to make significant revisions on a page or two of prose while waiting for spaghetti to cook. I can't figure this out, except to note that there is so much to prose composition that requires *management*—he said/she saids, insertions of descriptions, etc. But every word of a poem—indeed, every blank space—is crucial.

Topics differ too. Anything is a fit subject for a poem, any conflict is the germ of a story. I like to stretch the limits of both genres. So many of my poems occur in sequences— thus, the poems are lyrical but, taken as a whole, the sequence tells a story. Many stories concentrate on the breaking or evoking of a mood—like a James Joyce story (I hope!), there is little actual action. The stories are more psychodrama than gripping adventure.

Language Is More Clay Than Stone

Susan Swartwout / 1989

Susan Swartwout's interview was conducted in 1989 at Knox College in Galesburg, Illinois, where Rita Dove received an honorary degree. The interview appeared in *Farmer's Market*, Vol. 6, No. 2, 1989. Reprinted by permission of Susan Swartwout.

Swartwout: When you were talking about *Thomas and Beulah* I realized that the story was writing you—that it was a way of dealing with personal history, or a way of asking about your history. You said of *Museum*, on the other hand, that it had to deal with certain artifacts in your life. Explain that: artifacts.

Dove: *Museum* was a much more constructed book, I think, now that I look back on it, than *Thomas and Beulah*—though in *Thomas and Beulah* things seem to fit together—in the sense of consciously looking for moments and people and events which become frozen and emblematic. That's what I meant about artifacts, that they reflect this moment, whether it's a person like Benjamin Banneker or whether it's a fossil, like in "The Bowl, a Fish, and a Stone," or whether it's "Nestor's Bathtub," or whether it's memories of my father and my childhood. All these things become frozen like emblems of certain kinds of events which shape consciousness. In the whole section, for instance, childhood exists almost as though in a bell jar. You remember it very well, but also it is a closed-off area.

I had the title for the book *Museum* very early, before I had written even a third of it, almost. I had a sense of where I wanted it to go. But I didn't want to have only museum pieces, not just the kinds of things you'd expect in museums. But as the fossil of a fish can suggest to us a whole prehistoric area (you have to re-imagine yourself back to that moment), in that same way, I wanted to look at some of these figures, who may not be the most important people in history, but certainly are indicative of things in our history. So Rafael Trujillo as a villain in that sense is indicative of all of the kind of arbitrary cruelty that can happen.

Swartwout: So these kinds of artifacts are the touchstone you weave into these lack-of-self-consciousness poems that you write? I was going to ask you about that, too, whether the self-consciousness really does mean anything. You called it "the worst thing that could happen to a poet." How do you focus on your poem's body language without being self-conscious?

Dove: Well, everyone has their tricks. I keep myself from becoming self-conscious—though I can get self-conscious—by trying to direct my attention other places. It's like not looking directly at the poem, you know, not looking at it too hard or it just disappears. You just can't get to where you want to go because you're trying too hard. For instance, in *Thomas and Beulah* as I mentioned yesterday when I started on the story that the book was a single poem. I really honestly thought at that point, when I wrote the first poem, that I was only going to write one poem; I thought at the time I wrote this poem, This is a story about my grandmother and I'm gonna write it, and that's it. I thought, OK, that's over.

A couple of days passed, and I felt a little dissatisfied. I said, "This isn't it. You can't just end and disown part of a story." Then I said, "Well, maybe I have to write a group of poems, about six." I kept talking about writing a suite of poems. I was going to write this little suite of poems about Thomas and the mandolin. I had about six poems—I even sent those six poems off, I remember, to the *Ohio Review*—and I thought it was a nice little group. Luckily I was in Europe, and it takes so long for things to get back and forth. After a couple of weeks, I realized this wasn't enough either. So I wrote them and I said, "Forget it. Just forget that one," and I began filling in some of the gaps. At that point I thought, OK, a section of a book.

Part of it, I think, is that no matter how much you love writing, you have to admit that it's frightening too. It's also hard work, and you'd much rather it be easy. I was really hoping that I wasn't going to have to write that much. When I finally realized that it was going to have to be as long as a whole book, I was really depressed for a while. I said, "Oh no! I don't want to do this! This is too hard." So that's the moment when I became self-conscious, when I realized that it was going to be a whole book. Up to that point, I was just not thinking about it too much.

When I wrote the poem "Dusting," I realized that it had to be a whole book. When I first wrote that poem—it came very early, I think—I didn't realize that it was part of the group. It came before I had even written six poems. When I wrote "Dusting," I thought, Oh, this is just a poem about some woman like my grandmother, just dusting. But I didn't connect what the unconscious was doing until much later, and I said, "Oh God, this is my grandmother!" She was saying, "You can't tell one side of the story," and it was just that simple, suddenly. At that moment I began to feel self-conscious.

With every poem there is a different way you might have to use to get over the self-consciousness. What I did was to begin to concentrate on the images. In other words, do not think so much about the entire thing (I've got to tell their two lives. What do I choose? all that kind of stuff). I began to look at the poems that I'd written and ask, "What do their lives revolve around?" This is, in a sense, a technical question, too. It's also looking at the poem intrinsically. As images go into the poem, you think, What happens in Thomas's poems that seems central? For him it was the mandolin. With Beulah, it started out with the color yellow, which happened to end up as a goldfish, something which is locked up and has to get away. Then the yellow scarf. And then it changed into a bird, it became the canary. So that was a kind of wonderful transformation; it's not that I thought all that out: I'm going to make this goldfish turn into a bird. My grandmother had parakeets, but I didn't want parakeets because they're blue, so I changed it to a canary because it was yellow. That led me to another place. It kept me from becoming too self-conscious about what I was doing, which was, in a sense, taking my grandparents' lives and transforming them into poetry. Which was a kind of scary thing.

Swartwout: Christina Rossetti talked about having a dream where the sunlight turned into yellow canaries and all the canaries in London gathered in the park, and then flew back to their cages. One thing that I noticed in *Thomas and Beulah* is that they have these almost counter-images: Thomas has the mandolin as his music, and she has the canaries for her music. Images in "Dusting" and one other poem where Beulah, "obedient among her trinkets," and Beulah's "secrets like birdsong from the air," and then her ballerina image and the tutus exploding. Were you thinking consciously of gender differences there that are more general than just, say, your grandparents?

Dove: I wouldn't say I was thinking of it consciously; you know, I've never approached a poem in that sense. In fact, in a poem I'm never consciously thinking of gender or race, but obviously it's going to be contained in the poem somewhere. When I was writing that book, I would go back and forth through Thomas's section and Beulah's section. I was very conscious of the fact that the poems moved in different ways, that there was something different about the way he thought and the way she thought. I still don't know to this day that I could ever explain it any better than that. I probably would resist trying to list the ways I would think she would think, and so forth. But I did feel that there was a very different way in which they looked at the world. There also are some similarities. I think that her poems are quieter, the lines are longer, but I don't know what more that means. Certain things—the fact that he has a mandolin that has been out in the world and he hangs it up on the wall, and that she has the birds that sing but are in their own cages, they were at some point conscious, but not when I was writing them.

Swartwout: We have been talking about self-consciousness versus not being self-conscious. It reminded me of what you said about the language being like an unconscious current, and that you just have to sort of write, and not think about what you're putting down, kind of like writing with your eyes closed. I wondered if you thought that some of your writing was to encourage that kind of mental process in the first place, to get that language going.

Dove: Do you mean in myself?

Swartwout: Yes, just to get yourself started with different words and images.

Dove: It's very hard to say what comes first, you know, the chicken or the egg, or in terms of the poem, whether it's a line or whether it's an image, which is not language, or an emotion. Different poems start with different things. It's always dangerous to think about your process, but I could say I do believe that very early on for me the language clicks in.

Let's put it this way: if I'm working on a poem and get stuck (it happens a lot), my first recourse is to go to the language. In other words, instead of thinking about where I want to go, I think about the cadence. Very often I think that I can feel the cadence of the next line, but I don't know any of the words in it. That can happen, and I think that can be particularly useful in a poem where in fact you know a lot about the theme of the poem. And partially that helps out an awful lot, but the problem with that poem was that I knew what was going to happen. The event was there—I mean it was a fact—and that's what I wanted to write about. The poem was always circling around that moment, but how do you get through it? It was sound that carries me through most of the time, and images which recurred.

You see, language—I've said it somewhere else before, but it's the best comparison I can come up with—language is really like clay. And it's more clay than it is stone. I don't want to use the idea of sculptors and that kind of resistance. It is something you put your fingers into and form and squish around. You can switch things around. There are many ways of giving a powerful effect. But to have the chutzpah to manipulate the language, too, to really try to get it out of its commonplace syntax—because that puts you to sleep; I mean, it's the stuff you hear every day—without making it too strange, to get out just enough so that someone is aware of its cadence, instead of having it be just white noise—that's part of the job of a writer.

And it's part of a way to jog your perceptions so that they come out; it's part of the way to keep from thinking ordinary kinds of things. That's why I really can't emphasize it enough. It's not that I undervalue or devalue emotion; obviously, all the language-play in the world is nothing without the stuff behind it. But sometimes in cases of extreme emotion, the trick is not to rip yourself apart and put your liver on the page. That often doesn't work, to try to force it out that way. But to try another way. Say, I tried to write about this death and it bothers me very much, and I can't really do it. Let me try a villanelle, for instance. Or I'm writing these really long lines, and it's just kind of spilling out and spilling out and I have too much on the page. Instead of saying consciously, "I've got to write myself insane," I'll make the poem skinny, use the same words and break it up. But then it's a back and forth thing, too, because then you try to break it up into smaller units, and suddenly by breaking it into smaller units, two bricks come together that wouldn't normally have been on the same line, and it jogs something in your memory. Then you go with that, and go back and forth.

Swartwout: So you're talking about the form in your poetry. What do you see as the relationship between that and what you're actually writing about? Again, is that conscious?

Dove: Well, the question of form and content is absolutely unanswerable. They all make sense, and they all sound great, and no one knows what any of them means, I think. They are, I think, in the ideal poem, absolutely inseparable. The form must feel inevitable. In that sense, there is no such thing as "free verse," whatever that is. A poem determines it's own . . . I don't want to say cage . . . maybe latticework or something like that, something that you weave in. And it's not enough to say, "This is a skinny poem, a poem of long lines," or as blocks or there are internal rhymes, or whatever; it's also how fast it moves down the page and if there are a lot of one-syllable words in the poem and if they're crisp or not, and at what point do you slow the poem up? Is it a poem where the line endings make you go on to the next line or is it one where they make you stop? All of these things have something to do with the way the entire body gets engaged in pronouncing the words. Even if you don't say the poem out loud, even if you are reading it, you are still putting it through your body; you're putting the words in your mouth and imagining that. The whole body gets involved, and in that sense the poem really becomes a dance, and form is just the positions that we all move through. I have no idea if that makes sense.

Swartwout: I have a question about self-consciousness: as a Black writer, do you find yourself, in the process of writing poetry, feeling that you have an obligation to the Black community to convey certain things or certain ideas? Do you feel that's something that cripples you or enhances you?

Dove: It doesn't have to temper self-consciousness. I think—and this could go for a Black writer or a woman writer or whoever—but I think I would say very provocatively now that really the writer has no obligation to any group. What the writer has an obligation to is to themselves and whatever it is they are trying to say, and to be absolutely honest in whatever it is, and to say it in the best way possible. But what that means ultimately is that if one does that, one is in a certain way, serving the interests of the people. What is the most important thing, I feel, about being a Black writer is that the things I would talk about in a poem or a book like *Thomas and Beulah*, the kinds of emotions they go through, some of them are absolutely informed by Black experience, some of them are informed by being a woman (or a man), some of them are informed by being an American in a certain situation, or being poor; others can be absolutely universal. But if while I was writing it I had thought, Well, I want to serve this group, then I think I would have been crippled. Because then the feeling is, once you try to imagine what any group would like you to say (it's like trying to figure out the marketplace), you stop up something inside.

There is a wonderful essay—I think it came out in 1926—"The Negro Writer and the Racial Mountain." It said that what the Negro writer has to do is write from their own Black selves, and if that pleases white people we're glad, and if it doesn't we don't care; and if it pleases Black people we're glad, and if it doesn't we don't care. Basically, this is what your duty is. But that also means that one is bound to disappoint, and also that once they are out there you cannot control your writings anymore, other than to make sure each poem has its own integrity. If at any point you compromise the integrity of the poem because you're trying to please some people, take something out because it might reflect negatively, then you've taken away the integrity of the poem. And it's very often those kinds of sequences which can easily be excerpted and used by any group one way or the other for propaganda, whether for or against a cause. It's tricky. It's the kind of thing where I would love to be able to say to a group (and I certainly wouldn't say to my grand-mother's Evening Star club), "No, I'm not writing for you." I mean, you don't say it because that's not what they mean when they ask that question, "Are you writing for us or not?" What they mean is, "Are you telling our story?" So that's a different question. But it does make you self-conscious.

And it's been something that I've been wrestling with because after the Pulitzer Prize, people would ask me, "Are you a Black writer, or . . . ?" The implication is that if you say you are a Black writer, then you aren't some other kind of writer. Obviously I'm a Black writer, and I wouldn't say I wasn't a Black writer. I'm a woman writer. If someone asks me that, what they're asking actually is, "Do you align yourself with . . . ?" And you don't know exactly what book they mean when they say that. I find it is that kind of drawing lines.

Swartwout: Do you think the poet needs to disassociate to create? And if so, how? In what way? Completely physically or spiritually?

Dove: I don't believe in the poet in the ivory tower. I need quiet when I write, and I need to be alone as much as I can be. But I can't stay in that place, I can't live in that space. Poetry is about life, which does not mean, on the other hand, that one doesn't sometimes draw back from life and think about it. But I think there's a kind of a give-and-take and dipping in and out. I guess poets get that reputation for being kind of other-worldly and, you know, "dippy" and other things, mainly because when you start thinking about very ordinary moments, when you start looking around and observing very closely, you simply get out of sync with the rest of the world. We're trained to walk across a campus on our way to class, let's say, and not see anything 'cause you gotta get there in ten minutes and you don't have time to hear the birds and to smell. So you automatically select certain things, block out other ones, and go. When a poem slows down that process and you can freeze every moment—a small moment that at some point in your life you've had that moment coming and you do see something that jumps out and reminds you—when you start doing that and closing to it more and more often so that you start thinking like that, then you get to class late. You're just slightly out of sync, and I think that that is what just happens: one starts to slow down.

But on the other hand, too, I feel very strongly about poets being in fact "in" the world: that one has a life. One can be a poet but you have to have a life. If you don't have a life then I don't see where you're going to write your poems from. And you don't live in order to write either. I mean, you don't go out and have experiences just so you can write about them. Because the only way I feel that you can write about experience is if you experience it deeply. Which means that while you're experiencing it, you aren't thinking about poetry. I don't know if that answers your question, but I hope it does.

Swartwout: How long was your stay in Germany?
Dove: It was a full year, from July to July.

Swartwout: Did you continue your writing while you were in Germany, and how difficult was that?
Dove: I did continue writing. When I went to Germany, I went (supposedly) to better my German, and I wanted to translate their poetry. So I took lots of courses at the University of Tübingen in literature, and I studied a lot of German poetry. I was writing while I was there, and I wrote afterwards.

It's an interesting question, because we were talking earlier about what happens when you're in a foreign country and you finally notice that you're dreaming in that other language, and that you're actually speaking it without translating it in your head. I began to let go of my English—not that I couldn't talk; I mean, obviously I could use language, but it was self-conscious. I don't think it happens to everyone, but I think for me it happened maybe because I do tend to be so musically oriented, and I went for the cadence of German.

As I tried to write, I couldn't remember what was normal English. The syntax was very different than in German. Now that happened at the beginning, and in fact I was glad when the year was over so I could get back and immerse myself in English again. For a while I felt very schizophrenic. It was like I'd immerse myself in German or English, and there was nothing in between.

The second time, I went to Europe for a longer period of time. I went for a year and a half in 79–80, and my husband already knew West Berlin. I was writing *Museum*, and the short stories. And I started writing short stories because I thought my poems were beginning to sound German; the verbs were all at the end, and it was just weird.

The point is, now I can switch back and forth. I think that has a lot to do with just getting comfortable with the language, and you'll end up being able to switch back and forth.

Swartwout: Do you think there was any element of that experience which carried over to improving your writing? Not their experiences, but just the use of language?

Dove: Definitely. Definitely. It's hard to pinpoint, but I think that German had a great deal to do with some of the things that happened in my poems. In German, very often when you have a past participle, a participial phrase, or something like that, the verb ends with an "-en." So you have something like, "He used to the store to go." And these sentences can be pages long, and the verb is at the end, which means you have to spend all that knowledge and all this energy to hold it there, and you don't know what to do until you get to the verb, and then everything kind of goes PHLOONK! Now when that happens, it's a wonderful magical moment when everything finally makes sense. I think that notion of trying to suspend for as long as possible different pieces of a puzzle, let's say, until they come together at the end of an image is something I got from the feel of German. I think that it has happened in some of my poems—I wish I could quote them, but I can't think of anything right now—where the last line or two lines tie it all together with an epiphany at the end. I think that happens more often after the first book of poems.

Swartwout: You were talking before about being so musically oriented, and you've been talking about cadence and that kind of thing. Because you write a lot about music and musicians, I was wondering if music has ever inspired you to write.

Dove: I'll start back a little bit. I played cello for about fifteen years. I was really very serious about it, and then decided in college that I really didn't want to be a performer. I really didn't want to get out there on stage; I was very shy. I didn't know I was going to end up on stage anyway. I decided that wasn't really for me, but I've always played an instrument or been in-volved in music, not only just listening to it, but doing something with it. Right now I'm playing in a gamba group. A gamba is an early instrument, like a cello. I also sang in a choir this year in North Carolina after taking voice lessons for the first time because I'd always wanted to take them.

In a sense, that does inspire my book, but not in any direct way. I need music; it makes me happy, and I want it in my life. I do play music while I'm working, but in a very odd way, that music has to be almost like white noise. It can't have words in it—I want instrumental music, please! I love jazz and blues, but I also love classical music, early music particularly. It just depends on my mood.

Writing for Those Moments of Discovery

Steven Schneider / 1989

Steven Schneider's interview with Rita Dove took place in Tacoma, Washington, just after she had won the Pulitzer Prize for *Thomas and Beulah*. It appeared in the *Iowa Review* in 1989 and is reprinted by permission.

Schneider: How does it feel to be the first Black woman poet since Gwendolyn Brooks to win the Pulitzer Prize?

Dove: My first reaction was quite simply disbelief. Disbelief that, first of all, there hadn't been another Black person since Gwendolyn Brooks in 1950 to win the Pulitzer Prize in poetry, though there certainly have been some outstanding Black poets in that period. On a public level, it says something about the nature of cultural politics in this country. It's a shame actually. On a personal level, it's overwhelming.

Schneider: Did you feel you had written something special when you completed *Thomas and Beulah*?

Dove: I felt I had written something larger than myself, larger than what I had hoped for it to be. I did not begin this sequence as a book; it began as a poem. The book grew poem by poem, and it wasn't until I was about a third of the way through that I realized it would have to be a book. So I grew with it and I had to rise to it. I started with the Thomas poems because I wanted to understand my grandfather more—what he was like as a young man, how he grew up and became the man I knew. To do that, though, I realized pretty early on that I could rely neither on my memories of him nor on the memories of my mother or her sisters or brothers, but I had to get to know the town he lived in. What was Akron, Ohio, like in the '20s and '30s? It was different from the Akron I knew. That meant I had to go to the library and read a whole bunch of stuff I never counted on researching to try to get a sense of that period of time in the industrial Midwest. On the other levels, I had to enter male consciousness in a way which was—well, I knew I could do it for one or two poems, but this was an extended effort. I was really, at a certain point, very, very driven to be as honest as I could possibly be. Also, I didn't

62

want to impose my language or my sensibility upon their lives. And things
got . . .

Schneider: Things got very complicated?
Dove: That's right.

Schneider: Did you have a different kind of satisfaction about finishing
this book than your other two books?
Dove: It was different. I am not going to say I was more satisfied; I don't
think I have a favorite book of mine. But there was a feeling of relief because
I had made it through.

Schneider: How long did it take you to write *Thomas and Beulah*?
Dove: About five years. I was working on the *Museum* poems in the middle
of that, too. So, altogether five years.

Schneider: You've mentioned to me that your life has been quite hectic
since you won the Pulitzer. How does this affect your life and your writing?
Dove: First of all, the act of writing is such a private, basic matter. It's you
and the poem, you and the pencil and the paper in a room under a circle of
lamplight. And that is the essence of writing. A public life, then, becomes
schizophrenic; on the one hand, you have to extend yourself and talk to people about your writing, an experience which you cannot really articulate. To
talk about private experience to total strangers is very schizophrenic. Once in
a while it's good to get out and do readings because the shadows on the wall
grow large when you are writing. But in this past year and a half, I sometimes
feel I have been a little too public—or let's just say I feel the public encroach-
ing on the private time.

Schneider: Are things getting back to normal now? Do you find you are
able to work on a regular schedule?
Dove: Things are getting back to normal for several reasons. One of them
is that I think I've learned a little bit how to live with the public life and not
let it affect the private sector. Also how not to feel guilty about saying "No."

Schneider: For some writers, winning such a prize so young can block
their creative output for years to come. How do you respond creatively to the
pressures of fame?
Dove: I remember when I first got the Pulitzer, the question that came up
in every interview was: "Does this put pressure on you now for your next

book?" And in those first weeks afterward, the question always hit me out of left field. What did they mean?

Schneider: You didn't feel pressured until they started asking you.

Dove: Exactly. I didn't feel it at all. So in a way, it is an artificial pressure. It's particularly artificial if one really sits down and thinks about the number of people who have gotten Pulitzers and how many of them stayed "famous." If you look at the list, it's very interesting. Nothing's guaranteed.

Schneider: So some Pulitzer winners have declined in reputation?

Dove: Sure, some Nobel Laureates as well.

Schneider: So that takes some pressure off?

Dove: Right. And taking that further, what does it mean? I mean, it's wonderful, but in the end, what is important to me? When I go into the room and try to write a poem, the Pulitzer doesn't mean a thing. I am still just as challenged by the blank page.

Schneider: Much has been said about the number of Black writers who seem to have been ignored by the literary establishment. This surfaced again recently when James Baldwin died. Do you think the literary establishment has been unfair to Black writers?

Dove: Of course it has been unfair. This is true not only for Black writers, but for other minorities as well. It is outrageous that James Baldwin never got a Pulitzer Prize. It's outrageous the Ralph Ellison didn't get every literary award around for *Invisible Man*.

Schneider: There have been recent attempts to revise the canon and to give more attention to women writers and to minority writers in America. Are you gratified by these attempts? Are they going far enough?

Dove: I think they are absolutely necessary. I can't say whether they are going far enough: it depends on where, in what context. But it's important to try to round those things out. Let's face it: if Gwendolyn Brooks and Toni Morrison are not on the reading lists for Ph.D. dissertations, students aren't going to read them.

Schneider: So what do you think your winning the Pulitzer Prize for poetry means to other young Black American writers?

Dove: When I was growing up it would have meant a lot to me to know that a Black person had been recognized for his or her writing. *Thomas and Beulah* is a book about Black Americans, and two very ordinary ones at that.

Nothing spectacular happens in their life. And yet this "non-sensational" double portrait is awarded a prize. That's what is important.

Schneider: You mentioned you talked recently with some South African writers. Does winning the Pulitzer Prize give you more political leverage and visibility?

Dove: The Pulitzer does carry international credentials. In the past year and a half I have had increased opportunities to talk to and meet with writers of other countries and to see how they live. Because of the Pulitzer, I got the chance to do a conversation via satellite with some South African writers. I may have the chance of going there, which is certainly not going to be a pleasure trip. I feel the need to see the situation there for myself, if it's possible.

Schneider: Let's talk about *Thomas and Beulah.* Your interest in these characters resulted from a story your grandmother told you as a child. Is that right?

Dove: Yes. That story actually became the first poem in the book. I was about ten or twelve when she told me about my grandfather coming north on a river boat; it seems he had dared his best friend to swim the river, and the friend drowned. This was, for me, a phenomenal event. My grandfather had been a very gentle and quiet man. Frankly, I couldn't see how he could have carried that kind of guilt around all those years. I found it incredible that I had never heard the story before. In the writing, I had to confront several problems: How could he have borne it? How does anyone bear guilt that is irretrievable?

Schneider: Did you set out consciously on a quest to reclaim your roots?

Dove: No. Not consciously. Though it was a conscious attempt to under-stand someone who had meant a lot to me, who was part of me. And in doing that I got drawn more and more into my family history which was perfectly fine and kind of wonderful. It gave me a doorway into my history. I had a hinge, something that I could work on and through. I ended up talking to a lot of people about my grandparents; I learned a lot about my roots that doesn't appear in the book.

Schneider: Certainly that knowledge becomes meaningful to you and who you are today.

Dove: Yes, exactly. I think I was always working toward that. Now when I look back on the three books that I have done and see how they move, I understand that old adage about coming back to your own backyard. But it is almost as if I started out in *The Yellow House on the Corner* with a very domestic scene, a real neighborhood. The second book, *Museum*, was experience against the larger context of history.

Schneider: There are some family poems in *Museum* too.

Dove: Yes, but the family poems in that book constitute one section only; the overwhelming majority are portraits of individuals in their particular historical context.

Schneider: How did you go about recreating the era of Thomas and Beulah's migration?

Dove: I read everything I could get my hands on about the migration from the rural South to the industrial North. The WPA books that were done on each state were especially invaluable.

Schneider: So there were lots of details you had to track down.

Dove: Exactly the stuff that will drop out of the next edition of the *Encyclopedia Britannica*, right? I was trying to get that feeling, that ambiance, so I talked to my mother an awful lot about what it was like growing up at that time. She was remarkable. At first she asked, "What do you want to hear?" But I didn't know what I wanted to hear. I just wanted her to talk, and that's what she did. I amassed so much material; then I had to kind of forget it all in order to write the poems.

Schneider: You have said of *Thomas and Beulah* that "less and less did it become based on my grandparents because after a while I was after a different kind of truth." What is the larger truth you were after?

Dove: I was after the essence of my grandparents' existence and their survival, not necessarily the facts of their survival. That's the distinction I'm trying to make. So when I said it became less and less about them, I meant I was not so concerned about whether Thomas in the book was born the same year as my grandfather (he wasn't, incidentally) or whether in fact it was a yellow scarf he gave Beulah or not. What's important is the gesture of that scarf. One appropriates certain gestures from the factual life to reinforce a larger sense of truth that is not, strictly speaking, reality.

Schneider: Is there something especially significant about a generation like Thomas and Beulah's which had to uproot itself—in this case, from the South, in order to work in Northern cities?

Dove: Yes, of course. Only very recently have historians begun to explore that entire era in any depth and what impact the Great Migration, as they call it now, had on not only Southern communities and Northern communities but a host of other things. So much has been done or talked about the uprooting of the Black family through slavery, but this was a second uprooting and displacement. It's the first time that Blacks in this country had rooting and displacement. It's the first time that Blacks in this country had any chance, however stifled, of pursuing "the American dream." Obviously not with the same advantages as whites, not even as the otherwise ostracized European immigrants, and so it is a very poignant era. I never heard very much about it when I was a child. I wondered why my cousins from Cleveland spoke with a Southern accent, but we didn't. It wasn't that unusual that entire communities were brought up and resettled around each other. It's a major population movement in our country that just went largely unrecorded.

Schneider: Did you begin with the notion of writing such a closely knit sequence where many of the poems depend upon previous ones?

Dove: As I said earlier, when I started out I did not think in terms of a book. I did start out with a single poem. Then I thought, "This isn't enough," and I went on. I thought I was going to have a suite of poems, a group of six or seven. At that point I did want them narrative; I thought there must be a way to get back into poetry the grandness that narrative can give, plus the sweep of time. Lyric poetry does not have that sweep of time. Lyrics are discrete moments. On the other hand, a lot of narrative poems can tend to bog down in the prosier transitional moments. I didn't see very many long narrative poems that really weren't smaller poems linked together. So one of the things I was trying to do was string moments as beads on a necklace. In other words, I have lyric poems which, when placed one after the other, reconstruct the sweep of time. I wanted it all. I wanted a narrative and I wanted lyric poems, so I tried to do them both.

Schneider: Some of the poems seem more capable of standing alone than others—"Jiving" and "Lightning Blues," for example. Many others depend on our reading of the previous ones.

Dove: At the beginning of the book I warn that these poems are meant to be read in sequence. I put that in there because the poems make most sense when read in order. But even though some of the poems are absolutely dependent on the others, in the writing I was still trying very hard to make each poem wholly self-sufficient, of a piece. In other words, a particular poem may be dependent on an earlier poem for its maximum meaning, but in itself it is a complete poem. It just happens to need another beat to make the best connection.

Schneider: A few of the poems have italicized song-like rhymes that sound like they might derive from Southern minstrels or gospels. I am especially thinking of "Refrain." What's the origin of those lyrics?

Dove: I made them up. They are in the spirit of the country blues. They are also influenced by spirituals and gospels. The poem "Gospel" begins as a takeoff on "Swing Low Sweet Chariot." It starts off: "Swing low so I / can step inside." Both "Refrain" and "Gospel" are written in quatrains, and I think there's quite a kinship between them. The roots—no, let's say the connections—between gospel and blues are very close.

Schneider: Were you listening to recent blues recordings?

Dove: No. Mostly older blues recordings, though I have listened to recent ones too. While I was writing this book I was playing a lot of music, everything from Lightnin' Hopkins to older ones like Larry Jackson or some of the recordings that Al Lomax made of musicians, all the way up to Billie Holiday, stopping about in the '50s. It seemed to be the music for the book.

Schneider: Let's talk about Akron, Ohio, the town where Thomas and Beulah lived. Your book serves as a commentary and history of that place with its zeppelin factory and Satisfaction Coal Company, and its impoverishment during the Depression. This kind of social realism in your work seems striking and in some ways a departure from your earlier work.

Dove: At some point in the writing, I knew the poems needed background; I realized that I had to give a history of the town. I can't say I approached this task with joy. After all, Akron is not a tourist attraction. Let's face it: few of us were born in beautiful places. Yet I remember Akron, Ohio, as a place of beauty. Rilke says in his *Letters to a Young Poet*, that if you cannot recount the riches of a place do not blame the place—blame yourself, because you are not rich enough to recall its riches. When I read that again, I realized that I'd be doing Akron injustice if I would just dwell on its industrial ugliness, and if I could not explain or bring across some of its magic or make it come alive to others, then it was my problem, certainly not Akron's.

Schneider: Does *Thomas and Beulah* feel like a different book from your earlier ones?

Dove: I think it is a departure from my other work—rather, I came home.

And, rather than a collection of poems, each working out a discrete universe, *Thomas and Beulah* is a string of moments that work together to define a universe much in the way a necklace defines the neck and the shoulders. In my first book, *The Yellow House on the Corner*, there was an entire section dealing with aspects of slavery. *Museum* is somewhat of a hodgepodge of various social and political realities and how individuals work within them. *Thomas and Beulah* is the first sustained effort at sequence.

Schneider: It seemed to me that especially in *Yellow House* and in places in *Museum* there is more of a surrealistic feeling to some of the poems. In *Thomas and Beulah* we don't get as much of that. It seems much more grounded in the place and in the time and in the people.

Dove: The word "surrealistic" has been used quite often in describing my work, and I must say I have always been amazed by it. I never thought of myself as being surrealistic.

Schneider: Maybe "deep image."

Dove: No. Obviously, though, this is what people think of it. So now I kind of smile; I'm not going to escape this world. I mean, I accept it as a fair judgment. To me magic, or the existence of an unexplainable occurrence, is something I grew up with. One shouldn't try to explain everything. I learned to live with paradox, to accept strange happenings. I listened to older people talking about, for example, a person who refused to die easy and came back to haunt. In terms of memory and guilt, that makes a lot of sense to me. Now I'm not talking about ghost stories; I'm talking about growing up in America, a lot of surreal things are going on all the time.

Schneider: One interesting thing about the Thomas section of the book is that Lem really haunts Thomas throughout. I find that very moving. Is this based on the story you referred to earlier from your grandmother?

Dove: Yes, yes. And you know the only facts that I had in the story were that my grandfather had come up the river with a good friend and that the friend had died. I knew nothing about the man. In fact, my grandfather never mentioned the story to us as children. The idea of Lem haunting him grew out of poems—it actually grew out of the character of Thomas and what I felt he would have done.

Schneider: Another question about Thomas. He comes across in some ways as a real lady's man. How did Beulah tie him down?

Dove: I don't know! I mean I think that . . . he might come across that way, but his being a lady's man was constrained by the death of his friend. In a way, he is trying to play his way out of hell.

Schneider: Of course, the other side of it is he is very dedicated to his family.

Dove: He's a classic case in that he mourns the youth he had, but he can't get back to it anyway. I think it would be untrue for any of us to say we haven't felt that at some point. You feel you want to let go of all the stuff that starts attaching itself to you as you grow up, but you can't do it anymore.

Schneider: The bills have to be paid. What is it that you admire about Beulah? And what is it you would like to honor in her?

Dove: I think of Beulah as being a very strong woman, who still has no way of showing how strong she could be. She is the one who really wants to travel, to see the world. She is curious, she is intelligent, and her situation in life does not allow her to pursue her curiosity. If there is anything I want to honor in her, it is that spirit.

Schneider: The sense of sacrifice?

Dove: Certainly that too, but lots of people make sacrifices. It's the way one handles sacrifice that's crucial.

Schneider: She did it gracefully.

Dove: She did it gracefully, but not too gracefully—that is, not without spunk. It's important that people know there's a struggle involved, that the sacrifice is being made. You have to learn not to be crushed by what you can't do.

Schneider: Both Thomas and Beulah seem relatively free of gnawing bitterness toward their environment, toward whites, despite some difficult circumstances, very difficult circumstances. Is there a lesson in this?

Dove: A lesson? Let me take a different tack. We tend to forget that there were generations upon generations of Black Americans who did not have the luxury of bitterness. I don't mean to suggest that there was no bitterness, just that you had enough to do with surviving. You had to eat first. This drive for survival above all else could lead to a certain autism; one's personality freezes.

The civil rights movement and the rise of Black consciousness in the 1960s made the release of emotion—anger, elation, fury, righteousness—possible. One could get emotions out without being poisonous and so still be able to go on with life. But Thomas and Beulah came from a different generation, from an era when there was no point in talking about what white people had and Black people did not. That was a fact of life—it didn't mean they liked it, it didn't mean they thought it was right. But there were a few more pressing matters to talk about. Inequality was a given. I know how impatient we became with our grandparents in the '60s and our great aunts, when we would call ourselves Afro-Americans or Black and they would continue to say "colored" and we'd go: "AHHHHH, come on." The impatience of youth. Why aren't Thomas and Beulah furious? Well, they were, but they had a different way of expressing it.

Schneider: Both Beulah and Thomas grow old together, and sadness overtakes the readers as we read of their health problems and their demise. But they stick together and support each other. Is there a commentary on aging here for a society which is accused of neglecting its elderly?

Dove: Yes. Certainly, one of the things I learned in writing *Thomas and Beulah* is that all of us are guilty at one time or another of not assigning other people their full human worth, for whatever reasons—men having preconceived ideas of women or vice versa, racial prejudice, misconceptions about the young and the old. In order to be able to understand my grandfather, or how my grandmother could be the woman she was, I had to go back and revision their youth. It was a humbling experience for me. And there are certain satisfactions with age that we tend not to think about.

Schneider: Thomas and Beulah are there for each other to the very end. That kind of commitment through thick and thin, as sappy as it may sound, is a striking part of the book.

Dove: I received essays written in the form of letters from students at Brown University. One student thought Thomas and Beulah didn't like each other at all, that the marriage was very sad. I was absolutely amazed at that notion. It must have something to do with our concept of love—that if we are young it is going to be romantic all the way through. In the poem "Company" Beulah said: "Listen: we were good, / though we never believed it." I remember that absolutely calm feeling that my grandparents had, a sense of belonging together. Today I see young lovers struggling to find earth-shattering ecstasy in every second. That's part of love, but it's a small part.

Schneider: There is a kind of ripeness about their love that is unusual and that only comes with age.

Dove: Absolutely.

Schneider: What does the future hold for Rita Dove? Do you plan on writing more poetry or trying a novel?

Dove: More poems, of course, and I definitely plan to write more fiction. I'm writing a novel right now. Why not?

Schneider: Will you be doing a lot more teaching? Or traveling in the next couple of years?

Dove: I have this year off, but I will be going back to teaching in the fall. I enjoy teaching. Travel is always in my life. I'm always traveling, it seems.

Schneider: We mentioned fiction, and you do have that one book of short stories (*Fifth Sunday*). Do you find the two activities—writing fiction, writing poetry—mutually supportive or do you think of them as separate, unrelated activities? Is there any kind of schizophrenia about it? Or is it just natural?

Dove: I think that they are part of the same process. It's all writing; there are just different ways of going about it. I don't find them compatible in the sense that when I am writing poetry I am not usually going to start a story. If I'm writing a story I am in a slightly different mode. I can't explain what it is. It's not as severe as speaking another language. Still, I think the notion of prose writing and poetry writing as separate entities has been artificially created, partly as a result of fitting writing into the academic curriculum where it is easiest to teach them separately. That's valid pedagogical methodology, but there is no reason for them to exist separately outside the workshop. One of the things I deplored when I was in graduate school was just how separate the two were kept; the fiction writers and the poetry writers didn't even go to the same parties.

Schneider: This is the final question. It's actually two. Does writing poetry enable you to be more fully aware of who you are? Is it the bliss of writing that attracts you?

Dove: No. It isn't the bliss of writing but the bliss of unfolding. I was hesitating with the question because I wanted to consider how to go about making my answer clear without making it sound corny. I don't think poetry is going to make anyone a better person, and it is not going to save you. But writing is a constant for me. There's an edge that needs to be explored, the edge between being unconscious and then suddenly being so aware that the skin tingles. Let me be more precise. There is that moment in the writing of a poem when things start to come together, coalesce into a discovery. This is sheer bliss, and has something to do with discovering something about my-self. It doesn't mean I understand myself; in fact, the more I write, the less I know of myself. But I also learn more. Territory is being covered—excursions into the interior. I write for those moments of discovery really, but there are two steps in this process: one is the intimate revelation, and the second step is to take that revelation and to make it visible—palpable—for others.

It's one thing to experience strong emotion; it's another thing to communi-cate it to others. I do believe that an experience inarticulated will be lost; part of my task as a writer, one of the things I take on and want to do, is to articulate those moments so they won't be lost. I think there is no greater joy than to have someone else say, "I know what you mean." That's real corny, but it's what literature does for all of us, the reader as well as the writer. An active reader longs to be pulled into another's world and to comprehend that world, to get into another's skin utterly and yet understand what's happening at the same time. That's an immensely exciting thing. And that's what I work for.

Gifts to Be Earned

Mohamed B. Taleb-Khyar / 1991

The following interview is part of "An Interview with Maryse Conde and Rita Dove," which appeared in *Callaloo* 14:2 in 1991. © Charles H. Rowell. Reprinted by permission of the Johns Hopkins University Press.

Taleb-Khyar: You are a writer of tremendous talent. Beyond any considerations of race, gender, class or culture, your works belong to that common heritage of humanity called the classics. You enjoy already an international reputation. Your works have crossed national and cultural boundaries, and literary history is beginning to record you as one of the most articulate and genuine voices of our time.

My first question has to do with your background. It is always interesting to hear what a writer has to say about her or his background, but in your case it is even more interesting since your background has a direct relevance to your works. Could you begin this encounter by addressing your background; for example, how you grew up and how you came to writing?

Dove: I grew up in Akron, Ohio, an industrial town of about 300,000 people. Akron is called the rubber capital of the world because most American tire factories used to be located there; because of its industrial importance, especially in the first half of our century, it was a place where many Black Americans migrated from the South in order to find jobs.

That's what happened with my family, too. My father, like his father before him, worked for the Goodyear Tire and Rubber Company, except that my father became the only member of his family—he was one of ten children—who made it to college and then even through graduate school. The others in fact had decided that he was the brain, and they made sure that he could go to school. I think they sacrificed a lot for him. So he became the first Black chemist at Goodyear and, for all I know, the first Black chemist in the American tire industry. This, and all the things he had to go through in order to make it that far, I found out very late, actually just a few years ago, because he never talked about it when I was young. He got his master's degree after he returned from fighting in Italy in World War II, and he graduated at the top of his class, but by the time I was born in 1952 he was still an

74

elevator operator at Goodyear, taking former schoolmates from college, most of them inferior to him as chemists, up and down the elevator because the rubber companies wouldn't hire Black research scientists until well into the '50s. Today, when I hear the anti-affirmative action talk of people like George Bush and William Bennett, how they toss off comments about being anti-quotas and hypocritically advocate color blindness, I have to think of this tradition of white Northern racism, its recent history.

As children we were kept from those kinds of things, but we were told that we were going to learn, and it was just a given that we were to study, go to college, get a degree and strive for a professional position like lawyer or doctor or scientist. In that sense I came from a fairly traditional upwardly mobile Black family—upwardly mobile in the second generation. Both my parents had experienced the transition from lower- to lower-middle-class status, and though we were raised to be middle class we could still see the roots of that struggle. I grew up very shy, as one of four children, with an older brother and two younger sisters. I wrote at an early age. I started with stories and little plays featuring my classmates, but I never really thought of writing as something that could be an occupation, something that you can do for a living. It simply wasn't in the stars; it wasn't anything anyone I knew had ever done. So I did a lot of stumbling around, reading on my own.

To my mind at that time, real books had been written by people long dead, and what I was doing was just fun—I didn't consider it "writing." I didn't realize that writing could be a life-long passion until I was well into my teens. I had a high school English teacher whom I still see sometimes—Margaret Oechsner is her name—who took me to a little writers' conference one Saturday afternoon to meet some real writers. I don't know how she knew I wrote, since I had never shown anyone anything. But that conference changed my life, because I realized that it was possible to be a writer, alive and walking the streets, and I began to write with that perspective.

Taleb-Khyar: I take it that you have an experience of exile. How does exile inform your writing?

Dove: I did feel a sense of alienation when I lived in Europe, though that sensation got weaker over the years, from stay to stay. It wasn't necessarily a feeling of exile because my sojourns abroad, after all, were voluntary. When I first went to Germany in 1974–75 as a Fulbright scholar, I felt I had been plunged into something completely different from what I knew until then, even though I had learned the language and gone through all sorts of other preparations to make myself knowledgeable beforehand.

One of the major differences between my situation and that of a Black in France was that I was an oddity in Germany, especially in Tübingen, the small university town in Southern Germany where the Fulbright people had decided to send me. There were few Black women, and the ones who were there were African, not African American. Most Germans don't consider it impolite to stare, so they simply gawked at me or even pointed. It was amazing to me to be pointed out on the street like that, and it offended me in many ways—on a racial level, of course, but also on a cultural level because if someone stares at you in the States, it's impolite.

Even now, sixteen years after those first encounters, I'm still not used to it; sometimes I lose my patience and stick out my tongue. Once I told a group of children that I was actually a witch and their eyes would dry up like corn flakes when they went to sleep that night; that was a terrible thing to do, but I was so fed up with being on constant display. All the things that you think white people don't ask anymore about Blacks were said to me: Can you tan? Why are your palms light-skinned? Oh, your teeth are so white, all that stuff. But I also met good people, and then coming from a different culture could be quite fruitful.

There was also the matter of the language with a different structure, a different syntax, a different logic. In German the verbs often come at the end of the sentence, so in an argument you can sustain your energy until the very end and then throw in the verb that will suddenly make the sentence coalesce. At one point, that might have had an effect on my writing—I began to try to do that in English. I should add here that being surrounded by a foreign language does have something to do with exile, with the feeling of exile in language. One of the things that fascinated me when I was growing up was the way language was put together, and how words could lead you into a new place. I think one reason I became primarily a poet rather than a fiction writer is that though I am interested in stories, I am profoundly fascinated by the ways in which language can change your perceptions. When I was about nine or ten, each week in school we would get a list of spelling words to study, and each week I would take those ten new words and use them to construct a story, which continued from week to week. Thus language became discovery, a matter of seeing where the words would lead me—not necessarily what story I had in mind, but where the words would take me. That was an early indication, I think, that I would become a poet. But what has that to do with Germany? In Germany I began to feel that I was in between languages, and when I sat down to write I couldn't figure out what was really English or some amalgam of English and translated German.

Taleb-Khyar: Is that a wonderful or a terrible thing for a poet?

Dove: Both! I mean, it can be both for a while. I think it helped me in the end, but it was terrible at first. A lot of it certainly had to do with the fact that I hadn't grown up with German; I had learned the language artificially, in school, and so I wasn't used to switching between languages as someone who grows up bilingually has to be. The difference is evident to me when I watch my daughter, who speaks German with her father and English with me. Anyway, I felt caught between languages, and when I came back to the States I sometimes felt as if I didn't exist anywhere. Even back home, I was in a foreign country again, and for a while I viewed it all with the eyes of a stranger. Everything was so colorful.

Taleb-Khyar: And big.

Dove:: Yes! And Americans seemed more superficial. Also, my political awareness had increased dramatically. In Germany I began to hear things about the States that I hadn't heard about at home. That was my first realization that the "free press" we are so proud of is quite selective in its choices of information to pass on, and I became much more aware of the fact that this grand country I came from had some serious cracks in its marble. I realized that during my rather sheltered college years at Miami University, in the rural setting of Southwestern Ohio, I had filled the role of the striving, gifted Black student extremely well, but without much concern for the outside world. And now, suddenly, in Germany I was on display in a strange environment where some people pointed with fingers at me and others pitied me as a symbol for centuries of brutality and injustice against Blacks. So I felt simultaneously alienated both from my home country and from the place I was in. On the other hand, travel—serious travel, I mean, when you're trying to understand a place and not just passing through, taking pictures— serious travel can heighten the awareness a writer needs to see many sides of a story. Of course, as a minority we have acquired that binocular vision necessarily. As Du Bois said, to live as a Black person in America, you must learn to fit into the main culture even while you are not of it. Even if you come from an upwardly mobile middle-class background, you grow up with an awareness of *difference* and a set of cultural values rooted in the Black tradition, so in a certain way you are already bilingual.

Taleb-Khyar: You mentioned Du Bois's comment on being Black. I have two quotes on the subject I would like you to respond to. The first one is by Jean Genet. In his play The *Blacks,* Genet wrote as an epigraph: "One evening an actor asked me to write a play for an all-Black cast. But, what exactly is a Black? First of all, what is his color?" By this I believe that, for Genet, Blackness is not an essence, as some would have it, but rather a function that can be at any time inhabited by anyone who finds themselves in the position of the oppressed or, as you just said, in the position of the minority. The second quote is, in a way, a response to the first one. It is from James Baldwin's *The Evidence of Things Not Seen.* James Baldwin wrote: "White people [in this hemisphere] discovered Christ by way of the Bible. Black people discovered Him by way of the Cross." To Genet's question "What exactly is a Black?" Baldwin seems to answer, "A Black is somebody who suffers, at least in this hemisphere." What would be your answer to that question? What is exactly a Black person? What is his color?

Dove: The quotes by Genet and Baldwin approach the notion of being a Black in very different ways. Baldwin is saying that the American slaves embraced Christianity through their specific experiences of misery in a much more personal way than their white tormentors. American Blacks had been robbed of every cultural value—family, home. religion, unity with other people of their particular background, freedom of choice. In their despair they found metaphors for their suffering, and metaphors for transcending suffering, for spiritual survival, in the tales from the very book their oppressors cherished for the opposite reasons. But times have changed, accelerated by great movers like Martin Luther King; and we have gone beyond the image of the cross and the metaphors of heavenly redemption. In their push for earthly redemption, these leaders built upon the cultural values that had emerged from the African American experience and utilized religious motivation—in part because everybody understood that—and merged it with the basic human desire for freedom and equality.

Naturally, these changes led to new perceptions in the next generation. I came of age, whatever that means, at the end of the '60s; I was eighteen in 1970, when the Black Power movement was about to slide into an intellectual and political decline, especially on its fringes, though it had certainly achieved heightened self-awareness and pride in being Black, in being oneself. I remember during my college years feeling that I was Black with a capital "B"; that was Blackness as it had been defined in the '60s. For most of my age group, who hadn't rioted, or stormed the ramparts anywhere, Black

Pride was a rather abstract feeling, though it gave us tremendous self-confidence. Those who were just a few years older still had to fight for it, but we got our pride for free. Measuring Black Pride in concrete terms amounted to who had the largest Afro. Al Young has a wonderful poem called "A Dance for Black Militants," where he talks about being Black as a fashion statement.

Another truly positive result of that era is the re-discovery of our own literary tradition. Black literary writers were not yet part of the curriculum, so we dug them up on our own and the disregard among white professors for the best of these writers struck me not only as cultural ignorance, but racist discrimination. And as William Bennett and his conservative cohorts have proven in recent years, this kind of discrimination and ignorance is still rampant among certain so-called scholars. But we Black students in the early '70s, and also a few white ones, discovered an Afro-American literature shunned by most of academia, and that was very affirmative and constructive.

The '70s were also a time when Black Americans could dare to take a sabbatical from their collective psyche and try to explore who we were on an individual basis. After the furor of the '60s, that was good and absolutely necessary. In an ideal world, being Black should take on the same kind of significance or nonimportance as being white. Race may define a large part of one's identity, especially once one gets beyond childhood; and there are certain situations where it matters, as well as certain experiences that would not have happened to someone of a different "persuasion," but it shouldn't become a trauma that causes one to distrust people on the basis of their color, or to refrain from befriending someone else because of his or her racial origin. This, of course, is theoretical talk. In fact, we know that there's not much socializing between the races—a sad commentary on this society, isn't it? Not that I'd want to forget being Black, but I would love to walk through life without the anxiety of being prejudged and pigeonholed on the basis of my race. I am aware that at any moment I could be judged simply for my color alone. At any moment I could walk into a situation where it doesn't matter who I am—what I'm thinking, what I've written, published, whatever. I am seen as a Black person, together with whatever their preconceived notions of a Black person are, and that's it. Outside of my own house and my family I'm constantly on the alert, so as to be able to deal with such stereotyping as best as I can.

I might add that in the States, place and time are also of utmost importance for the perception of race. In Mississippi or Alabama, or for that matter, here in Virginia, growing up would have been quite different for someone my age from growing up in Akron, Ohio, simply because I would have gone to poorly funded segregated schools, instead of sitting next to white and Black kids, as equal among equals, in integrated and well-equipped schools. I would have had to sit in the back of the bus as a child and would have been treated as a subhuman during my encounters with the "dominant culture," instead of being encouraged, and handed the tools, to strive for excellence.

Taleb-Khyar: How about the African culture? What is Africa in your imagination? How does Africa inform your writing?

Dove: Oh goodness! This is far too big a topic. I have a complicated relationship with Africa because, like many Black Americans, I went through a period when Africa was a mythic place for me—like in Countee Cullen's poem "What Is Africa to Me." My image of Africa contained a few totemic emblems, and that was it. It had nothing to do with life as it is lived. As I said before, though, by the time I came of age and reached a point where I could have realized my teenage fantasies of visiting the "Homeland," a lot of disillusionment with Africa had begun to surface. Besides all the post-colonial political turmoil, there were stories of how Black Americans would go to Africa to be "among their kind," and the Africans would treat them like the strangers they essentially were. I realized that Africa is not a homogenous cultural entity, but a continent with radically diverse cultures and peoples, even if most of them would be classified as Black in the United States. And though our centuries-old connection might justify focusing extra attention on African causes, especially an emphasis on African history, it didn't justify cherishing a mythical Africa in my heart. In some ways, I might feel closer to my Cherokee and Blackfoot heritage because I can connect them to familiar geography, and the oppression of my Native American forebears is a clearly defined part of my own country's inglorious history.

Any response I could have about Africa today has to be woefully uninformed, since I have never been there. Well, perhaps I still harbor some special sentiment, but I don't want to romanticize this. Yes, there is a feeling of loss. There's a hole somewhere, you know; I feel like I came from someplace—that a part of my ancestry sprung from a place that is irretrievably lost; but as I said, I don't want to romanticize that. I mean, I can't go back and find it.

Taleb-Khyar: You are fascinated by history. In a book of poems such as *Museum,* for example, history is an utterly trivial, yet utterly tragic affair. It is at the same time intimate and objective, its heroes ranging from your own father to a Dominican dictator. It is made of moments rather than times. A series of sketches instead of frescoes, it is always discontinuous. Could you comment on your use of history?

Dove: You're absolutely right that history's portrayed as something ultimately tragic in *Museum.* One of my goals with that book was to reveal the underside of history, and to present this underside in discrete moments, because for me as a poet the apprehended moment is of supreme importance. That approach has to do more with the genre, then, than with my political assessments of historical events. In *Thomas and Beulah,* these moments are tied to the lives of the two protagonists and interwoven with events of their time; those moments are strung together to tell their stories. What fascinates me is the individual caught in the web of history

Taleb-Khyar: You said somewhere that it is an unusual thing for you to do, putting a chronology at the end of your book.

Dove: Well, in a certain way it's also a parody on history because private dates are put on equal footing with the dates of publicly important happenings. But significant events in the private sphere are rarely written up in history books, although they make up the life-sustaining fabric of humanity.

Taleb-Khyar: You contrasted in a poem the march on Washington with a picnic that was more important for your characters.

I would like you now to address the question of feminine discourse. You write extensively about women. Do you feel that there are things a male writer could not express, or ways in which he could not express things?

Dove: He tries to get us in every way.

Taleb-Khyar: You get this question everywhere, don't you?

Dove: Well, politically I consider myself a feminist, but when I walk into my room to write, I don't think of myself in political terms. I approach that piece of paper or the computer screen to search for—I know it sounds corny—truth and beauty through language. Writing, though it is always a struggle between words and rhythm and concepts and topics and characters, has to be fun, and a challenge, to be worth it. As a writer I just happen to be a Black and a woman, and those perceptions may appear on the page more often than not because those are the viewpoints I'm most intimate with, and so I filter my intentions, my subject matter, through them. As an artist, I shun political considerations and racial or gender partiality; for example, I would find it a breach of my integrity as a writer to create a character for didactic or propaganda purposes, like concocting a strong Black heroine, an idealized so-called role model, just to promote a positive image. I'm interested in the truth. And the truth is that if a character turns out to be an evil Black person, or an evil woman, then that's the way it's got to be.

I'm not sure how interesting it is to readers—and it shouldn't be important for the appreciation of an artistic work—to know what's happening in the artist's private life, but since I've identified myself politically as a feminist it might be meaningful to put the personal into perspective. I lead an unspectacular family life. I feel that life for me would not be complete without my husband and our daughter. But I also believe that people can feel complete without a mate, and without children. If there are women who are silent because they are afraid to speak, or if their personal conditions are such that they're unable to write, though they would love to, then I feel concern for them. And I believe their stories must be heard; their circumstances must be improved so that they can tell their stories. But if I decided to fight for a cause, I'll do that off the page. I'm not going to bring my arguments into my work, unless they happen to fit the situation of that particular character. That doesn't mean that it isn't thrilling and absolutely legitimate, in a poem like "Dusting" for example, to show how domestic chores figure in the turning of the globe. These may be considered political acts; I consider them artistic acts. Attacks against chauvinism and sympathy for the downtrodden don't have to fall victim to agitprop, though one certainly has to watch out for the trap of didacticism. In general, I think anything is possible, so I would never say that there are certain topics that a man cannot write about, or topics that a woman cannot write about. And I can admire a writer for her or his craft and abhor their narrative choices. In some men's fiction, for example, you never see women except as they impact on the masculine sphere.

You can't judge feminism by its extremists. For me, feminism means righting the wrongs of gender inequality—the inequality that goes beyond the physical distinctions between women and men. In our household the roles are so interwoven, so meshed, that if our daughter had to write an essay in school on what her mommy does, and her daddy does, she wouldn't know how to begin. We both write. We both cook. We both wash. A few role-specific differences remain: he doesn't iron, I don't climb on the roof. I can live with that.

Taleb-Khyar: You mentioned earlier politics, political things. I would like you to address what Chinua Achebe likes to refer to under the title of "the

Prince and the Poet," and that is the writer and politics, the writer and the dominant ideology or the center of power. Could you elaborate on where you stand politically?

Dove: Well, it's a very different situation in the United States, because it has become part of the system to treat political trends like fashions: protest is absorbed; it is subsumed and marketed. Protest is treated as a joke or made into fashion; it can be printed on t-shirts and even become an excuse for the denigration of whole groups of people, like the despicable *machismo* in some rap songs. Literary writers, poets especially, who care about subtlety and are sensitive to the intricacies of language, can't compete when it comes to mass appeal. Therefore, we writers become irrelevant, unless some wild fluke turns one of us into a celebrity. Anyway, it's usually short-lived. I think my notion of what my "role" is or what it is that I'm trying to do in a social sense is to constantly remind myself, my students, and my readers of our individuality. To me, one of the greatest dangers for people in this country is the temptation to think in terms of groups rather than to extol each person's uniqueness, and it is extremely difficult for young people—the ones who could affect change the most—to resist this outside pressure. There is a great urge among all Americans, and not only Black Americans, though I'd like to address them specifically, to fit in, to be like everybody on television, to share a style, to compromise themselves behind a media-approved "lifestyle" instead of leading an independent life. The Melting Pot.

In my poems, and in my stories, too, I try very hard to create characters who are seen as individuals—not only as Blacks or as women, or whatever, but as a Black woman with her own particular problems, or one white bum struggling in a specific predicament—as persons who have their very individual lives, and whose histories make them react to the world in different ways. One could argue that insisting upon that individuality is ultimately a political act, and to my mind, this is one of the fundamental principles a writer has to uphold, along with a warning: don't be swallowed up. Don't be swallowed up!

Taleb-Khyar: Asking a writer to choose among her or his works amounts to asking a mother to choose among her children, but everyone knows that mothers have their secret favorite child. So if you were to look back on your careers and select a text as the best representative of what you want to achieve, which one of yours books would you select?

Dove: I don't think I have a favorite. Maybe because I feel like I haven't done yet what I dream of doing. I mean, my own favorite is the one in the future, the work that's always perfect before you write it. Also, I don't like to look back; my passions are best served when I push ahead. Nevertheless, when I'm forced to look back on my work, I tend to like different poems and even whole books at different times and for different reasons. *The Yellow House on the Corner,* my first poetry collection, can still excite me because of the tremendous discoveries I made about myself and my relationship to language when I wrote those early poems. *Museum* has always been a favorite of mine because I like the cynicism—no, not exactly cynicism, but its dispassionate eye. Still, I would not want to have it without *Thomas and Beulah* afterwards. As my latest book, *Grace Notes* contains poems fresh enough that I feel immediate passion for them. And it is true that public reaction has nothing to do with my own preferences. In fact, the point that so many people mention or want *Thomas and Beulah* has made me begin to get tired of the book, because I think, Have they read anything else? Are they only reading this book because of the Pulitzer? It may be the easiest of my books to understand, especially for someone who isn't a regular reader of contemporary poetry. So I'm suspicious of that popularity, though I still like the book.

Taleb-Khyar: Intertextuality is now a favorite theme both in creative and in critical texts. It was with Borges, I believe, that fiction began to incorporate books as subjects of investigation, fantasy, and wonder. That trend continues today in various degrees, for example, in the works of writers as different as Umberto Eco, Hélène Cixous, Daniel Maximin, John Barth, Guy Davenport, or Raymond Jean. Do you write in consciousness of other texts, as well? What is the importance of books in your books?

Dove: The way you phrased the question frightened me so much that all my thoughts immediately flew out of my mind! Let me approach it this way: When I am writing, particularly when I am writing poetry, I do a lot of wandering around the house. I do a lot of disconnected things while I'm thinking, while the poem is brewing. Sometimes I pull books off the shelf and I read them, and I'll read a poem here or there, or I'll read a novel in one sitting or just snatches of a novel. But I never think, I want to read a Derek Walcott poem, for instance, to see how he handles scenery. I don't operate like that. I just go to the bookshelf almost like a sleepwalker, and kind of imagine the book I want to pick out.

I don't want to know why I choose to read a certain book. I prefer to keep that at a subconscious level, and I will resist any kind of probe into that process. What I can tell you are a couple of things that spurred me on in the past when I was writing. When I was working on *Museum*, I had a poetry collection on my desk by the German poet Hans Magnus Enzensberger, called *Mausoleum*. His book is a museum of sorts, too, dealing with various lions of industry and other makers and shakers. I don't think my poems look anything like his—the subject matter is quite different and he writes in very long lines, while the poems in *Museum* are very skinny. But I was intrigued by his way of looking at history, and it inspired me to find my own perspectives.

When I wrote *Thomas and Beulah* I had other works of literature close by. One of them was Robert Penn Warren's *Audubon: A Vision,* a book-length poem written in parts. Another one was Aimé Césaire's *Return to My Native Land,* which I had read before, in high school, and which had had a tremendous impact on my perception of the world. Was there anything else? Charles Wright's *Bloodlines.* I tend to bury this kind of information. I mean, I don't try to remember it because it doesn't help with writing the next book. But I read all the time—although I find that I read less while I'm working on prose than when I'm working on poetry. I don't know why. When I'm working on poems, I'm reading all the time. Now that I'm trying to finish a novel, I find that a week or two may go by without reading anything other than some factual information, perhaps, that I might need for the timing of a scene.

Taleb-Khyar: What do you like in contemporary writing?

Dove: What I find exciting in Afro-American literature today is its diversity. We've come a long way in the '80s—particularly in poetry, where I watch developments more closely than in prose or theater. Especially among Afro-American women. Toi Derricote is writing amazing, painful poems about the violence in her childhood, very personal poems, that manage not to shut the reader out—poems having sometimes to do with race, and sometimes with family. There's nothing you can pin down and say, this is distinctly Black, this is distinctly female. Nothing fits snugly in categories; instead, the poems are informed by both the experience and the pressure that craft—the language—has applied to that experience. On the other hand, you have someone like Elizabeth Alexander, who is writing very graceful and elegant poems that range all over the place. And there are others—Marilyn Waniek, Thylias Moss, Karen Mitchell come to mind. The sensitivity and the ease with which these women are writing about whatever happens to interest them, and their confidence this will be interesting to others, their disregard of social pressure to write about "the Black cause" or "the female cause" in predictable ways—that's what I find exciting.

Of course we find this artistic liberation in prose as well; it's an amazing time for Black women writers. In the '70s, in college, I practically considered Toni Morrison a personal savior. When her first novel, *The Bluest Eye,* came out, I thought, Finally, someone who's writing about where I come from. It was a breakthrough that a Black writer was writing about growing up in a Midwestern town, rather than dealing with the South or with urban decay. In order to get published in the '60s, it seemed like you either had to be from the rural South, or you had to have suffered horrific experiences of race discrimination—which allowed for a rather oblique view into Black life.

Nowadays we're getting closer to the whole picture. Of course it's not perfect—it will never be, and there is still a lot of terrible and often self-congratulatory stuff around posing as "the real Black thing." What I find distressing, for example, is the notion that if you're Black, you're going to write in the blues mode. Half the people who are writing these bluesy-jazzy poems really have no appreciation for the blues as an art form. They think, in a very superficial way, that if you're Black, then you're blue, so let's get down to it. That's fine, if the writing is good. What I don't like is the kind of poetry praised in certain cliques and journals for its " Blackness" or cultural verisimilitude, when so much of it is just badly written. It's extremely frustrating to read a poem that has wonderful ideas and a few interesting images, but the whole doesn't cohere because the writer is so caught up with being hip and clever. But let me get back to the Black writers whose work I admire.

Charles Johnson's novel *Middle Passage* [which won the 1990 National Book Award] is an absolutely astounding book, beautifully written and intellectually dazzling—I wish I could write prose that well. In poetry, I have to be thankful to Derek Walcott and Michael Harper; their works have always nourished me. Michael Harper, by the way, often uses blues and jazz idioms, and he uses them very, very deftly—what a difference to the would-be poets of the Black struggle and their contemporary successors! Harper is proof that one can write cogently and compellingly in those idioms. You have to know what you're doing.

At Arizona State University, where I taught for eight years before coming to Virginia, I would step out of the English building and accost Black students and say, "Why don't you come into this building? It won't bite you." And they'd answer, "Oh, English. Yeah, well, we're scared of English." I'd say, "Well, you're speaking it every day. How in the world can you be scared of it? How are you going to succeed at anything in life if you run from it? Now come in here and take some classes, learn a few new riffs!"

But this basic attitude of dismissal continues all the way up the academic ladder. I rarely have more than one or two Black students in my creative writing classes, though nothing and no one keeps them from enrolling. It's one of the hardest things for creative writing programs to find Black students with a genuine interest in the craft of writing and enough courage, self-esteem, and determination to wrestle their fears to the ground. I've had students say, "Well, 'they' don't understand the way I write." My reply: "Then, either make them understand it, or see if they have some suggestions worth thinking about." Criticism, however flawed and biased it may be, is part of a process that can help you reflect upon and improve your work, especially when you are in the learning stage. I find this unwillingness of many Black students to go into an English class and challenge the professors in an informed way very regrettable. The same holds true for creative writing. If you want to write a poem informed by blues or jazz rhythms, perhaps because these are original Black art forms on which you feel inspired to expand, then go ahead—write, and if necessary challenge the teacher who has been dealing in his or her own particular brand of poetry, and educate them. But also give them a chance to show whether or not they can learn. And if you can learn from them. I lose my patience with students who think poems come full-blown from some magical source; that gifts needn't be earned. And I find it odd when people accept the fact that in order to be a musician, one has to practice and practice—pianists learning their scales and so on—but somehow the same doesn't apply to writing. When I hear of Blacks who want to be writers but refuse to take creative writing classes for fear they might somehow be tainted by another cultural impression, I lose my patience. Do you want to write? Then sit down and practice.

Having the Picture Coalesce in a Kind of Whoosh!

Wayne Ude / 1992

This interview was conducted during the Associated Writing Programs Conference March 1992 in Norfolk, Virginia. The poet Maurya Simon attended the interview and asked some of the questions below. The interview appeared in *AWP Chronicle* in October/November 1993. Reprinted by permission of Wayne Ude.

Ude: After four books of poetry, your latest book is a novel. How did you come to write *Through the Ivory Gate?*

Dove: It began with the main character, Virginia. I had the idea for a young, black female puppeteer; and like most of my ideas, I can't possibly explain to you where it came from. But once she popped into my head, she wouldn't go away. I knew right away that, if I were to develop this character and get to know her better, it would be a novel.

The next step was to convince myself that I really could do it, and that took some years. I wrote an early draft many years ago and put it away because I really didn't know how to do it, but I kept returning to it. I threw away a hundred and fifty pages at one point—just stripped it down to its essentials. I think I had to learn where the shape of that particular novel was hiding. It was a long process until the last four years when I began to sit down with it every day.

Ude: When you began working on the novel, you had been writing stories for a while, though your 1985 collection, *Fifth Sunday*, hadn't yet appeared.

Dove: Yes, I was working on the novel then, but I was shaping it in small, short-story-like sections. I think short stories are much closer to poetry, so the transition was easier. Stories seem to have the same concentration of energy, the same sense of radiating from one event or one moment. The images that are used in stories, especially the images that really serve the story, tend to be compact and all of a piece in the same way that most lyric poetry is.

I discovered the shape of the novel through writing and came to realize that time was going to be much more fluid than I sensed at first. So I wasn't

88

going to write the novel as I first imagined it, where each chapter is a short story. It wasn't going to be that manageable.

Ude: Your book of poems, *Thomas and Beulah*, focuses on two characters' life stories, and the poems interweave. Perhaps after that book, a long prose narrative wasn't so great a leap as it might have seemed before.

Dove: I'm sure that was the case. While living through the research and writing *Thomas and Beulah*, I certainly didn't think about this kind of thing *while* I'm writing. But I'm sure that after *Thomas and Beulah*, I felt more comfortable working with various forms of extended narrative.

Ude: The puppeteering in the novel is delightful, especially Virginia's first appearance as an artist-in-the-schools before the grade-school classroom. How did you come up with a puppeteer? Have you worked in a puppet theater?

Dove: It's mostly imagined, something I would have loved to do but never have. My experience with puppets only goes as far as making puppets for my daughter when she was three or four, and staging little puppet theaters in the back yard for birthday parties.

I think part of the desire to use puppets came from being profoundly moved by adult puppet theaters such as the Bread and Puppet Theater. Their performances tap our primal need for drama and gesture and pageant. To combine street theater with these puppets puts the adult at odds with childhood, and that idea developed into sending Virginia into the classroom. Having taught a bit of poetry in the elementary schools, I've often wished for props, like puppets.

Ude: You weave in Virginia's own early memories of her parents and grandmother giving her an African American doll. It was a wonderful risk to have Virginia as a little girl reject the first Black doll her grandmother had given her in favor of a white doll she's had long enough to love, though the doll is so unlike her.

Dove: But the white doll is also well manufactured and sold as a more desirable goal, corresponding to people Virginia has seen in magazines and on TV, whereas the Black doll is so poorly made that it doesn't seem to correspond to anything in life. The moment is risky, and I've taken some flak for it. It's very important distinction to make, because part of the subtle effect of racism and marginalization in this country comes from exactly that kind of tokenism in media—the representing of Blacks in a slipshod way, which says subtly that the media-moguls don't care enough to present Black culture completely and accurately. "We're gonna do a little bit; are you happy?" they say and throw a bone. One may feel one should at least accept the bone in order to get more, even though it's not what you want, and it's not what most of the others have. It's a sad compromise.

Ude: Did you do a lot of research on puppets?

Dove: I did a lot of research on Bread and Puppet Theater and how it evolved. I also read lots of puppet plays, from children's plays to Garcia Lorca's puppet plays and marionette plays just to see how dialogue changes when puppets are involved. And I read books on the theory of puppetry, which was wonderful. And then I *stopped*. Because it was overwhelming—I knew too much about it; I really didn't want to get too encyclopedic or esoteric about the nature of puppets.

You know, Virginia does that once, when she gives a speech and tries to explain her vocation to the parents at an open house. She's justifying puppetry to them, and they look at her as if they're thinking, Oh dear, where did she come from?

Ude: I was a little surprised at first that you gave Virginia both puppetry and the cello—two art forms. Why did you decide to give her both forms of expression?

Dove: When I was a young woman going through college, I met so many people who were practicing more than one art form. College is time for exploration, and I had many friends who were playing an instrument and acting, or who were doing gymnastics and painting. This mix is diminished in graduate school when suddenly we're all specialized, beating one drum rather relentlessly.

It does seem to carry over as almost an unspoken rule that you shouldn't let your characters have too many interests; you should give them one trait, or one obsession; but I thought, No, no, that's not the way life is.

I just turned forty last year. I suppose I have to start considering myself as a person of middle-age, or a poet in her middle period or something; and I notice that quite a few of my friends have turned back to earlier passions, like suddenly taking up the piano again. You know, the passions we gave up around graduate school; and I thought, the human spirit can't be confined in easily manageable spheres. The mind is a connector; the mind will connect *anything*, but the connections among the arts are very natural. I don't want to suggest that everything comes to some kind of coherent conclusion, but that the mind is a natural integrator. The mind will take all the events of a day and join them one to another.

That's part of what I was trying to show in the novel, too—the sense that as we walk through Virginia's world we're going to be able to eavesdrop on her mind, to sit in on all of the connections she makes.

Ude: The connections of family and the past are important throughout your work; but here in the novel, near the ending, Virginia learns something with which she may not be able to connect, when she finally hears Aunt Carrie's story of the relationship with her own brother, who's also Virginia's father.

Dove: I thought a lot about that part of the story. Before I wrote the ending, I wasn't sure how Virginia was going to react. I was fairly confident that she was her own person enough to be able to tell me.

When I reached that point in the novel, Virginia still didn't know what to do with Carrie's story, how to react to it. At first I thought, But that's not a reaction, not knowing what to do—but then I realized it *was* a reaction, it's the reaction she's capable of now.

One thing that disturbs me sometimes about the form of a novel is its tendency to wrap everything up—the compulsion to bring the main character to a big realization so all the pieces fall into place, and the story can deliver its punch. Life just ain't like that. Life sometimes offers little revelations, and their consequence may never find any kind of dramatic fruition, or their drama may be played out so late in the characters' lives, after so many other events, that it would ruin the shape of your novel. So I realized that I was actually fighting against a convention I had accepted through years of reading, a convention which sparked my uneasiness when Virginia didn't quite know what to do with Aunt Carrie's revelation. So I thought, OK, this is the way it has to be. She doesn't quite know what to do.

Ude: In your poems you use many different points of view, particularly in *Thomas and Beulah*, and in the other books as well. Yet in *Through the Ivory Gate*, you hold to a single point of view.

Dove: When I was writing the novel, I didn't want it to be a poet's novel. I didn't want it to be like my poetry. It was a chance to do something new, to do something that I couldn't do in poetry, which was to hold this one point of view for a long time, through a varying string of events.

Ude: How difficult was it as you worked on drafts of the novel to keep strictly to the first-person so that we see the world only through Virginia?

Dove: It was a relief to do everything through Virginia's mind. The novel began with Virginia, it was her story, and that stayed the same through all those rewrites, and those deleted pages. The sections I took out of the novel were false starts that I wrote to get to know the character, material that just wasn't necessary anymore. I wanted to leave the reader with that feeling of what it's like for Virginia to be in her mid-twenties. In your mid-twenties, life is possibility. You have no idea what's going to happen. Friends who are thirty-five or forty or older will say, "Gosh, when I was younger, I didn't know what in the world would happen to me; there's no way in the world I could have predicted this life." So I wanted that sense of openness, too.

The hardest part was handling all of the flashbacks and switches; to keep the chronology clear was agony, as was getting stuck in verb tenses—"Now this is past, so this has to be— OK, now I've got to back up into the present, how do I do that? How do I sort out my *would*s and *would have*s and *had had*s?"

Ude: Do poets do less of that kind of time management?

Dove: Well, poets do it—we just do it without a lot of past participles. Everything exists—not on the same plane, but on many planes simultaneously—and it's almost an unspoken understanding that time travel is instantaneous in poetry.

Ude: Your short stories often have a surprising shift at the end. In "Fifth Sunday," for example, we're watching a young girl go through a Sunday thinking about a boy who's starting to show an innocent interest in her. Then she faints; and suddenly at the end, we have a nurse saying that this very naïve young girl probably fainted because she's pregnant. The nurse hasn't checked carefully enough to realize that the girl's period has just begun, which means she can't possible be pregnant. The girl's absolute fury in response is the kind of twist I mean.

Dove: Yes, it's a real switch; it's a shock, and she grows up in that moment, or let's say, she toughens in that moment. But then my youngest sister once said to me, "Rita, I just don't get it. Your poems are going along so nicely; and then, in the last two lines, you do something radical, you go off the wall."

I think I can draw an analogy between that and my passion for crossword puzzles. I really enjoy seeing things come together in the end—I mean, pieces of a puzzle or aspects of a situation that are interesting, but you can't quite make out the sense of them, or you have a partial sense until the final piece pops in and you discover a new meaning. I'm almost an addict when it comes to crossword puzzles. It's really terrible; I have to limit myself to one or two a day. The pleasure of having the picture coalesce in a kind of whoosh! is something that I think informs my poetry and also the short stories. It's the sense that at the end, if you look back at the story, the indications were there. The clues were there.

Simon: Do you feel less certain about writing prose?

Dove: Yes. If feel more uncertain about prose because I haven't been doing it as long, and because I wasn't "trained" as a prose writer. The only things I can carry into my prose writing are a reader's love of it, my sense of writing poetry, and what I've learned as I go along. I haven't had as much time to think about the process of prose writing as consciously as I have about poetry.

Simon: You have such a strong sense for developing a narrative line. It seems to come naturally.

Dove: I never realized there was a strong narrative element in my poetry until someone told me. By that I simply mean that while I'm writing, I try not to concentrate on the poem's components, like narrative elements, too consciously—as paradoxical as that sounds. But I grew up with all sorts of relatives telling stories all the time, so a story well-told is something I learned to appreciate early in life.

Simon: Some of the poems you read today were about your daughter. Or at least a reader assumes that, since you have a daughter. Do you think of her when you write? Do you imagine her reading the poem?

Dove: No, I don't. It's probably self-protection that I don't. In fact, I don't think of any audience at all. Or if I think of an audience, I think of one person reading. A group is too big; that's not intimate enough. I do think of *her* as I'm writing, but not of her reading the poems.

Ude: In the poem "Summit Beach, 1921," from *Grace Notes*, your character is confident that the world will be wonderful, and yet the final image of the scar on the young woman's knee reminds us of her earlier confidence that she could fly. The scar and the memory of stepping off the roof have the feel of an actual, remembered story.

Dove: My mother did that when she was a child. She thought she could fly, and she climbed up on a shed roof—kids do that sort of thing—she stood up there with an umbrella and thought she could fly. Of course I laughed when she told me. My mother always said she was more disappointed than hurt that she couldn't fly.

But in "Summit Beach" the character isn't my mother; so as I was working on that poem, I was not quite sure how things were going to end for *this* character. I was working toward the ending, and the scar was there, and I didn't tell you if the scar was there before the idea to include the flying. I think it was. I think the scar was there, and I didn't know how she got the scar. I'm almost positive that's how it happened.

And actually during the composition, when my mother's flying attempt came into the poem, it was a way of getting to a feeling of both hope and despair at the end of the poem. I wanted to have this feeling in remembering that event, you could still feel the exhilaration, right before she's going to hit the ground. And since we have the scar already, we know what's going to happen. I wanted that kind of ambivalence at the end. So up until that point, I felt the poem was on the ground and she was being stubborn, she was not allowing herself to blossom and open up, and the music begins to overwhelm her. It opens her up to this memory of the moment before flying, the first time, before the fall. It's right before the fall.

Ude: "Fantasy and Science Fiction" seemed very different from your other poems. The title suggests that it's a more surreal, associative poem.

Dove: It's very different. When I was a kid I loved science fiction. I have an older brother, two years older. We were very close as kids. We did all sorts of thing. In the summer when we weren't allowed to watch television, we read and we wrote our own science fiction stories. I wanted to capture some of the surreal quality of science fiction, the way that science fiction has of altering reality without apologies, and without really getting very deep into the psyche. I wanted to write a poem that was light, and yet emulated the feeling I had whenever I read science fiction. So it was fun to do, and different.

Ude: What about the ending, where you say it's not the sort of story you would tell your mother?

Dove: Well, science fiction is incredibly moral and outrageous at the same time. The stories are parables. What the science fiction I read said about modern life, about the evils of automation, seemed incredibly sophisticated and bleak—and of course lots of fun to read at the same time. I always thought that if my parents knew what these stories were saying, they wouldn't let us read them. They didn't know this stuff was subversive literature!

Ude: Family history allows many of the poems to resonate between past and present. That also seems true in your poems which are set in other countries.

Dove: Oh, the present is so little of what is actually in the world. In my life, I guess, the present is a very complex thing that is fed by the past continually, almost every instant. Add the anticipation of the future, and it's all there. Travel, in a way, is a metaphor for living in the present or present tense. First of all, by being cut off physically from your roots and everything that you take for granted, you become hypersensitive to everything around you. I don't want to make this sound grand, but there's a sense of continual survival when one travels: "Gosh, I managed to find lunch." There is this intensified feeling of constantly walking through the present.

And yet, when one is traveling, one is constantly coming up against the past, some extrapolated sense of one's own culture's past. At the same time, all these foreign places remind one of home. When I travel I'm thinking constantly of home. It's very strange.

Ude: How is this affected when you're in a country where you don't speak the language?

Dove: That's even stranger, because then you become all eyes and ears, and the interior life become very discrete, contained, and unsullied in a funny way. Because you aren't communicating with anyone else, unless there's another person with you, in which case there's another kind of intimate life that's a bubble you walk around in. I like going to places where I don't speak the language or speak only a little bit of it, because it redefines everything that I know about perception. Sometimes we edit out perceptions through the way we articulate them, even in conversation. If you don't have the opportunity to do that, experiences have a chance to make their connections and resonances inside you before words, and they grow in a different ways, come out in different ways.

Simon: You've lived in Germany for a fairly long time.

Dove: The longest stretch was a year and a half, I think. When I'm in Germany, I speak German, I think German. It takes a week to get to that point. So in fact the English language then has this space inside—it gets to germinate in the darkness for a while.

Simon: Does the sound of the German language tend to influence the poetry? Do you write poetry when you're there?

Dove: That's a difficult question. If I'm there for three months I don't write as much. When I was there for a year and a half, I wrote a lot. And at first it was mentally soothing to have an island of language to go to, with all the other language around me. After a while it became difficult because more and more German idioms began to creep into my English usage. I don't mind that necessarily, but I couldn't tell any more what was standard English. I couldn't remember what was ordinary and what would be charged language or unusual diction.

And I think German syntax has crept in at times. This idea of having a poem or story come together only at the very end has some of its origins in the way that German syntax is construed, the way that in German the verb occurs at the end of the sentence. You have to gather all the information of the sentence and wait for the verb to make sense of it. "Wolfgang to the store around the corner from Detlev's house while it was raining *had walked*."

Ude: In the poem, "In Which I Refuse Contemplation," the speaker is visiting in Germany and hears news of the death of a cousin. You give us all sorts of layers of connection to the past, to home, in the midst of this foreign language and place.

Dove: Yes. It's that layering, too, the simultaneity of experiences, and the layering of worlds. The speaker of the poem is standing in Germany, with that life going on around her; she has to attend to it in some way, but she has just received this letter about the death of a cousin. In a certain way she's conducting her life on two levels at that moment.

There's also two levels of the language, and I've had that experience a lot, this feeling of thinking or living in one language and then something comes up in another language and I have to do them both. I can get short-circuited very easily. Every time I come back from Germany, or go there for that matter, there's a week of not really being one place or the other, in terms of language, and not really being able to think very clearly. I'd never be a simultaneous translator. I don't have that gift.

Ude: You do another kind of traveling in other poems. In *The Yellow House on the Corner*, the entire third section is set in the time of slavery. How difficult were those poems to write?

Dove: Yes, history is a kind of travel in its own way. It was difficult. What helped me in the writing of those poems was the language. I had been reading slave narratives, and those accounts became especially powerful because of the contrast between the horror and brutality of the experiences and the language in which those experiences were recounted, which was very refined, very restrained. There was something in that rub that made it that much more compelling.

The abolitionists had done this intentionally. They transcribed and helped with the editing of these slave narratives; they felt that if the language were inflammatory, that would be overkill and they would not convince people of the horrors of slavery. They wanted to impress upon the reader, subliminally, that these were noble human beings. The language is noble, and what's being described is far from noble. I wanted to have the kind of rub in the poems as well. Having the language be restrained helped a lot in coping with the horrors of the content.

Ude: Often the horror emerges through your dramatization of what happened to family. In "Mississippi," for example, the daughter is being left behind and her mother is being sent down the river.

Dove: I think you're right. The whole obsession with family is rooted in the essential African American trauma. And it's one that I think we can't even begin, to this day, to understand thoroughly. It goes back so far, and it's not only the fact that we don't know our roots.

There was always the unspoken agreement, I think, among my family, both immediate and extended, that family is sacred and no matter what anyone in the family does, they're still family. This is a way of keeping the family together or keeping the clan together. It's not oppressive; it's not as simple as having to do this or that to be a credit to the family, though that can be there, too. But there was a sense that, even if someone screws up royally, you take them in. There is no excommunication of a family member; and that means that there's always some place to go, where someone will love you.

I've always felt that. I'm sure that it's an important connection, and it goes all the way back to that trauma—when you not only didn't know whether you could keep a family together, but you were practically guaranteed that you couldn't.

Ude: In "The Transport of Slaves from Maryland to Mississippi," the slaves revolt en route and free themselves, and then some of the freed slaves make it possible for their companions to be recaptured. It's tremendously honest to say: this too happened.

Dove: That was based on an actual event, and the slaves betrayed the rebellion because, as the one woman says, the slave driving the wagon—the one responsible for guarding the other slaves—"could have been a son of mine." The flip side of this coin is that if you don't know who your family is, everyone is your family.

Ude: In all of those poems you take me some place I haven't been—and maybe don't want to go, either; but I need to go there.

Dove: I wrote the first one, which actually was the prose poem, "Kentucky, 1833," when I was a graduate student at Iowa. And I remember when it came up for discussion, someone said, "Well, I feel like someone told me that in order to be healthy, I had to take a spoonful of medicine a day, but I'd rather take an apple a day."

It was a moment when I realized that for some people the horror of events and the political aspect of a poem make it impossible for them to see any aesthetic merits. This is far afield, but I think it is a real problem in workshops, and one reason poetry with a political or sociological content often gets short shrift. It's very hard for people to be able to discuss that material in a technical sense. At the same time, that comment was the first indication I had that I was onto something good.

Simon: How about the other poems in that section? Did you get much response to those?

Dove: Some responses, but not very good ones. I was the only Black person in the Iowa workshop at the time, and I think many Black writers who have been in workshops will have had the same experience: you're always the only one. There falls the burden—and it is a burden, whether you choose to bear it or not—the burden of other people's guilt. I discovered in that workshop, though I did get some valuable comments on some poems, that the poems dealing specifically with my heritage always got the worst comments, because people could not find a way around the guilt; they couldn't quite figure it out.

It's disheartening. Being a student in a creative writing workshop is a very naked experience and as the only person representing any other culture, you're setting yourself up doubly. Which is why I think it's so important—my God, we've just got to break down these barriers.

Inevitably in this country when someone regards you as a hyphenated poet—as an African American-woman-poet, or a Latin-American-gay-poet, or whatever—then for some reason your peers and the critics start making allowances, the rigor drops; it's this condescension which is so insulting, because as a serious writer one approaches the art with all the rigor of non-hyphenated poets. And the rigor does drop. I've seen it happen time and time again. A reviewer won't talk about the book or a student won't talk about the poem in terms of its techniques or its aesthetic; they'll only talk about the subject matter, and my God!—we're talking about a writer, you've got to treat the book as you would any other writer's work. Use the same standards, please.

Ude: Your poems, like those in *Thomas and Beulah*, often present different versions of the same world.

Dove: I'm fascinated with taking a moment, or a moment's truth, and viewing different facets of it. I'm sure part of that comes from growing up as an African American where, as with anyone who comes from a non-main-stream group, I had to learn two versions of the world. I mean, you have your version, and then the mainstream has its version, and in order to surface in the mainstream you learn that version too; it's on television, you pick it up.

It's almost like being bilingual, and there are these other parallels too. We don't have anything that covers all the different ways a single person might need to learn, but when DuBois talks about having second sight, or binocular vision, that's what it's like.

I think I had a second shock—realizing that there are many different truths and all of them can be viable and operating at the same time—when I went to Europe for the first time in 1974. There were lots of anti-American demonstrations then because of our role in the overthrow of the Chilean government, and I was startled that Europeans had a different view of our involvement there, that my dear country, home of the free, was just as good at giving out propaganda as everybody else. So I am really very interested in seeing more than one side to a story. This happens in *Thomas and Beulah*, where two different lives sometimes connect and cross, and sometimes they don't; but you also see each person in different lights, different perspectives.

Ude: This may be coming back to that twist at the end of your poems. Many of your poems end with strong, lovely conclusions. In "His Shirt," for example, in *The Yellow House on the Corner*, you give us images of the beloved's shirt, and then conclude with the possibility that it "could be mistaken / for something quite / fragile and / ordinary." And of course the shirt is both very important and quite fragile and ordinary. Very quotable lines.

Dove: Sometimes I worry about that. I worry that the click is too loud at the end. I don't want to blow someone out of the water. One of my life-long quests probably will be to write a poem that doesn't do that at the end.

Simon: But I don't think you do blow people out of the water. The closure is open enough to make one thoughtful and not hit us over the head. The lines feel as though you as the poet discovered them, that you came to them suddenly, as we do.

Dove: I did discover them. I don't think I've ever had the ending when I began a poem.

Simon: How do you see your own poetry changing or evolving, or do you try to stay unaware of that as you're working?

Dove: I know it's evolving. But I'm not really aware—and again this is very deliberate stupidity I'm cultivating for myself. I've noted a tendency to longer poems, a few longer poems, something which I think in the first or second book I couldn't do yet. I wanted to but I couldn't.

I have noticed that I'm not daunted anymore by a poem that I know is going to be a longer poem, which is going to take some time to reach its own satisfaction. Part of this certainly has to do with writing a novel, because there's so much delayed gratification you must endure when you're writing a novel. So now I'm willing to float a little longer. But I can't tell, really, how my work is evolving. I'll let others tell me.

Ude: Is your day different when you're working on a novel than when you're writing poems?

Dove: It is different. With poetry I tend to work for three or four hours at a stretch, but I will do a lot of hopping around between poems. I don't work on one poem only for weeks. I will work on several poems for weeks, or months.

There's much more of a sense when I'm writing poems of just having associations, jumping between associations. I can be working on a poem, working on the third line of the second stanza and trying to get the stanzas to fit together, when a line or a few words for another poem will hit me, and I'll write them on a separate sheet of paper, finish what I'm doing, go and work on that for a little while, then go back to the first one. So I'm doing a lot of juggling around, and coming out after a day's work or a week's work with no poem yet, while all these poems just seem to be building themselves. I tend to finish two or three poems at once, but I have long periods where everything is in abeyance.

With the novel, particularly as it neared completion, it took over. I would work very much from the beginning of a scene to the end. For the last four or five months or so I just couldn't write any poetry, I had to live in the world of the novel. I didn't like that very much.

I was much more regular about my writing schedule, too. I would get up early in the morning and work until one or two. I would never be able to write poetry first thing in the morning. With the novel, in those early hours when I was a little fuzzy, I could trim things. I could work on "he said/she said." I could work myself into the work, whereas with poetry, I need to be able to jump right in.

I found I could work for a longer period of time on the novel without feeling as exhausted. With poetry, after three hours I'm drained. I could work up to six hours on the novel without feeling the same kind of exhaustion. I could take breaks while working on the novel and say, Well, let me go back to this scene, or let me look up and find out if this date was actually a Thursday in October 1974, so that I can develop the chronology.

Simon: Do you write in longhand?

Dove: I start out in longhand, and I use college-ruled notebook paper. So it's almost like going to school again. I like that red line on the notebook paper, I like what it gives me—I write in the margin all the time, write little ideas or extra words—and when it gets to the point where I can't see the shape of the poem after several drafts longhand, I'll type or do it on the computer. Then I print it out and immediately start tearing it up again.

I try not to let it sit on the page too long in black typescript before I start revising, because typescript can really freeze up on me—with poetry. With prose, however, I wrote the novel directly into the computer, printed it out, and then revised, except for a few scenes near the very end where I noticed that I was waxing poetic. "Get on to the end!" I had to prompt myself. Sometimes I had to slow it down, so I had to write longhand.

Ude: How do you juggle writing poetry, writing fiction with the longer hours, and teaching?

Dove: Not very well, I'm afraid. I don't know how anyone does it, and I'm always asking people, how do you manage? I try to balance it, first of all, by looking at students' poems in a different part of the house. I don't let their poems, or anything that has to do with the university, enter the room where I write. Otherwise I find myself thinking about it constantly. Students' poems can sneak into your head, and you suddenly think, That's an idea, they should try it this way. Also I try—and it's very hard to do, but I try—to confine my teaching homework, preparing for classes, to specific days. I teach on Monday and Tuesday. The University of Virginia has been wonderful; they let me do this kind of thing, teach one part of the week. And I hold office hours on Wednesday. So on Monday and Tuesday and on Wednesday, I work on student things, I prepare my classes.

On Thursday I start to write but I give myself a little bit of time to decompress; on Friday and during the weekend I don't do anything but write. I'm constantly feeling guilty. But it's the only way to do it for me. I don't think I'm any good to my students if I'm not writing, first of all. You know, most of the good writing is confined to spring breaks, leaves, summer.

If I'm really working on something, when a poem or a story or whatever takes over, as they do, that just means I don't get sleep. That's what gives. I love to work at night, but I haven't worked at night for years because of the demands of daily life. I teach in the afternoons, my daughter has to get up and go to school. Though my husband and I trade off weeks—one week I get her off to school, the next week he gets her off to school. That's the one major difference in the way I'm working now and the way I used to work, that I have to work at times that I don't like to work.

Ude: What general advice do you most often give to your creative writing students?

Dove: Read! And write, even when you're tired, scared, discouraged. Never settle for a word or phrase if you know there's a better one out there.

A Chorus of Voices

Steven Ratiner / 1992

Steven Ratiner interviewed Rita Dove on Friday, 13 November 1992, at Mount Holyoke College, just after the appearance of her novel *Through the Ivory Gate*. The following text is reprinted from Ratiner's collection *Giving Their Word: Conversations with Contemporary Poets* (University of Massachusetts Press, 2002). Reprinted by permission of Steven Ratiner.

Ratiner: One of the central features in your poetry and fiction is the power of history and memory. Where does that drive to tell the story originate in your life?

Dove: Well, it really begins with two feelings I had as a child: first, that *I* wasn't represented in History—I'm talking of History with a capital H— neither as a female or as a Black person. And second, the nagging sense that ordinary people were not represented in history, that history gives you the tales of heroes, basically—and not what happens to "ordinary" people who live through the events. You are right that the twin poles of history and memory have certainly not only fascinated me—I'd almost say haunted me all these years. Because I think history is a very powerful weapon. If you can edit someone out of history, then the next generation—those who do not have a personal memory of certain events anymore—won't have anything to go on.

And cultural memory is remarkably short in our day and age because communities are disintegrating, so there is no oral or communal sense of carrying on a tradition. Everyone is focused in on media, which means that the media has the power to tell them what to remember—which brings us to memory, that other focus. I use memory more in the sense of personal recol- lection—although there is the power of communal memory, too. It's intri- guing how particular yet inaccurate we are in remembering things; we remember what we want to or need to remember. Put five people in a room who have seen the same traffic accident, and you'll get five different versions of the story. I find this process fascinating.

Ratiner: Are you consciously trying to preserve glimpses of history for the next generation? As a poet, are you a carrier of history?

Dove: A carrier of history of a particular sort. In *Thomas and Beulah*, I was hoping to hand down a sense of two very normal people living through a period of incredible change in the United States. I am very interested in how an individual behaves in the flux of the larger history, but also I am interested in recovering the sense that we—as individuals, as human beings— can connect to the universe. The heroic sagas that we get in history books may be necessary to provide the overview, but they do make you feel like you don't count.

Ratiner: What I love in your writing is your astounding sense of the par- ticular. We feel we can almost live through the experiences of the poems. And some of the moments provide us with a small glimpse of a Black America we'd otherwise never see.

Dove: I believe we live our lives in the particular; we blossom through detail. We don't walk down the street thinking: here I am, forty years old, walking down a Midwestern street. We look at *that* flower, smell the breeze. Sensory detail is how we experience the world; and the deepest way to con- vince someone of your reality, that you can understand someone else's world, is through the particular.

Ratiner: But there are things that I can never experience—especially being white, being male—and suddenly to have some small entrance into this other life is quite a moving experience.

Dove: Well, that is marvelous, because I believe if, as human beings, we can enter those other worlds even for an instant, then it becomes a little more difficult to hate that other person simply because they are different, to treat them badly or to kill them.

Ratiner: But you mentioned specifically the way history wields a certain power. Tell me a little bit more about that. I know poets shy away from proselytizing through their poems, but I can't help but think that your inten- tion was more than making the beautiful object on the paper.

Dove: Definitely. My primary intention has never been to make the beauti- ful object on paper, although I think that beauty beguiles us so well that no matter how horrific the topic, if the poem is beautiful, it convinces. It's true, poets tend not to proselytize. Let me approach it this way: in my first book is an entire section of slave narratives; what had impressed me about the slave narratives I had read was the fact that they were a witnessing, a witnessing of horror. Some of them had been written by ex-slaves, others dictated and transcribed by abolitionists.

Yet how modest the language was! All they wanted, it seemed, was simply to get it down on paper, so people would know what happened. That feeling of not being able to trust any larger power to do the right thing—that you just have to bear witness to the experience—that, I think, is the extent of the proselytizing I am doing. Witnessing is very powerful; in a way, each poet does exactly that every time he or she writes a poem—witnessing a little piece of life. I don't think about the poems in terms of the grand sense—well, I am going to remake history or revamp it—but perhaps more a feeling of chipping away at history as a whole; I don't think of history as orderly, as some kind of entity that we can even understand.

Ratiner: Your poems, with great delicacy, bear witness to the lived experience of history. Two examples from *Grace Notes* come to mind: "Summit Beach" seems to bring back the figure of your grandmother Beulah again; and "Crab Boil" centers on a girl I took to be a young Rita Dove.

Dove: Yes, I am the speaker in "Crab Boil." I will admit that poem as autobiographical, though that recognition is not necessary to an understanding of the poem.

Ratiner: In each poem, a small personal experience is depicted center stage with just a hint of the larger historical forces churning in the background. The phrase "the Negro beach" is enough to conjure the racial climate in the 1920s. But Beulah seems hardly aware of this when she "climbed Papa's shed and stepped off / the tin roof into the blue, / with her parasol and invisible wings." If not the tide of history, there must be something else that supports this woman, gives her the confidence to take that brave step.

Dove: In that particular poem, the "something else" is a sense of self, a wellspring of love that comes from family and the community. I keep coming back to the community. What will always keep you going is that sense of being supported by others, others who understand, others who care, who have been through similar experiences. The girl in "Crab Boil" doesn't quite understand the segregated beach business, but she has learned, even at that young age, to look and pay attention to her elders. Elders are very important in African American families; in fact anyone older than you in an African American community has the right to tell you what to do, to dispense lengthy advice. But this girl has enough acumen to look around and to watch and so learn how to behave, how to survive in a world whose rules are absolute for her. On the one hand, such alertness can cause you to become very reserved and distrustful; on the other hand, you learn to rely on those around you who have "been there," and then you are strengthened by this support system.

Ratiner: But you create an interesting tension between the communal sway and the will of the individual. The girl keeps questioning, "Why do I remember the sky / above the forbidden beach, / why only blue and the scratch, / shell on tin, of their distress?" She almost empathizes with the crabs captured in the pail, especially after Aunt Helen's comment, "Look at that——/ a bunch of niggers, not / a-one get out 'fore the others pull him / back." They tell the girl the crabs will feel no pain in the boiling water, and she finally accepts their claim. "I decide to believe this: I'm hungry." There's a conflict of two sorts of knowledge: the wisdom of the culture set against the girl's innate understandings, almost a wisdom of the body.

Dove: But we get the feeling that she goes along with their wisdom yet she doesn't believe it totally. She decides to believe for the moment, and in this moment, as you said, the individual comes into conflict with the community. I think, really, she bows to the exigencies of the situation. Even so, I think it's the best possible relationship between individual and community. We are all individuals who may share certain things which make us feel that we are a community—but the individual should never be obliterated or even blurred by that connection with the community. Even Beulah in "Summit Beach, 1921"—she wants to fly!

Ratiner: Although at the end of the poem, the girl thinks of her aunt and reasons: "After all, she *has* / grown old in the South. If / we're kicked out now, I'm ready." What has changed inside her?

Dove: What has changed is that she now understands how to gird her loins in a moment of survival. She understands when to stop feeling in order to get through the moment. It is a sad epiphany, because this kind of revelation dulls children's eyes when they are faced with injustice that doesn't make sense—unless you just give up on people, declare the human race evil. And this is especially tragic for her, a little Black girl who is extremely perceptive, who looks at everything, the sky and sand and even hears the sounds of the scratching claws—who was like one big nerve ending. She decides to muzzle her emotional responses because she must survive; she has to eat, she is hungry. Whereas at the beginning of the poem she might have been devastated if the whites had come and chased them out, now she is ready to not feel a thing and go.

Ratiner: I wonder if that dramatic break with the world is particular to minority experience in this country? Does that moment dovetail with the scene [in *Through the Ivory Gate*, Dove's first novel] where young Virginia is thrilled over her first straight-A's report card, and the response of her white friend is to push her down, call her "nigger." With that one word, her sense of the world is shattered, and you describe the beginning of that survival mechanism the girl will adopt.

Dove: Well, yes. Of course it would be ideal if it had never happened to her, but it does. And I don't think it's something particular only to racial minorities; it happens to all of us on some level as we grow up, as we change from children to adults. I think it is more consistent and perhaps less explainable when racism or sexism is the cause. It really is horrible, but it happens. So to try and make others see how betrayal shatters reality and how one may shut down in order to survive would bring us a long way toward explaining adult behavior in certain situations. It all depends too when this shutdown occurs. For people not in the mainstream of society, it may happen at a younger age, which is potentially more damaging.

I remember a poem by Yehuda Amichai in which he talks about his grandson using the metaphor of a hatching egg—how he has come out whole and how miraculous that is, until some tragedy, some hurt occurs. Then, says Amichai, the boiling begins; we just don't know if he is going to come out hard-boiled or soft-. You see children of all ages, all colors: you see them at age five and they are glorious; and you see them at age eight, and half of them are still wonderful but somewhat muted. I've seen this because I've watched my daughter grow up; she's nine now. But I also see older kids when I visit classrooms to teach poetry, and when they get to be about eleven, there is very little openness left. It's just incredible; but something has happened along the way.

Ratiner: You've talked about the intellectual discipline in your household, the knowledge that your parents tried to armor you with as a girl. There's the father's admonition in "Flash Cards": "What you don't understand, master."

Dove: It wasn't a rule that was laid down, though there were other kinds of rules—a prescribed amount of television per week, and always doing your homework first thing after school—but there was a feeling in our household that the only ticket to a happy life is to do the best you can, no matter what you do. You can't cheat on that kind of commitment. But it wasn't a stern warning; it was an expression of love.

The one place we were allowed to go practically anytime was the library. The only stipulation was that we had to have read all the books we got before returning for more. I remember my parents asking, "Have you read all these books?" And then they would say, "Well, you aren't through yet; you can't go back until you finish reading these books." You know, finish what you have done.

My siblings and I, we enjoyed learning—maybe because we weren't allowed to watch too much television. In the summer that was agony! We had to find other things to do: so we read a lot, and wrote radio plays and rock 'n' roll songs. My brother and I started our own summer newspaper. He was always the editor-in-chief because he was two years older, and I always quit to form my own magazine called "Poet's Delight." I never got further than designing the cover; I'd spend a week drawing every single autumn leaf on a maple tree. And then I would write one poem, and that would be it. We went through this summer after summer, the same scenario. But it forced us to invent entertainment, to use our inner resources. On the other hand, there was this great feeling of trust our parents instilled in us, as if to say, "Well, we raised you this way and we'll stand behind you."

And I remember once coming back from the library nearly in tears; I was about eleven or twelve or so, and they wouldn't let me check out Françoise Sagan. I had read something in a magazine about this seventeen-year old girl who had written this risqué novel, and of course I wanted to read it. I think it was *Bonjour, Tristesse*, and the librarian said, "No, you can't read it, you are not an adult." It was the first time anyone had forbidden me to read. So I went home and told my mother, who wrote a note that said, "Let her check out any book she wants." I think my parents felt if any book was too old for us, we would get bored quickly. That moment had a great impact on me; I realized they trusted me.

Ratiner: Turning your mind loose—that's quite a brave step for parents, a test of faith in the learning process. And neither of your parents—am I remembering this correctly—had been to college themselves?

Dove: My mother had a scholarship to Howard, but wasn't allowed to go. She was sixteen when she graduated high school. She had skipped two grades and her parents were afraid to let such a young girl go to Washington, D.C., alone, so she didn't attend college.

My father was the first person in his family to go to college. There were ten brothers and sisters, and they were poor, so during the Depression when they didn't have shoes, they made sure that my father had shoes in order to go to school, because he was intellectually inclined and they believed he had *the chance*. I didn't learn about this until I was an adult. This was his burden, and he carries it still—all hopes were pinned on him. He got a master's degree in chemistry and became the first Black chemist in the rubber industry in Akron, Ohio, so he became the battering ram that opened the door.

Ratiner: That has become a common immigrant tale—parents pinning their hopes on their children. So there is the communal handing-on of their dream. And even if it were never mentioned, you knew you were being given not only a chance but a responsibility. Were they happy when you turned to poetry for your life's work?

Dove: It wasn't the career they expected. I don't recall any conversations where they tried to steer us toward a certain career; I just *knew* I was supposed to be a lawyer or a doctor, you know, that kind of profession. But doctors had to cut people up, so I thought, OK, a lawyer, then. When I entered college, I declared a pre-law major until my first class in government, and that was the end of that! I guess I felt sufficiently afraid of what my parents might say so I claimed an English major as preparation for law school, and I kept up this pretense until I was a junior. That was the point I decided to try and become a writer. I went home at Thanksgiving and said to my father, "I want to be a poet," and to his credit, he simply put down his newspaper and said, "Well, I've never understood poetry, so don't be upset if I don't read it."

I remember feeling immense relief at that moment, as if he were handing me the reins. He was saying, "I accept that this is what you want to do; I just want to let you know that I am not showing any disapproval by not reading it." Since then he has read my poetry, of course, but at the time I considered it a perfectly honorable pact.

Ratiner: For any family, the prospect of their children pursuing a life in the arts creates a certain anxiousness: how will they make a living, and will they be safe? Let me ask you, then, about the burden of family. There are many times, especially in *Grace Notes*, where you talk about the pain you carry as a result of the family experience. One that caught my attention was the wonderful "Poem in Which I Refuse Contemplation." There is a skipping back and forth from the speaker's consciousness to that of a letter from her mother. And the letter blends all the anguish of family life with the comforting business of everyday life.

Dove: It is a difficult burden. When you move out of the family's physical reach, you begin to grow into a different person. And every time one returns to the family, one slips into an old role only partially; a subtle feeling of alienation occurs. In that poem, I am the one who went away. My brothers and sisters all still live in Akron, Ohio; they're professionals in chemistry and computer science, but they stayed there in the family, while I went off to all these places. I always felt they didn't really understand why I needed to see the world. What is she doing out there? That's what I imagined them thinking. So I think there is a sense of . . . not really alienation, but a sense of difference, of distance that experience creates—and though one may long to go back home, to return to the womb, it isn't possible.

Ratiner: And even if memory attempts to bridge that distance, something has been surrendered. The poem contains the lines "but I can't feel his hand . . . /" and the closing "I'm still standing. Bags to unpack." And I just wondered if it seems to you that language is the way we can unpack our bags, let go of some of the burden, and at the same time re-establish some kind of a bond?

Dove: Language and poetry are not going to save anybody. Poetry can make the hurt a little bit more comprehensible and hence bearable, but it is not going to "make it all better." I have never felt that. Poetry can bridge some of that distance, but the distance is still there. In that poem the invisible bridge of support, a remedy for alienation, is the way in which the mother's words reverberate and inform the thoughts of the woman standing there with her bags. In the end she can say, "I'm still standing. Bags to unpack."

In a way, the mother's letter has given her a lesson. In one sentence, she mentions that the cousin has been strangled; the next, she complains about those raccoons in the crawl space—so life goes on. "I want to let you know what is going on in our end of the world," the mother is saying. "Take care." So there is a connection; there are people out there who love you.

Ratiner: I think I skipped past that meaning too quickly. I was struck by the weight of the bags, the burden, and not the reassurance of the mother's love. I guess that double-edged sword is present throughout. I think of the poem "Flash Cards," with the father drilling the math lessons into his children's brains. His injunction comes in the line, "What you don't understand, / master," but the weary child counters at the end, as if it were the answer to one of the arithmetic problems, *"Ten,* I kept saying, *I'm only ten."*

Dove: My brother and I would get together to figure out our math homework. We would spend hours trying to figure out a difficult problem on our own before giving up and approaching my father because, well, he was a *real* math whiz, and if we had a question about algebra he would say, "Well, it would be easier if we used logarithms." We would protest, "But we don't know about logarithms!" but out would come the slide rule nevertheless and two hours later we'd learned logarithms, but the whole evening was gone. So it did force us, number one, to try and do it on our own. And in the end, you also realize that they love you, since they are spending all this time on you. My father was very stern in those days; right before bedtime those flash cards had to come out. I hated them then, but I'm glad now.

Ratiner: But his challenge, "what you don't understand, master," goes beyond math homework. I thought that was one of those examples where he was trying to armor you with a way of approaching your life.

Dove: Yes. And yet there is still that individual spunkiness of the ten-year-old who says, "Yes, you are supposed to master it—but give me a break, I'm only ten years old! Let me be a child a little longer." On the whole, though, this advice has served me well. I don't have any real sadness about that. I am grateful that my parents were as strict as they were, because the mind is at its most malleable and absorbent at that age; you can cram as much into it as you can bear. It gets harder and harder the older you get.

Ratiner: Knowing how you feel about this, I thought it was curious how often you touch on the sense of "forbidden experience" in your writing. There are Uncle Millet's stories in one poem, the sort of racy tales of women and whiskey, which you weren't supposed to hear but somehow memorized. Then there is the sense of unbridled fantasy in another, "Fantasy and Science Fiction." There seems to be this tension between the civilizing influences of family and community versus the sheer forcefulness of the imagination which asserts itself through language.

Dove: Forbidden stories are powerful stories. They are forbidden for certain reasons, and those reasons are keys to navigating the maelstroms of human relationships. Forbidden stories can change your life.

Now in the poem, "Uncle Millet," the forbidden quality lies in the idea that one can actually step out of the boundaries of rules and survive. And as wonderful as my childhood was, there certainly was a sense that the adults were watching carefully to make sure we would not stray from the narrow path. To think that one could escape blame by running off to Canada and still slip back home every once in a while to say, "Hi!"—you don't want to let children know that such a thing is possible! But in the poem "Fantasy and Science Fiction," the kind of dreaming that takes you out of the influence of the family is not something you would tell your mother because you instinctively know she will start tightening the reins. The individual's imagination can be a dangerous thing for the community. I'm not trying to say communities are all like this—it's a give and take.

Ratiner: In the last several years, we've had an experience where the larger community wants to censor individual imagination. Society is not willing, as were your parents, to turn over complete responsibility to the individual. Instead, governments attempt to control, not only what kind of art you can make but what kind of art you will be permitted to view.

Dove: It is extremely dangerous. It is dangerous for the spiritual health of the world. You cannot keep a mind sequestered; it will break out some way.

Ratiner: And by offering a mind its freedom—even if it entails a certain element of danger—what does this confer upon an individual?

Dove: It is offering people a certain faith that they will be humane. First of all, what is danger? This is something everybody defines in their own way. The idea is that if a child is brought up with honesty and compassion and discipline, then no knowledge is dangerous because that child will take that knowledge, think about it, and be able to decide what is wrong or right.

Ratiner: This would seem to be an argument for poetry, the arts, as a vital element in the health of the individual mind as well as the society at large.

Dove: The arts *are* vital. In an age when we find ourselves being increasingly compartmentalized, where information bombards us but meaning is practically nonexistent, or expendable, the arts are perhaps one of the most necessary elements in society to remind us of our humanity.

When photos can be altered so that you can not even tell whether it is an original image or not, we need to be connected to—all the words sound corny—but we need to be connected to our soul. We need to remind ourselves why we are here on this planet, what kinds of responsibilities we have—not only to the planet but to each other as well. And no other discipline that I can think of is doing that work except the arts.

The poet began as the person charged with carrying on the legacy of the race; she was present at all official functions and rites of passage; he provided the songs and the music for these rites of passage, and so served as a conduit between ourselves and the universe. And that still holds true today; that is what a good poem or a novel or play or dance or musical composition does—it connects us again.

Ratiner: I'd like to ask you about music, which is another pervasive presence in both your fiction and poetry. Was that also something inherited from your parents?

Dove: Music was always being played in our house. There was Bessie Smith and Josh White, but there was also Fauré's flute sonatas. My maternal grandparents both played instruments, the mandolin and the guitar. My parents never learned an instrument; it was understood, though, that when we reached the age of ten, it was time to pick an instrument. So I chose the cello, as Virginia does, and played cello all through college and even beyond. I've since switched to the viola de gamba. Music offered me my first experiences in epiphany—of something clicking into place, so that understanding went beyond, deeper than rational sense. Since my parents were not musicians there was no one to ask, "How do I get this melody to sound right?" So I just kept plugging away until the things my music teacher had said made sense. At a very early age, music was my private sphere of discovery. It was a journey I was taking on my own. For a brief time I considered a career in music, but I knew I didn't have the kind of discipline necessary for a concert performer. But music remains a great source of pleasure to me.

Ratiner: In the novel, when the character of Virginia plays the cello again for the first time in years, you write that "the high notes in each phrase insinuated themselves into her blood: above the treadmill of chordal progressions a luminous melody unscrolling and floating away, high in the upper ether, where there was no memory or hurt." How does music or art accomplish such transformation?

Dove: If I knew how music did that, I would be one up on everybody! One of the magical things about music—and you're right it's not just music, but any art—is the pleasure of its making. The journey that it takes you on transcends not only the painful memories, but the pain contained in music's very expression as well. An incredibly sad piece can be exhilarating. One of the secrets of art is how it can help us not exactly digest the pain, but accept it. It lifts you up, over the pain, but it doesn't let you forget it.

Ratiner: So there's no question about the music as an escape or a suspension of the gravity of daily life?

Dove: I don't see it as an escape. I don't see escape as very desirable because if you escape history—if you escape anything—then what you are actually doing is abdicating a part of your humanity. You are saying, "I don't need this, I want to forget that"—but to me, part of being human is precisely this push and pull, this ambivalence. It makes life three-dimensional.

Ratiner: How does this connect with the ideas in a poem like "Dedication," where the speaker says, "What are music or books if not ways / to trap us in rumors? The freedom of fine cages!"

Dove: Poetry is a wonderful "fine cage" because a poem, particularly a lyric poem, has as its cage all of its sounds, even its shape on the page. And to fashion a full-fleshed poem in as tight a space as possible is, to me, the real electricity of utterance. Of course, narrative poems take larger spaces but even so, there is no room for fluff in that context, either. To me, poetry is very musical. It is a sung language; it is also a way of—not capturing, not reminding us—no, letting us *relive* the intensity of a moment. Moments slip by as you go through life and sometimes a moment is sharp enough and arresting enough to make you stop and remember it; but the smaller moments, even the ones that affect us, are followed by yet another moment, so they get lost. Poems recover those moments—a very small moment, perhaps just an instant, but in a fine cage indeed.

Ratiner: So the word cage does not carry with it the connotation of imprisonment, loss of freedom, in that poem?

Dove: That poem is a tricky one because the narrator is duplicitous; you can't trust a person who begins, "Ignore me. This request is knotted— / I'm not ashamed to admit it." Although she says "ignore me," she actually insists upon the opposite. The narrator chafes a bit at the things that music or books can't do. They can't do everything, obviously. We still need human contact; we still need love. So that quote is a poke in the ribs at those who would insist that music and art are ethereal and can make you a better person. This poem is saying, "Art? It's not so hot."

Ratiner: It reminded me of a Bill Stafford poem entitled "The Day Millicent Found the World," where the girl travels into the woods until she finally reaches the longed-for state: "Lost. She had achieved a mysterious world / where any direction would yield only surprise."

Dove: Oh, that's great!

Ratiner: Your speaker declares, "I wanted only to know / what I had missed, early on— / that ironic half-salute of the truly lost." I thought it was

a delightful concept, this unspoken brotherhood or sisterhood of people hopelessly immersed in experience.

Dove: You don't even have to do a full salute!

Ratiner: Let me ask you about the music of your writing—not just
"music" as a motif but the musical textures you create with your words.
There's one passage in "Definition in the Face of Unnamed Fury" it almost
feels like a tenor sax belting out a bebop phrase. Tell me about the music you
hear when the words are coming to you.

Dove: The music is so important to me; I can't stress that enough. A poem
convinces us not just through the words and the meaning of the words, but
the sound of them in our mouths—the way our heart beat increases with the
amount of breath it takes to say a sentence, whether a line of poetry may
make us breathless at the end of it, or give us time for contemplation. It's the
way our entire body gets involved in the language being spoken. Even if we
are reading the poem silently, those rhythms exist.

There are times, in fact, when the music of language guides me as much
as any plot or meaning. In the poem you mentioned, Thomas is frustrated
because he tries to go back to the mandolin after long absence; he is rusty
and can't make it work the way he wants to. It's one thing to say that in plain
old language, but to make the rhythms jagged, the lines full of stops and
starts and aggravations that can explode in, as you said, a sax riff or a little
bit of blues—this conveys a deeper sense of frustration. So I pay serious
attention to a poem's music. "It don't mean a thing, if it ain't got that swing";
if there's no music, what's the point of a poem?

Ratiner: If there is a down-and-dirty feel of the blues in that poem, one
of my favorites from *Thomas and Beulah* has a completely different musical
sense and, with it, a different emotional sweep. I'm thinking of "Gospel."
The poem flows with the rhythm and insistence of gospel, and hearing it
spoken aloud does seem to carry a listener away, rising up on that ship of
voices. It set me wondering if you—like Beulah stepping off the roof in
"Summit Beach"—feel as unbound and protected by the presence of this
music.

Dove: True, I am carried by it, I am buoyed by that music, absolutely—
"No sound this generous can fail." But first you have to get there, you have
to reach the point where the sound is that generous, no one can help you. It
is comparable to Garcia Lorca's description of the *duende*; he has a wonderful essay which mentions a famous singer who comes back to her native

Andalusia to sing in front of her people. She has this beautiful, well-trained voice, and yet they all declare they don't want to hear merely beautiful singing: where is the *duende*? they ask. So the singer gets back on stage and tears up her voice in order to achieve the *duende*—and I think this is soul—the moment when the song, the words and the emotion are wedded unto death and nothing, not beauty, nor propriety, nor genius, can get in the way. A great poem is possessed by the *duende*; you cannot dissect it.

Ratiner: Let me shift the context a bit. Yours is an interracial marriage, am I correct?
Dove: Yes.

Ratiner: If I may, I'd like to ask a question about how that experience has altered your perspective as a writer. One of the rare criticisms I've heard about your writing concerns the lack of raging anger in your work. I heard one poet say, "Of course Dove's poetry can be accepted comfortably by white academic society because she doesn't have the edge, the raw angry passion of a poet like Ai. So her work doesn't threaten the safety of that intellectual distance." I wondered if being in an interracial couple—and probably having to deal with more challenges day by day than most of us are ever confronted with—if that hasn't tempered the old angers, re-channeled that energy toward some other end?

Dove: Oh, the anger is still there. The way I function best in the world is not through anger but, as the father says in "Flash Cards," to master it, to be on top of situations. It is very hard to think when you are angry. That doesn't mean that you aren't angry, but it means you are trying to find a way around the anger so you can do something about it. Certainly, as a partner in an interracial relationship, I have had my share of things to be plenty angry about. But the best revenge is to be as clear as possible in my poetry. I agree that it may be easier for the literary society to accept poems like mine rather than those of, say, Ai. There is a point, of course, where I cannot control how someone wants to use or interpret my poems. Most of the poems, though, are differentiated enough; they are not easy answers.

My feeling, my mission if you will—though I don't usually think of it in those global terms—is to restore individual human fates to the oeuvre. Literary portrayals of women and African Americans have been flat, and since the '60s they've been predictably angry. This stock characterization allows the reader to fall into certain categorical thinking. I want to resist that. I don't want you to think of a particular character simply as "this Black angry person"; I want you to think of him as Joe or Mary or Martin. Take the speaker in the poem "Genie's Prayer Under the Kitchen Sink": he's been summoned by his mother to unclog the pipes; he's angry because his life is going nowhere, it's as clogged as his mother's sink. I want you to see him not as "just another angry Black male," but as a man with a stultifying job, who suffers from a paralyzed leg, whose sister died of cancer, whose anger is against fate and circumstances but who is so possessed with the urge to create that he pours his energy into building cheesy rec rooms for prurient entertainment. Now—if you can see this man as an individual, then he cannot be lumped into a group and dismissed.

I think the poet Ai's dramatic monologues also insist on individualities, very distinct human predicaments—most of them angry personalities, perhaps, but distinct nonetheless.

Ratiner: And to my reading of it, both poetries offer us different tools, different approaches.

Dove: Exactly. We needed a Martin Luther King and we needed a Malcolm X.

Ratiner: But when I heard that comment, I had just gotten your new novel and I came across the scene where Virginia says, "I didn't ask for respectability. I can't help it if it dogs me wherever I go." I thought this might be biographically accurate. Maybe it has to do with the quality of your family background. It seems to have given you a very stable base from which to speak, and if your voice is not going to be the one putting the torch to certain old ways, perhaps it is implicating a new ground on which to build something new.

Dove: Yes, we do need fire, but we need more than fire, too.

Ratiner: Some of that difference involves a motherliness, if I can call it that, that appears in some of the new work. There are three or four poems in *Grace Notes* that are specific explorations of a woman's body, and often the focus is on passing that knowledge on to your daughter.

Dove: I have gotten very surprised reactions from readers too: "Can it be that Rita Dove is actually writing about *that*!" I had gotten a reputation for being a genteel poet; I've never understood how. But I am deeply grateful to the women who really blazed the way—poets like Anne Sexton and Sylvia Plath and Maxine Kumin.

When I was in graduate school and just beginning to write seriously and send out my work, a good poem was one that sounded like it had been written like a man. It had to have a certain toughness, a certain screening-out of emotions, clear and linear writing—which went absolutely against the way I lived my life. In fact, one of the reasons I wrote so slowly when I first began writing seriously was because I had this mistaken notion that I had to finish each poem before I could go on to the next—sort of like finishing your plate at dinner. When I finally began looking at the way I live my life, I realized that I never did anything linearly. I would juggle several tasks at once: if I was walking downstairs, I would pick up a couple of things along the way, talk on the phone, make a mental note to thaw out the chicken. Wait a minute, I thought. I don't live my life that way, why am I trying to write that way?

So I began allowing all those errant voices, those scraps of poems and stories, to surface in whatever fragmented form they chose, and my work method found its balance. It's a method, I think, that women find more comfortable than men, perhaps by virtue of the way most women have been trained to manage our lives. I really think it is much more akin to the way our minds work, in starbursts—the way we walk down the street and see a thousand different details at once and yet contain them all, so that they kind of bounce around inside.

Ratiner: Instead of creating an organized map to where you are going.

Dove: Right. Just studying the map in order to head straight toward a prescribed destination. How boring!

Ratiner: I also wondered, in a political sense, whether this was a way for you to reclaim the body, to repossess things that were perhaps barred from the way you were allowed to think, to write?

Dove: Absolutely. It was liberating to be able to write about the body, childbirth and breast-feeding, without reticence or lingering.

Ratiner: Was it an act for your daughter's sake as well? We've talked about the giving-over of knowledge from one generation to another. Was this a writer's need to hand something down to her daughter?

Dove: Yes, it is intended to be handed down. And my daughter has read those poems; she is nine now, so she thinks they're pretty neat. I can't guarantee what she will say when she is fifteen—teenagers are usually mortified by such personal confessions—but I hope the idea of a mother and daughter being able to share these kind of intimacies is something that will sustain her.

Ratiner: This idea of passing things on extends beyond the mother-daughter exchange to the way we attempt to educate the younger generations. With all the debate about educational priorities, I would think the arts possess one of the most vital sets of learning tools we could offer. The challenge is to pass on to young people this sense of the tradition—poetry as a place for discovery, as the reservoir of our common story. How do we do that? How do you pass on the intangible, those openings where music takes you to another reality, where a lyric poem can perform its sound-work, its sense-work all at once? How do you introduce someone to these transcendent experiences without resorting to that rational linear map?

Dove: You do it, I think, by going at it in as many different ways as possible. I really don't know how the mind grasps the intangible, why something clicks. We make educated stabs in the dark until something ignites. It's important not to be afraid in these situations—to read the poem and let it linger in the air, without engaging the left side of the brain. Instead of saying, "Isn't it wonderful how this certain image fits into the general conceit?" we should first simply read the poem aloud and let them claim it for their own.

Another way is to connect the act of writing or reading poetry with other kinds of art. Show the student that there is indeed music in poetry, and a kind of a dance of words. More than anything else, when students see that you are exhilarated by the language—when they see you lose your shyness, the reserve a teacher adopts in front of a class—then they know something is there, some secret worth unearthing, and they want to get in on it.

Ratiner: I've even had the question framed this way: what good is it? Because students have been taught that something is good if you can make a lot of money doing it, or because it carries a certain prestige. So I'll hand that question on to you: when you make a poem—what good is it in your life, and what good do you hope it might create when a reader receives it?

Dove: As human beings we are endowed with an incredible gift: we can articulate our feelings and communicate them to each other in very sophisticated ways. To write a poem in which the almost inexpressible is being expressed is the pinnacle of human achievement. So, in a sense, it's silly to ask what good is it to reach the pinnacle!

Every time I write a poem I imagine a solitary reader—the reader that I was as a child, curled up on the couch. I remember the moment of opening a book and feeling the world fall away as I entered an entirely different realm;

I remember the warm feeling of another voice whispering to me, a voice that was almost inside of me, we were so close. I write a poem and offer it to you, the reader; and if, on the other end, you can look up from the page and say: "I know what you mean, I've felt that, too," then both of us are a little less alone on this planet. And that, to me, is worth an awful lot.

Tricking the Muse by Taking Out the Trash

Steven Bellin / 1993

This interview took place in Rita Dove's home near Charlottesville, Virginia, on 14 December 1993. It appeared in the *Mississippi Review* in 1995. Reprinted by permission of Steven Bellin.

Bellin: I wonder if you'd mind starting by telling us how you came to be a writer, and why. Were there experiences in your childhood that were key ones?

Dove: I grew up reading; that was the first step. Our television viewing was rationed. There were books in the house, and we were encouraged to read as much as we wanted and anything we wanted, which was an important element. I would read everything from comic strips and comic books straight up to Shakespeare, and I didn't see any problems with the transition. At first, I didn't distinguish much between high and low literature. Books were places I could go to, where I could be anywhere in the world. Writing was a natural next step—to want to do the thing itself instead of allowing it to happen to me, to create my own world of possibilities.

I began by imitation-doggerel verse, Easter and Christmas poems, stuff like that. Around the fifth or sixth grade I began writing plays—satirical musicals à la *Mad* magazine, with new lyrics based on the tunes to popular songs. My brother, who is two years older, loved science fiction, so I would read his science fiction books after he was finished and then try to write my own stories about robots and Venusians and suspended animation, that sort of thing. I didn't think any of this was unusual. I never thought to myself, Oh, I'm going to be a writer someday. Writing was simply another way to pass the time, another way of having fun, of playing.

I think there were a number of reasons for that lack of literary ambition. First of all, I didn't grow up in a literary household. My father was a chemist (he's retired now); my mother, a housewife; my sisters and brother all ended up in the sciences. Oh, there were lots of books on the shelves at home; but no one ever said, "Wouldn't it be great to be a writer?" I knew nothing about the personal lives of the authors I was reading; I really didn't think about the authors that much at all. The stories were what gripped me, though most of

121

them had no discernible similarities to my own life, and none of the characters ever looked like me. So becoming a writer wasn't something I thought about; it wasn't even a blip on the radar screen.

Then, when I was in eleventh grade, my English teacher took me to a book signing at a downtown hotel. I hadn't told her that I liked to write; I had shown her nothing beyond the critical papers we were required to compose for school. She must have suspected something, though, because she called up my parents for permission to take me and another student to this book signing, and that's how John Ciardi became my first walking, speaking, breathing author. I didn't know who John Ciardi was, but I was sufficiently impressed to buy a copy of his translation of Dante's *Inferno*, and for the first time in my life the author's photo on the back of a book meant something. Personally, Ciardi was a bit of a curmudgeon, but the point was that that experience first put the notion into my head that writing could be a viable vocation, that one could consider a life built around writing.

Then I went off to Miami University, in Oxford, Ohio, and stumbled into my first creative writing class. And I do mean stumbled! I had tested out of Freshman English, and since most literature seminars were reserved for upperclassmen, I had signed up for a sophomore-level Advanced Composition course. Now, I wanted to read, not compose; but Advanced Composition was the only class open, and it filled a requirement to boot. Well, about three weeks into the semester, the professor fell ill and had to be hospitalized. Another professor was asked to take over the course—and that was Milton White, the fiction writing instructor. So fate gave me a rather significant shove. I remember Milton White striding into class that first day and announcing, "Now we're going to tell stories." And I was hooked.

Bellin: Did you begin with poems, or with stories? Was there any separation at that point?

Dove: In college I would take fiction writing one semester and poetry workshop the next; I never took both in the same semester. Earlier, in my childhood, there was no separation at all—I'd write a poem one day, a story the next. But there had been indications that I preferred poetry. For several summers, for instance, my brother and I would start a neighborhood newspaper. We never finished an issue because we would get into an argument: I wanted to be editor-in-chief, but my brother declared himself chief by virtue of seniority, so I would quit and form my own magazine and call it "Poet's Delight." Every year, it was "Poet's Delight," and I'd write one poem, design a meticulous cover with a woman reclining in the shade of an autumnal tree, and that would be it. I don't think I ever finished a single issue, but the evidence was damning: if I could be my own boss, I would always choose to be a poet.

I must stress the fact that none of this was conscious at all. Living poets simply didn't exist in the world I grew up in. Becoming a poet was not only unrealistic; there wasn't even a question of such a thing being remotely possible.

Bellin: How about now? Is it difficult to alternate? Are there special requirements for each genre that you have to go through?

Dove: Each genre has its own routine for me, its little demands and particular problems. I don't have as much difficulty switching now, particularly between the short story and poetry, or between poetry and drama. Going from short story to drama is a bit of a stretch, and the novel is an entirely different matter altogether. I've only written one novel, so my conclusions are based on insufficient data—but there was a point, at the beginning of writing the novel, when I could switch back and forth between prose and poetry; the closer I came to the final draft, however, the harder it became to switch, because I had to devote all my attention to the fictional world to make sure that everything fit. At first this was simply a technical necessity—making sure that everything happens on the day that it's supposed to happen, making sure the characters stay "in character," can be an all-consuming task—but in the end the problem is one for the imagination, because the only way to do right by the creation, without being a civil servant about it, is to live, breathe, and dream the novel's world. Only then do you have a chance of getting it right.

Bellin: There's always been a strong narrative trend in your poems as well. Do you see connections between what you were doing with the novel and what you were doing with the poems?

Dove: It's hard for me to see the connections. The first book was a kind of hodgepodge, but after that I've always tried to stretch the limits of whatever genre I was working in. I'm curious how much narrative can be sustained by a lyric poem, how much lyricism can float through a narrative poem. Initially, when writing short fiction, I was attracted by two kinds of short stories: those that pivot on epiphany, like in James Joyce's *Dubliners*, and the traditional tale à la Thomas Mann, which builds its world like a nineteenth-century novel and then unscrolls on a bed of accumulating details. My story "The Vibraphone" unwinds in that manner, whereas a story like "Zabriah" is a string of epiphanies. When writing my novel *Through the Ivory Gate*, on the other hand, I consciously tried to avoid writing a "poet's novel." I wanted structure, character development, a firm narrative base—not an extended tone poem.

Bellin: You're Poet Laureate this year. Obviously, you're a very prominent public figure for poetry now, but you have a novel out at the same time. I'm assuming you have to make some kind of connection between this public persona that you have, and then having a private life at the same time. Are there difficulties with that, or is it possibly productive?

Dove: It is very difficult, and it's not productive at all. I didn't think it would be productive, and I made a pact with myself that I wouldn't get uptight about not writing. In other words, rather than trying to be Super-woman by squeezing in an hour of writing between airplanes or interviews and being continually frustrated, it would be better to give myself leave not to write so that any writing that might happen would arrive as a boon. That my time is so fragmented makes it difficult to get any decent writing done; but the worst part is exactly what you mentioned—switching between public and private personae. I've discovered, as Poet Laureate, that I've assumed the mantle of the public servant. I find myself dealing with people who have little concept of what a poet does, how poems are made or read. They may have liked poetry at some point in their lives—I'm not saying they're utter Philistines—but they're frightened of being thought stupid, which means that they tighten up at the mention of any word over two syllables. And they've been brought up to believe that reading poetry means interpreting it, that talking about poetry is going to be an elaborate intellectual ritual, a game of one-upmanship. Trying to get through all those layers of fears is crucial, but it's exhausting, too. So there's a "Poet Laureate" persona I find myself employing in self-defense. I catch myself thinking, Forget the private person, cut out the self-reflection, and just deal with the situation on a public level.

That, more than anything, stops the writing. Since becoming Poet Laureate, I've written a few poems—and though the ideas are there, there isn't the right kind of time nor the right mind-set there to nurture those initial sparks into a blaze. Interviews for newspapers and slick magazines and radio talk shows are the most tiring because I have to say the same thing over and over again. That kind of repetition is deadening. But if I can implant the word "poetry" in people's minds, if I can bring poetry into the common discourse, then I will have accomplished something significant.

And the way to do it, for better or worse, is through the media. The other
day I was listening to the car radio, and the announcer dubbed some physicist
"the Poet Laureate of Science." Say what?! A few years ago, that wouldn't
have happened. Poetry's making a comeback; it's been coursing under the
surface all the while, and every little bit of media attention is one more
increment in the elevation of the water table.

Bellin: With the last few Poet Laureates, there seems to have been a lot
more media attention given to you, than I've seen.

Dove: It's mind-boggling. I expected there to be a little more interest because I represent a break with tradition, which is news; but I also thought it
would die off fairly quickly, too. I think the whole country is poised on the
lip of change; with the change in the Administration there's a generalized
excitement in the air, a feeling that things are beginning to happen once more.
My appointment might be part of that new wave.

Bellin: Can you talk some about direct influences on your styles? Are
there any poets in particular who have nourished your work, any that you
feel that you have to face down, the way Harold Bloom says poets have to in
The Anxiety of Influence?

Dove: *The Anxiety of Influence* is such a male-oriented book. There's so
much of that "I'm going to wrestle you down and take your style." Certainly
there are influences on me; but I never have a pat answer to this question
because I resist cataloging my creativity. My list of influences is constantly
changing: as soon as I become aware of their influence, it means that I'm no
longer being influenced by them. There are poets I return to again and again
for sustenance: I read them, shake my head and wonder, How did they do
that? I go back to figures like Emily Dickinson and Thomas Hardy, for example, and Langston Hughes and Shakespeare, and some prose writers as well—
James Baldwin, Toni Morrison, Gabriel Garcia Marquez. I love Derek
Walcott's work, but I don't think I'm influenced by it. I don't know about
Elizabeth Bishop. Elizabeth Bishop is someone I can't read if I intend to
write that day.

Bellin: It's very intimidating!

Dove: She's so completely her own. Nabokov is like that, too—so utterly
Nabokov that you must either give yourself over to his aura, in which case
you can't possibly write an original phrase, or you must resist succumbing
and stand outside the spell thinking, How clever, how amazing!—terrifically

envious but somehow unmoved, because you haven't permitted yourself to give in entirely—and then you can't write anything, either.

Bellin: In Bishop's work there's such modesty—almost as if the poem itself doesn't even come from the poet; it just exists as a modest piece of writing that exists on its own strength. I've always found that interesting.

Dove: That's very well put.

Bellin: There's a very strong sense of history in your work, an almost intimate sense. The past is very close to the present, or coexists with the present, almost side by side at times. I was wondering if that was a conscious intention of yours, or whether or not it was just an integral part of your way of looking at the world.

Dove: Sometimes it's conscious, other times it's not. I think there are two main reasons for my looking at the world that way. First of all, when I was growing up, relatives would gather and tell stories about our ancestors—some great-great-grandmother or great-great-grandfather. I enjoyed a sense of intimacy with these "characters," because they were part of the family. Years later, while studying history in school, it was all very abstract, you know: "This-and-that occurred in 1846, this-and-that transpired in 1898." But if we're lucky, something happens to bring the dry facts to life. For me it was the simple realization that a hundred years is really not that long ago. In 1965, I was in junior high school. The year 1865 sounded ancient then. But if you say "one hundred years ago the Civil War ended," it becomes an entirely different matter. After all, more and more people live to be over one hundred, and many of us had grandparents who were alive one hundred years ago. So that's when it hit home for me. I began to understand that history isn't merely facts and isolated events to be memorized, but that it is lived through people. Trying to fit my own history, and the history of my race and gender, into the Grand Chronicle—History with a capital H—led me to the realization that the underside of History, as it were, was infinitely more interesting. So in my work I make a conscious effort to treat History and history equally.

Bellin: History, with a small h, in comparison with History with a capital H, it's kind of a method of offering different interpretations, presenting different sides of this one story we think of as the historical one.

Dove: History with a small h consists of a billion stories. History with a capital H is a construct, a grid you have to fit over the significant events in ordinary lives. Great historians, those who can make history "come alive," realize that all the battles lost or won are only a kind of net, and we are caught in that net. Because there are other interstices in that large web. Whereas History is a chart of decisions and alternatives, history is like larding the roast: you stick in a little garlic and add some fat, and the meat tastes better.

Bellin: Has it been difficult working in that area of Washington? It seems that you're right in the middle of History-with-a-capital-H's stronghold.

Dove: I'm having a blast. Everyone keeps saying, "Oh, Washington's so sterile; it's such a power node." I'm enjoying myself—maybe because I look at its machinations with a certain measure of bemusement. The Poetry Office at the Library of Congress is tucked in a corner of what is called the "attic" of the Jefferson Building; someone once commented that the location was an indication of how the nation regards its artists, but I walk out on the balcony that looks out over the Capitol, the Washington Monument, the Smithsonian and even the Jefferson Memorial on a clear day and think, Best view in town. No, it doesn't bother me at all.

Bellin: In some of your earlier poems, I'm thinking specifically of "Nestor's Bathtub" or "Catherine of Siena," myths and legends, not exactly true histories, but those impulses are there as well. I was wondering what it is about myths or legends which make them such fertile ground for reinterpretation through poems?

Dove: Let's look at it this way. I have a more recent poem called "The Gorge." The gorge is what's left of the river that passed through the city; all kinds of stuff—a dead man's shoes, rubber inner tubes—has been left behind. I call this detritus "a trail of anecdotes." Myth begins in anecdote—telling a story in order to entertain—but it also constructs a narrative as a way of explaining our place and our progress in the world.

A myth or a legend becomes indispensable through the retelling. Generations repeat and elaborate upon the basic story; the really great tales are stolen by other cultures and changed to fit their new surroundings. You may ask what's so compelling about an anecdote that others had to steal it; why is it still provocative, even though we don't believe in the Greek gods, or Isis and Osiris, for that matter? Why do we still repeat these tales and listen to them with such pleasure? Because they touch the yearning inside us; they explain our impulses on a level deeper than logic but do not require blind faith, because they are allegorical. They explain some of the mysteries of our existence and our relationships with each other. Parables affect us in nonverbal ways, too, because of the resonances between the parallels.

For me, to work with myths is a way of getting at the ineffable. By exploring a myth—nothing anthropological or psychological, I'm not into rooting out all the extant variations or analyzing every symbol—but by re-imagining the myth, we can find so many resonances to our own lives. James Hillman's wonderful book, *The Dream and the Underworld*, talks about the dream not as a Freudian concept, as a tool to piece together the puzzle of just how sick you are, but as a realm with its own rules, much like the Greeks' idea of the underworld. Not quite an anti-cosmos; a parallel universe, an actual world deeper than we can allow our feelings to go . . . but it exists, it's there always, waiting. Myths tap into that well.

I've been writing a lot of poems lately around the myth of Persephone and Demeter. But let me backtrack for a minute. Donald Hall once said that sometimes when you're trying to write a poem and you get close to the source, everything shuts down. To you, that's when it feels like you're furthest away from the answer; but you're actually standing right outside the door. It's just been slammed in your face, is all, and you have to find a way to coax it open. No amount of sitting at the desk and beating at the page can get the door to open. What you have to do is to trick it—take out the trash, wash dishes, pretend you don't care. And suddenly the Muse thinks, Oh, she's busy doing something else, I can relax now—and revelation slips in. Myth, in an interesting way, can function in the same way as taking out the trash.

By following the trajectory of a myth, by re-imagining its principal characters or exploring a tangent, one can stumble upon the crucial stuff—what one really thinks and feels. My Persephone and Demeter poems, for instance, actually began as a technical exercise. One day I was thinking, I'm tired of all the male gods; what's a good female deity? Since Rilke had written sonnets to Orpheus, I decided to write sonnets to Demeter.

For a while I believed I had chosen Demeter because of Rilke's Orpheus. When I look back now, it's so obvious—my daughter Aviva was about five years old at the time, just about to enter kindergarten, to go out into the world. I had some readjustment to do as a mother. If I hadn't been oblivious to the actual reason, if I had tried to write about mothers and daughters consciously, I wouldn't have made it to first base. As it was, I simply decided to explore this myth which had attracted me for whatever reason, and I began by writing sonnets, not thinking at all of the personal implications. It really didn't dawn on me until— let's see, Aviva was five then, so I began writing these six years ago, and since then it's gone beyond sonnets to double sonnets and all kinds of strange things. Then, when Aviva was in third grade, she had to give a report on Greece, so she had been reading this book on Greek myths for weeks, just loving it. One day she came into my room with the book under her arm and said, "Hey! You've been writing about me!" I'd been reading her some of the poems, and she hadn't paid much attention; but when she read the classic version of the myth, it all clicked. She walked out of the room grinning, and I couldn't write a single word more that day. Wow, I thought, how blind can you be?

But it was a necessary blindness, I think. Some poets will use rhyme and meter in that way, and some use persona poems or journal entries, notebooks. In this particular case, it was the outer structure of the myth that I allowed to guide the writing. Exploring the ways in which I could work that structure into contemporary settings was very productive.

Bellin: Could you talk some more about what you've called "necessary blindness"? Is it a condition of writing poems in general, or writing anything in general, to not know exactly what you're up to before it reaches a certain point?

Dove: Well, yes, I do think that's true. It's very difficult, if you know exactly what you're up to, to produce a poem that surprises and enriches the reader—that, upon rereading, continually surprises and enriches. That doesn't mean I just walk willy-nilly into the poem, calling out, "Here I come, ready or not!" What I'm trying to say is best expressed by Roethke's line: "I learn by going where I have to go." I find that the more determined people are, the more supposedly aware they are of where they're going, the blinder they are. In other words, it's best to be open while pursuing whatever goal you've set.

Frankly, I wouldn't want to live a life where I knew exactly where I was going. Sure, you can have everyday goals, even five-year plans. You can say, "I'll go to the grocery store first, then the dry cleaners," but you have no idea what's going to happen to you on the way—what news report on the radio will change your perspective, what frustrating or dangerous thing will happen in traffic, who you'll see in the rice-and-beans aisle. And that's what makes life so damn interesting—what happens along the way. So the journey to the end of the poem is full of mysteries.

In the best poems, the mysteries will inform not only the ending, but will circle around and change the beginning, too. You may arrive where you thought you'd end up, but you're a different person when you get there.

Bellin: The experience of reading your poems is like that, too. There's the poem itself, and at the end there's an epiphany, a slamming of it home. Have you noticed that about your work?

Dove: Others have mentioned that my poems seem to turn in the last few seconds or so, but no one's said it quite that way before! Some of that is technical. Speaking in terms of craft, one of the biggest influences on my work has been my knowledge of the German language. In a German sentence in which a past participle or prepositional phrase occurs, the verb may be shunted to the end of the sentence. Example: "He turned to gaze at her hair upon which, with startling brilliance and a hushed, golden warmth, the reflection of the crackling firelight which Mimi had laid, glimmered." You have to wait. The first few times I was over in Germany, I'd have a headache at the end of each day. This is maddening, I would think: how can people communicate like this?

Then I gradually began to appreciate how this syntax kept the sentence energized. Could an English sentence be stretched to sustain suspense like that? Could I work it so that everything clicks together at the very end of the poem? Which is not to suggest that I treat the writing of a poem like solving a crossword puzzle, but that I'm trying to make the final epiphany happen grammatically as well as imagistically. I played around with this technique quite a bit in earlier poems, particularly those in *Museum*.

Bellin: I can see how that is replicated in the poems. After you've read the end of a poem, you have to go back and revise your notions of what's come before. I've always found that particularly enjoyable about your work.

Dove: Or you could have said, "Oh, no. Now I have to read it all over again."

Bellin: How has being Aviva's mother fed into your poems, or not? Do you imagine her reading the poems later and thinking about them?

Dove: You know, I never imagine that; maybe it's a kind of protection. Sometimes she asks what I'm working on, and she's been to some of my poetry readings and has her favorites. I know there are poems of mine that wouldn't have been written without her being here on the planet. It's not only the emotional aspects of motherhood, but the idea of watching another human being enter the world and knowing you are the lens through which this being receives so many of her basic perceptions. There's also the desire to widen her horizons without predetermining her future—all that handmaiden stuff. Teaching demands a similar kind of witnessing, but it's not as constant. It's really that profound moral responsibility that goes along with introducing another human to our planet—this is the ceaseless task of a parent, and it's an amazing sensation which has informed my work even beyond the notion of motherhood. I can't give you any concrete examples; I just know it has.

Bellin: I remember you telling me once that there was something you called the "tyranny of the articulate" in writing poems. I think it was that you think we're driven to say only that which can be said, only what's immediately understandable, and that's not exactly valid. Do you remember that, and could you elaborate?

Dove: It's a nice phrase; I hope I said it! The tyranny of the articulate is a particular problem in a workshop situation—the stakes are so loaded, yet the parameters are so circumscribed. Feedback is immediate, though it may not be accurate or well-informed or well-meaning; the specter of public humiliation looms so large that, rather than risk being misunderstood, the student is tempted either to entertain or to write "slick" poems, poems which resist penetration. In such a technically oriented, defensive atmosphere, what room is there for the notion of the poet whom Wallace Stevens calls "the priest of the invisible"?

I believe there are emotions that aren't expressible—I really do. And I think it's our duty to try to approach expressing these somehow. Being articulate is not the key. You might have a prodigious command of language, but it's what happens between the words that matters; so much happens in the leaps, the silences. It's something I'm still wrestling with; I'm endlessly fascinated by it.

Charles Wright is working in this direction—those long "journal" poems in which the mundane and the profound exist side by side, with all those ellipses, all that white space. And the cumulative effect, which is that the ineffable has somehow been given a shape. Rilke addresses the ineffable all the time. His *Ding-Gedichte*—the Thing Poems—are a testimonial to the fact that if you can capture the thing-ness of an object, you might also catch the inexpressible. What makes those poems like "The Panther" and "The Flamingos" so magnificent is that, although they try to be true to the object—the thing itself—the unspoken assumption is that there exists something above words, beyond words, that no language can touch. The sensation is brief; you feel it brush by.

Bellin: There's a similar sensation in a lot of your poems, I think. A lot of your poems are persona poems. Is there some kind of connection between having a speaker saying words that aren't ostensibly yours and getting at that which can't be expressed? I have a notion that persona poems are so effective because they resonate with something in our collective unconscious.

Dove: Well, the pronoun "I" is problematic. In fiction, it might increase the sense of intimacy; but poetry often sounds egotistical if the personality of the poet persists through the use of the first-person singular. A few poets have managed it: Frank O'Hara imbued his "I" with such a charming manner that we all want to be him, or at least near him. O'Hara's I/eye takes in everything indiscriminately to become this huge, generous consciousness. Walt Whitman has this gift too, as do Allen Ginsberg and Vladimir Mayakovski. But it's a very difficult thing to manage—whereas the third person, with its omniscience and omnipresence, gives us a wider portal to step through. A persona poem, on the other hand, is a vehicle for defusing the potential self-consciousness of the first-person singular.

Bellin: In *Grace Notes*, there's a poem called "Canary" about Billie Holiday, and the last line reads, "If you can't be free, be a mystery." And that line's a mystery in itself. Why did you choose Billie Holiday for that poem, and what does that last line say about her?

Dove: Ah, Billie Holiday, Lady Day. If you look at the circumstances of her life—how she prevailed against such debilitating odds to become this songbird—then you can see that her life was a study in ironies—you could even say parallel universes. She would step onto the stage, dressed to the nines with a fresh gardenia in her hair, and sing like nobody's business; then she'd step down after the show knowing she couldn't use the bathroom because it was a white nightclub. So what does a person in such a universe do? Billie had style. Even when she was really strung out on drugs, she exuded amazing presence; there was always an elegance to her musical phrasings. That insistence on style—not "style" in the sense of putting on a show, but how you carry yourself through the world—is what earned her the title Lady Day, why she's achieved the status of an icon. Lady Day not only refused to grovel—"grovel" wasn't in her vocabulary—she kept her head up even if she had to walk through shit. From the head up she seemed to be saying, "I'm smelling roses." At the same time, though, you could see in her performances a way she had of shutting herself off from the world, because otherwise it would have brought her down much earlier than it eventually did. That's what the last line of "Canary" refers to: if you can't be free, don't show it; don't let them get to you.

Bellin: Among jazz musicians of that era, there's so much of that, even among white musicians, that type of strength.

Dove: That's right; it just floors me. Because white musicians who wanted to be part of that music, that culture, had to go through similar humiliations, often at the hands of their Black band partners. It was a ritual hazing; it wasn't racist, but it was racial. They had to be tested; it was a crash course in bearing up under the consequence of their skin color. If they proved their mettle, then they knew what the blues was about. They'd do just fine.

Bellin: One last question. It's sometimes fashionable these days to characterize African American writers as being either Afrocentric or Eurocentric. Or male-identified, or feminist.

Dove: So many categories.

Bellin: How do you feel about these identifications?

Dove: I don't find the terms Afrocentric or Eurocentric useful. I think they're divisive; they're the province of frightened people who need to put things in categories in order to know who and where they are. Politically, they're calculated to pit groups against one another; linguistically, they preclude open thought. Nobody I know sits around all day thinking about whether or not he or she's Afrocentric. Life doesn't work that way. Such identity markers seem only to make sense with fringe elements on both ends—the doggedly Eurocentric, the Harold Blooms of the world who build a career on reinforcing their little fortresses of English stone; and the relentlessly Afrocentric who isolate themselves in their own schools and cut out half the knowledge of the world. I'm in favor of nothing that walls out knowledge in the name of purity. There is no way to keep yourself "pure," be it race-specific, gender-specific, or caste-specific. The most fascinating thing about life is its flux. Some critics persist in trying to define me, and it's tricky answering those kinds of questions. Newspapers are looking for a sound bite—something snappy—and they won't quote the entire answer because it's too complex, like life, so they will try to shorten the answer and they will get it quite wrong.

My favorite response to that line of inquiry comes from Langston Hughes, who published an essay in 1926 called "The Negro Artist and the Racial Mountain," in *The Nation*, I believe. The "new Negro" artists of the Harlem

Renaissance, he says, intend to express their "individual dark-skinned selves without fear or shame"; if white people liked the results that was great, but if they didn't that was fine, too. He then takes it one step further: it would be wonderful if other Black people liked what the Renaissance artists were doing, but if they didn't, that wouldn't matter, either. He ends with a declaration: "We build our temples for tomorrow, strong as we know how, and we stand on top of the mountain, free within ourselves."

Bellin: In academic circles, it seems that this insistence on labeling might be the worst by-product of deconstruction that there is. This insistence on identity has been making a lot of us writers uncomfortable.

Dove: Yes. One semester when I was teaching at Arizona State, a colleague in the rhetoric program, a prominent deconstructionist, was teaching a graduate seminar called Theories of Composition. One of his students interviewed me for her paper—she also interviewed a painter and a musician—and the questions were extremely aggravating because they were geared to reduce all nuance to statistics, to footnotes. I was constantly equivocating in my answers, dancing through the tulips. Well, I guess she must have turned in some kind of preliminary report, because one day when I was in the office getting my mail, the professor came up to me and said, "We're going to figure out how you do it!" And I thought, Who cares? The whole idea was so pigheaded and neurotic, there was nothing to say, really. As if anyone could pin any of this down.

Bellin: Let me come full circle. You mentioned Garcia Marquez earlier, and I was wondering if you thought there was such a thing as an international community of writers now.

Dove: There has always been an extended family of writers past, present and future; when you write, you are participating in the grand conversation. Down here on earth, however, writers travel much more today, so there's a chance to meet other writers and actually sit down for a talk. It's fun to run into old friends at writers' conferences in Paris or Toronto or Mexico City, even if there've been several years between reunions.

But let me return to this idea about the spiritual community. Rotterdam, in the Netherlands, has one of the oldest international poetry festivals around. One summer there I had a startling experience with language, poetry, and that spiritual community I've been talking about. Each evening four poets would read in their native tongues, followed by an actor who would read the Dutch translation for the audience's benefit. If you didn't happen to be Dutch or know the original language, you were out of luck—and those evenings went on for three hours. So, out of sheer desperation and boredom, the international poets would try to figure out what whoever read was reading. I knew German and enough Middle English and Latin to follow the Dutch translations a bit; other writers knew French, Russian, or whatever. One evening during a Japanese poet's recitation, when I was following the text of the Dutch translation and looked up in the middle of the reading, I found the other writers listening, rapt. It was a remarkable feeling; we understood. That's community.

Bellin: One last question, I swear. You mentioned Shakespeare earlier. What's your favorite play?

Dove: It depends what time of my life we're talking about. When I was a kid—this is really weird—my favorite play was *Hamlet*. This is great, I thought. Nothing happens; they just walk around talking to themselves. Then there was *Macbeth*, which was a serious contender to *Hamlet*. *Julius Caesar*, too. Today my favorite Shakespeare play would be *King Lear*. It's the most tragic thing I've ever read. With *Hamlet*, there's still the feeling that this string of tragedies could have been averted. The despair isn't absolute. *King Lear* is as empty, spiritually, as it gets.

Bellin: What gets me about those tragedies is how much they're concerned with epistemology. How can we ever be sure of what we know, and how can we even be sure we know anything? It seems a very modern question that art needs to address.

Dove: You're right. And yet it's a very old question, too. You'd think the questions raised by *Oedipus*—fate versus free will, mother love and blind power—would have faded by now, but they haven't. Those are the questions posed by great literature: unanswerable, yet forever asked.

Brushed by an Angel's Wings
Grace Cavalieri / 1995

This interview appeared in the April 1995 issue of *American Poetry Review*. Reprinted by permission of Grace Cavalieri.

Cavalieri: How do the poems in your new book answer the questions you asked in the foreword: why am I what I am rather than what I thought I'd be? For instance, does the poem "Flash Cards" partially speak to that?

Dove: I think "Flash Cards" does answer that in a way because the advice my father gave me is advice that led me toward things that really mattered to me. I always had the feeling, as a child, due to his advice, that if something seemed difficult or challenging, the thing to do was just to take it a little bit at a time and to work at it. And so the joy of working at something to find out what it means to me is what I grew up with. In writing I apply that all the time because in working on a poem I love to revise. Lots of younger poets don't enjoy this, but in the process of revision I discover things.

Cavalieri: So your father said, Take a monolith and crack away at it little by little. But aren't you really the person you always wanted to become? If anyone is, I feel it might be you. That would be a wonderful thing to think.

Dove: I think I *never* dreamed of becoming Poet Laureate, but I'm very happy to be who I am.

Cavalieri: There is another poem which I think is really important, and that is an autobiographical poem—the newest one you've written, I think— "In The Old Neighborhood." And I like it because it gives us so much information about your life.

Dove: It is an autobiographical poem in which I explore a lot of the impulses in my childhood, in the home life. That, in a way, made me the person that I am. The epigraph is important, "to pull yourself by your own roots."

Cavalieri: Let me go back to the white rock on the black lawn. Is the childhood home of your memory where you "reside most completely?"— another question you ask yourself in your foreword, that little girl curled up on the couch eating green olives, reading books. Is that where you feel most comfortable?

Dove: I do feel very comfortable there. I think all of us have moments,

136

particularly in our childhood, where we come alive, maybe for the first time. And we go back to those moments and think, This is when I became myself. And that's one of those moments—a feeling of finding rightness in reading—and thinking, I want to do this for the rest of my life.

Cavalieri: I have heard a rumor that you're starting another novel.

Dove: I've started it, but not officially. I've started taking notes on index cards. I don't anticipate that for many, many years down the road.

Cavalieri: Not this year, certainly.

Dove: Not this year for sure.

Cavalieri: But you did get that new poem "In The Old Neighborhood" written at the eleventh hour, and I thought, If someone becomes Poet Laureate of the United States, that may just give them the energy to write a poem. And you did.

Dove: Well, I did. I remember that I was working on the poem, actually, when I was asked if I'd like to serve as Poet Laureate, and I wasn't finished with it. In fact, I was stuck. And I said, "Well, fine, but can you give me two days." They said, "We can give you one and a half." And so it did give me a push.

Cavalieri: Did you do it in one and a half?

Dove: I did do it. I broke through my impasse.

Cavalieri: I have to talk about *Thomas and Beulah* because when I read that I knew that something very different was happening in American letters. And it is not the technical excellence you are cited for nor the breadth of subject matter which critics have cited. Something else is going on. I started calling you the Poet of Essence. We learned through that book to go for the breath of a poem. Here we have two characters who are like the figure eight: they just come together briefly in the middle at moments. So you just brush edge against edge, creating a brilliance for a second, very pointillistic, and yet it's more explicit than ever.

Dove: I'm very pleased that you recognize that. I didn't think of it as something new.

Cavalieri: I don't know of anyone else doing it.

Dove: I think it goes back again to that moment on the couch because I think that when we are touched by something it's as if we're being brushed by an angel's wings, and there's a moment when everything is very clear.

The best poetry, the poetry that sustains me, is when I feel that, for a minute, the clouds have parted and I've seen ecstasy or something.

Cavalieri: But, beyond that, to have faith enough that *we* would see it. That is the point. I mean we each have a private world. But you had enough faith in the reader to know you could touch the tips of all of these things and trust that the rest would manifest itself. I think that's something new, where you used a single word on a line and very spare words. You did not give us much information—not much linear thinking. Surely all poetry encompasses much of this. But I thought yours was a spectacular act, and I think it's something very new. I think it's influencing writing and teaching us how to write again—inventing poetry.

Dove: I know that when I was writing the poems that went into *Thomas and Beulah*, I felt that I was, at least for myself, doing something very new. I felt I was moving into a territory that I wasn't quite sure of, but it was immensely exciting, and the more that I wrote the more I realized that what I was trying to tell, let's say, was not a narrative as we know narratives but actually the moments that matter most in our lives. I began to think, How do we remember our lives? How do we think of our lives or shape our lives in our own consciousnesses, and I realize that we don't actually think of lives in very cohesive strands, but we remember as beads on a necklace: moments that matter to us come to us in flashes, and the connections are submerged.

Cavalieri: Now I guess is the time we need to give the vital statistics about *Thomas and Beulah*, just who they were, in your life.

Dove: *Thomas and Beulah* is based upon the lives of my maternal grandparents, and the book is divided into two parts: the first part is called "Mandolin" and basically sketches Thomas's life, my grandfather's life. The second half of the book, called "Canary In Bloom," traces my grandmother's life. So you have moments, and poems, which are complements of each other, and yet there are also places in each of their lives which have no counterpart in the other mate's life. I thought that no matter how close two people are, there are individual moments which are entirely intimate and individual.

Cavalieri: And that's why the figure eight is so important to me when I visualize that book. I think Helen Vendler asked you what you had to overcome to write that book. Do you think there was something to overcome? Actually I think she said, "Was there anything to overcome" and you said, "Yes." Now I would like to know—what was it?

Dove: There were several things. The first thing was—and I think this was the most difficult one, a moral issue in a way—was for me a question of Can I presume to write about my grandparents' lives? Can I presume to take on a voice and say, "This is they," and to take on a voice and to say, "This is what they would have said, had they had the opportunity"? And what helped me in that, actually, was my mother because I told her I was writing the poems. I began with the poems that formed Thomas's section and I asked her if she would tell me some details from her childhood, and she did. And she never asked to see a single poem. Her trust that I would not do anything to embarrass the family gave me confidence. If she thought it was OK, their child, then maybe I could do this. That was the first thing.

There were lesser challenges—a challenge, for instance, to decide how much was going to be strictly biographical and at what point to begin to invent, and I began to invent very early. And once that barrier was over, it was fine. I mean "invent" in a sense that, for instance, my grandmother's name was not Beulah, it was Georgianna. That was a decision I made—an aesthetic decision, actually—because Georgianna, though it's a wonderful name, was first of all too male for me, and second of all didn't have the Biblical connotations that I wanted for the book. Also, it's a long name, and a very difficult name to fit on a line. So once I broke through that, I didn't have to be absolutely faithful according to biographical truth. I could go after an inner truth. That freed me.

Cavalieri: Also, because our emotional lives are always partly imagined, the material is always valid. What does your mother think of it now? Does she feel there's anything in it that speaks to her? A truth beyond the truth?

Dove: Well, my mother said to me that she really likes the book, and she also said the one thing that moved her were the two poems that dealt with my grandparents' deaths. There's one poem, "Thomas at the Wheel," that deals with my grandfather's death when he was going to the drug store to get his heart prescription filled, and had a heart attack in the car. And there's a poem about my grandmother who basically took to her bed in the last year of their life. These were very difficult poems to write and the ones that I worried about the most because I didn't want them to be painful for my mother. But she told me it felt absolutely right, that that's what it was like. She seemed happy that it was recorded and down on paper.

Cavalieri: I can't remember, did you actually know your grandparents?
Dove: I did know my grandparents, and in fact the book began with a

story that my grandmother told me. When I was in my early teens my grandfather died, and I spent Friday nights to Saturday afternoons with my grandmother, for about half a year, and so she would tell me lots of stories. She told me the story about my grandfather coming north as part of a song and dance team on the Mississippi River on a paddle boat, and I had never known that he had this whole life before her, before me, and that's what sparked my curiosity. It emerged many years later, of course, and it took me some years to finally say, "I'm going to deal with this story that haunted me."

Cavalieri: And you chose that to be the spine of the book. One poem I mentioned I'm fond of is "Daystar." I felt that was Beulah's signature poem. Do you feel Thomas has a signature poem? I would choose "Variation on Pain."

Dove: It's difficult with Thomas because in a way his life both ends and begins with his best friend's death on the river boat.

Cavalieri: Perhaps you should tell us that plot, because there is a definite plot in this book.

Dove: He is a singer to his best friend's mandolin playing on a river boat that goes up and down the Mississippi—they're the entertainment. This is a story that my grandmother told me: my grandfather had said to his friend, whose name was Lem, "Why don't you swim across the river and see if you can get some chestnuts?" There was an island there, and his friend took the dare, dove in the river, and drowned. And that was the point where my grandfather gave up the river boat life, settled down in Akron, Ohio, and met my grandmother. In a way this was a turning point in his life. Most of the poems in Thomas's section deal with the fact that his life took a dramatic turn at that point, and he's always thinking back on that friend. The friend appears to him at various moments in his life, I think as a kind of guide through his life. And that, basically, is the trajectory that his life follows.

Cavalieri: And that's how you organized his pain, which is very important for it otherwise would have been free-floating. You gave it a center.

Dove: Exactly. And so in a way there's a moment after this event happens where Thomas decides to take his friend's mandolin and learn how to play it. That, in a sense, is his signature poem, because he's learning how to survive and carry on. The poem "Variation on Pain" is the second poem in Thomas's section, and his friend has just drowned in the river on a dare from Thomas, and there's nothing really left for Thomas to hold on to at that moment, but what his friend has left behind—his mandolin. So he picks it up and, in a certain way, picks up the responsibility of his friend's death. "Two strings, one pierced cry. . . ."

Cavalieri: How did you arrive at the pierced ears, and the ringing in the ears? How did all of that occur?

Dove: That's one of those mysterious moments in poetry that keeps me addicted to writing. I was trying to imagine the sound of the mandolin, which is a very curious sound because it's cheerful and melancholy at the same time, and I think it comes from that shadow string, the double strings, and that sound. And in trying to imagine it, the humming came through. The ear lobe, the fact that he, at the end, pierces his ears, was a total mystery to me. I did not know. I thought I was writing a poem where he was going to learn how to play the mandolin, but as I was moving through the poem and trying to imagine how he would feel and what he could do as an atonement for his friend, it just occurred, it just happened, and I don't know where it came from, but when it happened it was right.

Cavalieri: Because it went through him. And so it went through us. I guess nothing else will do. So the first section are poems about Thomas, and he's rather a dashing guy, kind of handsome, and you get the feeling, however tormented he is, that he's quite a dazzler. Then we have Beulah, who is a dreamer, an introspective person, a person with longings and yearnings that are never realized—the meaning in "Daystar"?

Dove: I think, of the two, Beulah was the one who longed to travel and had dreams of going somewhere. Thomas's traveling days were over. He had gone on the riverboat, and he really was just trying to get through his life. But Beulah, for lack of any other means, travels in her mind. In this poem, Beulah's trying to find a moment's peace from the children and resorts to drastic methods. That's what "Daystar" is about.

Cavalieri: The line "She wanted a little room for thinking. . . ." Well, that is about me. And that is about you. And that's why that poem will last longer than we do.

Dove: That was very important for the book.

Cavalieri: Among your other honors, you are a Literary Lion. That means so much.

Dove: Oh, it does mean so much because libraries are where it all begins and, of course, the New York Public Library is. . . .

Cavalieri: Where it all is.

Dove: Right. Those two lions out there. It was thrilling for me.

Cavalieri: Your opening at The Library of Congress taught me something. I had thought that writing a poem was more private than saying a poem, but then I realized that nothing more is at stake than in saying it. I felt that was the most significant gesture made by any Poet Laureate here at the Library of Congress and if we can talk about that poem, "Mickey and the Night Kitchen," I'll tell you why.

Dove: I asked my daughter if she minded my reading that poem and she did not.

Cavalieri: The poem discusses your daughter discovering her vagina and comparing herself to you. I thought, by virtue of reading that poem, that things are going to be different, that we don't have to be ashamed anymore, that you were saying, "I'm here to tell you that shame is all over with, that any part of a woman's body is a fine part to write about." However, in making that decision, if it were me, I would have said, "But I'm at the Library of Congress. I can't say *vagina* because it's so daunting here and so official." And that is where you walked through the white wall and said that who you are is official enough. That's what I took away from your opening reading. Did anything go through your mind such as . . . courage? Or did you just like the poem and want to share it?

Dove: Oh, I thought about that long and hard. I've made a kind of vow to myself to read the poem at every reading, and actually my daughter gave me courage too, because I asked her the first time she was in the audience. She's ten now. I said, "Do you want me not to read the poem?" and she said, "No, it's fine." And I thought, Well, we raised her not to be ashamed, so that's great. If it's fine with her then it should be fine with anyone. But I did have a moment, I thought, I am at the Library of Congress . . . and the Great Hall . . . and I thought, No, I've done it before and I will do it here. And it was very hard to do.

Cavalieri: I'm so glad to hear that because I thought, I'm laying a lot of stuff on this. But we really have not been anything, anywhere, where we're not anything anywhere else. That is how the world is changing, and that's why you're here to do it for us. However, I'm just that much older than you that I have a few more hangups. I had four daughters, and they remember me telling them the facts of life by my looking up at the ceiling a lot, and my telling the older one to tell the younger ones. So when you read that I thought, Oh, free at last, free at last. I wrote a letter to another woman poet and said, "She read *that* poem! She read the poem!" So you may go down in history in ways you never expected.

Are you still associate editor of the literary journal *Calaloo*?
Dove: Yes.

Cavalieri: And you teach creative writing at the University of Virginia in Charlottesville, as Commonwealth Professor of English. That sounds permanent.
Dove: Yes.

Cavalieri: Tenure. That's where you are going to be, then.
Dove: Yes, it's permanent. It's a wonderful place to live and to write and to be, so I have no plans to leave.

Cavalieri: And this year you belong to us. Among some of my other favorites are the women in your books. I think in *Museum* you take a look at some of the great figures in history who interested me, because what you did with *Thomas and Beulah* was to say, "History isn't just kings and queens anymore, you know; this is what history is." However, with *Museum* you did pay homage to the great symbols of our cultures.

Dove: That's true, and in a way I think that *Museum*, which is the book that preceded *Thomas and Beulah*, prepared the way for *Thomas and Beulah* because, though I did pay homage to important figures in history, we see another side of them. We see the side that no one sees when the lights are on. And then moving from there to the underside of history, looking at history through two "ordinary people," was a natural step.

Cavalieri: I am interested in your poems about the two Catherine saints: Catherine of Alexandria and Catherine of Siena. Let us look at "Catherine of Siena." The line "You walked the length of Italy. . . ." That was an important first line. Do you know how you got to that? And also tell me about why you focused on Catherine's clenched fists.

Dove: Partly through imagining or re-imagining what it was like to be a woman of intelligence and fervor in a period where women were not supposed to be any of those things, and imagining what kind of passionate inquiry, the need-to-know, was in these women saints; there must have been incredible tension as well. We are presented with a benign image of saints, but to me there must have been tension and so the fists came in. Even as she sleeps she has the fists—which are also the curled fists of a child. Also, the language itself, in a certain way, helped me to that moment. As the poem proceeds it becomes more of a litany so that at the very end there's this feeling of being very alone in the world. Even though she's been writing letters to people, there's this feeling of being, somehow, not understood except perhaps under the "star-washed dome of heaven," her heaven. So when I got to the line "no one stumbled across your path," I knew that the next line also had to start with "no one," and I don't know why, but I knew that there had to be an emphasis that there was no one there, and then came the fists.

Cavalieri: But it leads me to believe that you feel there's more available to us. You have more faith in relationships now because to have said that means that now there might be somebody who would unpry your fists.

Dove: Yes, I think you're right, there is this feeling that this is how it was then. Aren't we lucky, now there is more of a chance. Then there was really no chance that you would find someone.

Cavalieri: What permeates your work is an incredible trust in relationships, which is not an ordinary thought today. You really believe it's all possible.

Dove: I do believe it's possible. I'm not saying it's something that happens every time. My feeling is that, as human beings, if we really want to be full and generous in spirit, we have no choice but to trust at some level. That's not saying we should be gullible or foolish, but it's the "courage of your own tenderness" as D. H. Lawrence, I think, said in *Lady Chatterley's Lover*. We have the courage to be open to someone. It's the only way to get a relationship started. It's the only way to get a relationship going to keep it sustained. Sure, we can be hurt, but there's no way to even start unless we open ourselves to that.

Cavalieri: Did your parents' long marriage make you feel that people can have long marriages?

Dove: Yes, I think so, and the example of their marriage, the example of family life, a feeling of love and, well, unconditional love in that no matter what we do they would still love us, but they might tell us about what we did wrong. We had a feeling that love also means caring enough about someone to be honest with them, too, and being able to bear that kind of honest exchange. That has a lot to do with trust, too.

Cavalieri: Well said. If we are going to talk about another poem what would be your choice? What comes first to mind?

Dove: I think the poem that comes to mind is one called the "Island Women of Paris." It's a humorous poem and a poem of praise. Poetry so often gets this misbegotten reputation of being dour, of being melancholy all the time, and I like to show that it doesn't have to be that way.

Cavalieri: I think you always preface that reading by saying that in Paris you learned how to be looked at. How did you do?

Dove: It was difficult. I think I'd give myself a B-minus. It's really true that gazing at another person was not construed as being impolite in Paris. If you could bear up under the pressure of a gaze gracefully, you would win, in fact, admiring approval from passersby. It taught me something about being able to bear up under scrutiny with grace.

Cavalieri: Previously you mentioned that you were collecting index cards for another novel. When I read *Through The Ivory Gate,* I wouldn't have known that you'd written that. There was enough of your consciousness in it, but it was so different from your writing—of course, you were very faithful to structure, the classic way that a novel is presented. I was wondering what preparations you made for that book as compared to the preparations you make for the poem.

Dove: It's very odd with that novel. One of the things I wanted to do was to write a novel that was a novel, not a poetic rendition of something. I felt that the genre demanded that of me. Of course, I also tried to expand the notion of language and what I could do in prose, but the structure of the novel was very deliberate. It got me in a lot of trouble. I wanted to have a novel where the main character explores her options in life, and the main character is a puppeteer who is trying to create an artistic space for herself. She explores her prospects in life by flashbacks, by remembering things from her past, by filtering what she learns from people in her present. That's the way we go through life. So I thought I would be wrong to write this novel as a standard kind of plot with a bell-shaped curve that has a climax and a dénouement which seems to proceed in an orderly fashion. I thought, My life isn't like that. There is a sense of flux in our lives that's also peppered by flashbacks. So I entered into this rather difficult structure of having her move through a month's time and to have all the happenings of the past keep coming in and forming the present.

Cavalieri: You also got a chance to give some thinking to the politics of the '60s, which must have been floating around, waiting for a place to land. And we can't always do that in poetry.

Dove: This is true. It was a real pleasure to be able to get the ambiance of the times. In this case it was the late '60s, early '70s, to get that ambiance into the language, even.

Cavalieri: And where were you during the years.

Dove: In the '60s, in the '70s, I was growing up in Ohio and at Miami University in Ohio. I was a student there in the early '70s. My main character is a student at the University of Wisconsin in Madison, which was a real vibrant place at that time, so she was right in the thick of it.

Cavalieri: And, finally, we could not finish this conversation without talking about Toni Morrison and that Nobel Prize. What is going on? I tell you, when I read Alice Walker, *The Color Purple*, I thought, She is the Mark Twain of our time. Then with Toni Morrison's *Beloved*, I thought, she could write the Bible if she wanted to.

Dove: Yes. It's a phenomenal book.

Cavalieri: The layers of all our selves. The invisible and the visible, and the historical and the personal. Then Rita Dove, with *Thomas and Beulah*. Is that what eternity is, that each one transcends the other, and everyone just gets better and better and better? Is that the definition of eternity?

Dove: I think it's one definition of eternity—the feeling that we are not alone on this planet, that there are those who've gone before and those who will come, and that there is in fact a community of spirits, let's say. I don't mean spirits in a sense of ghosts. I mean a community of hearts, you could say, that's there. To me, that's immensely and profoundly comforting, and in the case of Toni Morrison I have felt for so long that we were having our own conversation somewhere. She's from Ohio.

Cavalieri: Did you know her in Ohio?
Dove: No, not at all.

Cavalieri: Did you talk to her since she won the Prize?
Dove: I have not talked to her since she won the Prize. I wrote her, I was thrilled, because I remember very distinctly when I first met her through her work, and read no blurbs because it was a library copy and the jacket cover was off. I had no idea who Toni Morrison was. When I started reading this

book I had the feeling this person was like my next door neighbor who had been talking to me, and in a way, she was. We grew up about 40 miles apart.

Cavalieri: Finally I want to mention the poem that is an homage to Billie Holiday. It's called "Canary."

Dove: Canaries are the birds that, of course, have a beautiful song; it's also a term that musicians use for the female vocalist. And the canary is the type of bird that miners take down to the mines to test for poison gas leaks, and if the bird dies they know that the mine is not safe for men.

Cavalieri: Thus, your line "Sharpened love in the service of myth."

Going Up Is a Place of Great Loneliness

Malin Pereira / 1998

Malin Pereira's interview was conducted at Rita Dove's house on the outskirts of Charlottesville on 12 January 1998. It appeared in the Summer 1999 issue of *Contemporary Literature*, Vol. 40, No. 2. Reprinted by permission of the University of Wisconsin Press.

Pereira: There's been a lot of excitement recently about your play *The Darker Face of the Earth* being performed at the Kennedy Center. I understand that you have made several revisions to the play and Story Line Press has issued a revised edition. What kinds of changes did you make? How substantial are they?

Dove: Well, the ending is different. The revision actually came about after I saw some of the scenes put on their feet, as they say in the theater, which means having actors read the lines and try to walk through them. The history of the play is very strange. I wrote it without knowing what the theater world was like, and there were other things happening in my life, so I finally decided, No one will do this play because it's too big, etc., and I put it away. It's only because my husband kept bugging me every five years or so to do something that I finally rewrote it, and Story Line Press published it in 1994. At that point I really did assume that the play was going to be on the page and that was it, and maybe someday when I was dead someone would do it out of pity or whatever.

When the Oregon Shakespeare Festival was interested in the play, I realized I had an opportunity to see if what I thought would work on stage would indeed work on stage. A lot of the revisions came about from my just not feeling comfortable with some of the scenes and the pacing. I did add a couple of scenes as I realized that certain characters were more stock than essential, and that we needed to feel that they had a full life, even if we didn't know what the life was. These are complicated human beings who are bringing everything from their past to the pressure of that moment. For instance, there is now a scene between Phebe and Augustus, because Phebe became embittered over being left, and I actually liked her as a character.

I was exhausted by the time I finished that version. I thought, OK, that's enough. Also, I did change the ending. It's essentially the same tragedy, except that Augustus does live at the end of the new version; it's just not a life worth living. With this version what happens is that Amalia kills herself; also Phebe is now in there too because I thought it was essential to have her there. As the three of them piece together, in this moment of craziness, what exactly the story is, that indeed Amalia is Augustus's mother, each reacts in a different way, and Amalia then kills herself to try to save Augustus, which means that the revolutionaries think that he did what he was supposed to do and he's a hero. But what kind of hero is that, who's just realized that he's lost everything that could make him happy?

That change came about because of my daughter, who had participated in all of the sessions at the Oregon Shakespeare Festival. She loved it and would sit through all these rehearsals and make suggestions. It was great. One night I was still perturbed at the ending. I had put Phebe in it, but I still didn't like the way the insurrectionists came in—bang, bang, everyone was dead. So I was fiddling with it, and she came down (she was supposed to be in bed), and I said to her, "I was just messing around with this ending." And she said, "You know, I think he should live. There are worse things than death." This is a twelve year old who really doesn't know what she's saying, but I suddenly realized, Yes, that's even worse.

It was interesting that in some of the workshops, that was one of the questions that was presented to me, because in the original Oedipus, of course, he does live. People asked, "Why didn't you follow the myth exactly?" I don't follow it exactly because I didn't want the play to be a kind of checklist against a Greek myth. I couldn't find the right way I could make it believable that he could live. I hadn't found the plot that would make him live and why that would be worth it for him, not just to fulfill the myth. And that was the moment that did it. So those are the major changes. Hector's part also has been deepened. I didn't want him to be merely a crazy man in the swamp; I really wanted everything that he said to make eminent sense if you knew the whole story. So he does have a couple of monologues, but the basic story is still the same. And that all came about working with these wonderful actors.

Pereira: So it was the putting the play into production that offered these realizations—it became apparent that certain things needed to be changed. I guess that's typical in theater.

Dove: Yes, it is very typical in theater, from what I understand. I found it really exciting, because as a poet, someone who's used to doing everything in one circle of lamplight, this was exhilarating. It was also exasperating sometimes—too many voices. I can really understand now how people can lose perspective in the theater, because there are a thousand things to think about. Most of the time I had to simply forget everything everyone said and go back out to my cabin and make my decision. It was a fascinating experience. As a poet (because I really think of myself as a poet), one of the things that I learned artistically in rewriting the play was how much power in theater a silence or gesture can make. It's very close to poetry and how what you don't say has to be contained in those white spaces, but also in the sound of the word. That's one of the essences of poetry that always thrills me and keeps me going back to it.

Pereira: Your earlier poetry often dealt with the historical past, but in *Grace Notes* and *Mother Love* you seem to have moved more into the personal present, and you've commented in other interviews about your willingness to now come into the personal a bit more. You called it at one point coming home, writing your way back home. How does *The Darker Face of the Earth*, which I read as a play about the historical foundations of American culture, relate to that?

Dove: Well, that's a great question. There are two parts to my answer. First of all, because *Darker Face of the Earth* has such a long history; in a very interesting way it's an early work that I came back to. I began working on that play about the same time that I finished my first book, *The Yellow House on the Corner*. So in that sense, all of the themes of *Darker Face* were very close to the slave narratives of *Yellow House on the Corner*, filling in the past, trying to get into the past as a person and to humanize it so that eventually I could get to my own past without being self-indulgent. However, trying to go back to the play and rewrite it for production felt like another kind of coming home, because now I had to inject a lot of my own emotions and takes on things in characters to make sure they were alive and not just mythic representations walking around saying their lines and getting off the stage.

The first version of the play is clean, but it's very quick, and it's more pageant than personalized. There's a little bit of me in every one of those characters that wasn't necessarily there in the first version, particularly Amalia, and it was very important to allow her to speak. In the end, I didn't want any easy answers: I didn't want anyone in the audience coming away thinking, These are the bad guys, these are the good guys; slavery is bad, slave owners are bad, look at the noble savage, and all that. I wanted all the characters to be fighting for their own individual realizations against the system. The big bad guy is the system, obviously. But that's all the kind of stuff I learned by finally coming around, coming home in the previous volumes.

Pereira: Interesting. So do you think that in some way the personal present and national history end up being connected for you?

Dove: They've always been.

Pereira: Why or how?

Dove: I think they both have something to do, a lot to do, with being female and being Black. From as early as I can remember, I always felt that there was a world with lots of "historical" events going on, and that my viewpoint was not a direct one, but I was looking at it from the side. I'm talking about when I was small. First it started out as a female issue, because I think for most kids there's a point when if they're in a minority, they realize they're a minority. It's very strange: "Oh, really, I'm not like you?" It usually comes from the outside somehow. But as a girl, growing up in a really traditional family, with a mother who was a housekeeper and a father who was a chemist, I always felt that there was this view of how the world should run, and then I was supposed to fit into this somehow, and I didn't think all the rules were quite right. Both my parents would say, "Education is the key," and "You can be anything you want to be," and then I'd look at the magazines and think, I can't be everything I want to be unless something's going to change. So that meant that I didn't take the historical at face value. Ever. Of course, W. E. B. Du Bois talks about the double vision when you're a minority. You see what the mainstream is immersed in, which is reality, but you also see the other reality. He talks about what advantage this kind of binocular vision gives you: it gives you perspective, it gives you depth.

As I grew up, I felt enormously lucky that, because of my circumstances, I had this vision. I never believed that the newspapers were true necessarily: that was just one version of the truth, and it's interesting, it's pretty good, but I'll wait to see what judgment is going to come in. So that's why the personal present and the historical past have always been connected for me.

On the other hand, language was always fascinating to me even from a young age. I think with most children it's fascinating at an existential level; the sounds that you make are wonderful, regardless of whether they make sense. There were several kinds of ways in which language was stylized in my life. I'm talking about storytellers in the family, the good ones, the ones who could tell the story you've heard three thousand times and suddenly it's a good story, from those to the kind of oral games you play on the street as a Black kid, from the dozens to what that implies and how the language becomes plastic, all of that and then also the literature. To read someone like Shakespeare and think, This language is part of the emotion, and there are all these different levels to language and different tones and qualities.

All of that, too, was experience which is perceived directly as one part of life, but if you're going to be a writer or are going to be an artisan, you choose a medium. The trick is to use this essentially artificial, made-up medium to try to imitate that immediacy, which it can never do because it's never immediate, but you give the illusion of immediacy. I was fascinated by that from a very young age. It was probably part of the reason why when I was in second grade I wrote this silly novel called "Chaos" where I took my spelling words and wrote chapter by chapter according to the list of spelling words. Part of the fascination with that was to see how the words themselves, the language, these symbols would build the reality.

Pereira: So in some ways writing your personal present is rewriting national history, adding the version that wasn't represented, or writing from the center that was marginalized.

Dove: That's one part of it. That's absolutely one part of it, with the understanding that my personal history is only one personal history. Also, I think that because I was acutely aware, even at a young age, that my perception of an "official" historical event was very different from that "official" version, I thought that that must be the same for every person, if they stopped to think about it. There's a war, and people can talk about casualties in the war, but if you've had someone die in the war, it takes on a completely different cast, and if you're a refugee from that war it takes on a completely different cast. All these kinds of things I think are fascinating, and in the end, unless you have a writer, or artist, or an oral history, the only version left is the one that is the official version, and I really resist that. I feel that all of us cannot ever forget that the official version is merely a construct that we may need to order our time line, but there are human beings, all sorts of individual human beings, to punctuate it.

Pereira: Which of course is what you're doing in *Museum*, writing poems of "unofficial" history. It reminds me of James Baldwin when he talks about how the sad thing about white America is that it often believes its own myths, believes the official version of history, and I find that somewhat true when I teach. So many of my students just hang on to those official versions of history.

Dove: And they can be utterly devastated when they realize that they're not true. I think that's why Vietnam and the '60s were so explosive and powerful. It was the moment when we realized that the myth didn't hold. Then the '70s and '80s became this retreat to "It's just me and I'm going to do this."

Pereira: How does it feel now not to have all of those responsibilities of being Poet Laureate?

Dove: It feels wonderful, actually. That's a terrible thing to say. It does feel wonderful. It also is not completely over, either, and I think that one of the hardest periods of time for me was right after it was over, because I naively assumed that when Bob Haas took it over I could go back to my life. But I couldn't go back to my life. There are residuals, and the letters and the requests keep coming, but I don't have the outside justification to say, "Well, I'm going to go on a half-time teaching load." So it took me, and it's still taking me, a lot of time to figure out how to conduct my life so that I have one. Since I was raised to be a dutiful daughter, I am someone who answers letters; I think Toni Morrison is the same way. We're Midwestern. We know how our parents raised us. In a way you get raised to try to fit into the Northern world. The Southern roots are very close: my grandparents came from the South. They came to the North and went into these factories and then had to build a new neighborhood, a new home, and the rules of social behavior were fairly rigorous. They say to the children, "This is how you have to be," and you do it because you honor yourself as well as your community, which really puts a double whammy on you. So there I was, trying to answer these letters and finally—I really think it took until about last year—I realized I don't have to answer all of these letters. I can actually just not answer, and they'll write again.

Pereira: It's apparent that music, your training in classical music, has been important for your work. It comes up thematically in so many ways. One thing that I'm curious about is how that training influences your work structurally. Have you thought about that at all?

Dove: Oh, I've thought about it. I haven't thought about it in any kind of critical way. First of all, at a very basic level, I believe that language sings, has its own music, and I'm very conscious of the way something sounds, and that goes from a lyric poem all the way to an essay or to the novel, that it has a structure of sound which I think of more in symphonic terms for the larger pieces. I really do think that sonnets to me are like art songs. That's one thing. I also think that resolution of notes, the way that a chord will resolve itself, is something that applies to my poems—the way that, if it works, the last line of the poem, or the last word, will resolve something that's been hanging for a while. And I think musical structure affects even how the poems are ordered in a book. Each of the poems plays a role: sometimes it's an instrument, sometimes several of them are a section, and it all comes together that way too.

Pereira: What we were considering in my class on your work, and I think we were applying this to *Yellow House on the Corner* and then to *Museum*, was that you often have five-sectioned works, and we were wondering if you were structuring them along the idea of five movements for longer symphonies. You have moved away from that, of course, in more recent volumes, but especially since those were your two first times structuring a longer piece like that, I was wondering if you just went to that structure.

Dove: This is fascinating, because the book I'm working on now has five sections, and I remember feeling, Oh, I like these five sections.

Pereira: Yes, comfy.

Dove: Really comfy. I think that three-sectioned books put too much emphasis on that middle section being solid and holding on to the ends, and when you have five sections it takes the edge off putting such great importance into the beginning. One of the things I do when I'm ordering and structuring the books is to try to thwart readers' notions that the first poem is going to give them the key and now here we go! But all it is is just an opening.

Pereira: I teach it that way.

Dove: There's also this sense that if you take it as the key, then what doors does it open further down? It's more like, Here's an opening motif, and then it's going to be embellished, and then it may change, and then it may go minor, and then it does all these things, so it isn't like this is the truth, but this is *one* truth.

Pereira: Very true of *Museum*, too. You play with the opening motifs along the way. It's really diverse; it's not like the answer is at the beginning. Well, you've published a lot besides poetry—short stories, essays, plays, and a novel—and I know from other interviews that you feel that crossing genres is very necessary and a good thing for a writer. I've wondered whether you find that there is a specific relationship between your poetry and your non-poetry that you'd be able to articulate. Do you think, for example, that certain subjects are inappropriate for poetry, and that then you turn to other venues?

Dove: When an idea occurs to me, sometimes it's an idea, sometimes it's a line, sometimes it's a word, sometimes it's a character, but at the moment when a piece begins, gets its genesis, and I feel that something is going to happen and become a piece of writing, I know what form it's in already. I can't think of an instance where I've tried it out as a poem and said, "Oh no, this should be a short story," or something like that. The only case I can think of where there are almost duplicates is the scene in the novel on a beach with guitar-playing, and then also in the poem "Summit Beach," but I deliberately decided to try it both ways. It was willed. The story came first, and then I thought I really would like to try this from a different angle, just that moment. There hasn't been that kind of crossover where I've said, "Oh, this didn't work, or that didn't work."

I think it must happen further back in the brain, in a series of thought processes, so that by the time it comes to my consciousness, all those decisions have been made. I think that has something to do with the way that the language itself gets used in various genres, the weight of each word, too. Because I remember when I was working on the novel, at first— and I knew it was going to be a novel—I thought, Oh, I don't want to write a novel—too big, too many words, it's such a waste. This is just how you think as a poet. Then, until I could figure out how the weight of each word and the weight of each sentence wove the story, I was just writing a lot of verbiage.

Once I figured out two things, the key signature and the time, then it became much easier. I figured out how each individual note—you've got me talking in musical terms!—how much weight each different note had and what kind of time signature I was going to have in this piece. All artists can fall into the traps of whatever we do well, and that for me is to write a poem. To write in other genres offers stretch and a counterbalance to that trap. The other genres help remind me that there's a value to length, there's a value to overload, there's something to lushness, too, and the work can be just as powerful as something austere.

Pereira: Which is mostly your aesthetic in your poetry.
Dove: It is.

Pereira: You don't tend to go on and on and on.
Dove: No, I don't, but someday. . . . If you go on and on, it has to have a

purpose. I get really frustrated with poems that go on, but the words can be sloughed away. I think there's a way to go on and on and still have it—the intent. But I do find, in relationships between the genres, that when I'm writing poetry, I very often read prose, and vice versa.

Pereira: You don't want to be influenced by the poets when you're writing poetry.

Dove: It's not just that I don't want to be influenced, because when writing a poem I will go to the bookshelf and get a book because I know there's something in there that I need to read again. But I don't want to sit down and read lots of poetry books while writing poetry. It muddies the water. It must have something to do with the musical training, because when I'm in another country I can pick up languages fairly quickly; I do it mostly, I think, through imitation and the intonation of the language, the way it falls. For example, I speak German fluently, but I have great difficulty if we go somewhere and someone speaks German with an accent, like a Swiss German. Or if someone speaks English with an accent, after an hour, I start to talk like that, and I have to go away! Wales and Ireland were a nightmare because I would start doing that, in part because I loved the way it sounded. So that tendency in me would mean that if I were reading exclusively Adrienne Rich for days, then I would start to write like Adrienne Rich. That's not my voice, that's her voice. So I have to not read much poetry while writing it, for self-protection.

Pereira: I've been interested in your recent focus on the work of Breyten Breytenbach. You just translated his Li Po poem, and I noticed you dedicated a poem to him in *Mother Love*, called "Political." I was curious, first of all, how you picked up Afrikaans. Did you go to South Africa, or how did this all come about? And I'm curious what interests you in his poetry as well.

Dove: A lot of it is just circumstance. First of all, I don't know Afrikaans. I know German and a little bit of Dutch. If I listen to Afrikaans long enough I can get into it. The way in which the translations came about was that I was at an annual poetry festival last summer in Rotterdam called Poetry International. Each year, they've had writers come from all over the world for this week-long festival, just poetry day and night. But also sometimes in the mornings they have a translation workshop for the week, and they choose a poet who writes in Dutch or a Dutch-related language, and all the other writers come in and translate the work, and the idea is to try to bring some of these works to their respective languages. Breyten Breytenbach was the poet for this last summer. It was great, because he was there, and the organizers had provided literal translations in a host of languages, in English, in German, in French, in Spanish. And he gave a reading. So I used the French and the German and the Dutch and the Afrikaans and the English, of course, to try to put it together. Again it gets to my fascination with trying to find the approximation in the language. Breyten Breytenbach I find interesting because of his linguistic standpoint—he knows so many languages. I like a lot of his poems, but there are also others that I'm not that crazy about.

Pereira: He's published a novel in French, as I recall.

Dove: Right, and he's lived in Paris all these years. I've met him at several conferences; when you go to these international conferences, you meet the same people all the time. I think he has lived in Spain, too. I can't help but feel that all those languages influenced his work. So that's where all that came from, and it's less a fascination with his work than just the way the circumstance presented itself. As for dedicating "Political" to him, that occurred after the first time I met him in Mexico. As I was working through those poems about mothers and daughters, I remembered a description from his memoirs, his *Confessions of an Albino Terrorist*, when he talks about the Black political prisoners singing as someone's being led to execution, and that really was powerful. I was trying to get into the sense of Demeter going down into Hell and what's going to sustain you if your daughter is going down into Hell. That image came back up to me.

Pereira: A writer you've mentioned throughout your work is Derek Walcott. What would you say has been important for you about Walcott and his work?

Dove: I'm still trying to figure that out. I love Walcott's work, but I don't think that it influences me. I find that his work is very different from mine. The first time I came in contact with it was through his play *Dream on Monkey Mountain*. I read the play—I must have been a junior in college—and I thought it was phenomenal: I never knew that theater could be like that. I was surprised to discover that he was a poet as well and thought, Whoa! I get a double treat here. Part of it is the fact that he's always dealing with—I don't want to call it a dilemma, but with this position of being in love with this island, in love with his people, but feeling also separate from them because he's gone off to school and he's writing these amazing poems that they won't read. He wants to honor where he comes from, but at the same time not be another colonizer of the experience; he's always very conscious of that. I think he is conscious of it all the way to the level of language, because he has earlier poems particularly where he puts in a lot of patois, and even in later poems, in the middle of this absolutely gorgeously constructed English, this British set-piece sentence, comes one of those "He no be this," which happens in the culture a lot. I think that he is an exquisite writer.

Pereira: But you don't feel that there is a technical debt there or any other kind of influence?

Dove: There is a debt in the sense that I wish that I could write that well. I think that the language is just gorgeous, and it's not my voice, not my style. But in general I admire his trying to mix in all levels of the language, because that is what he has grown up with, and he's making it work on the page. That was something that I aspired to. Trying to get syncopated rhythms into classic iambic pentameter.

Pereira: So it's that mixed heritage and the mixing of the traditions that you like.

Dove: I think it's a wealth rather than a problem, and it's so ass-backwards to say that there is a Black way of writing and then there is a white—that's madness. Every Black person I know speaks at so many different levels all the time, and why not use all of that? All of it. Why not? I do believe that people will come along: we've done it so long with other ethnic groups. If you think about all those attitudes and expressions that we've gotten from Jewish Americans, for example . . .

Pereira: It should be a both/and, not an either/or.
Dove: Exactly.

Pereira: Which brings me to one of my favorite poems.
Dove: Which one is that?

Pereira: "Upon Meeting Don L. Lee in a Dream," from your first volume, *The Yellow House on the Corner*. Critics have noticed this poem.
Dove: I know.

Pereira: You can't help but notice this poem. Arnold Rampersad points out that it might show a bit of hostility to the Black Arts movement. It's an early poem, and I wonder if you've moderated your stance toward some of the Black Arts movement aesthetic views or prescriptions, over time?
Dove: Moderated is a difficult word. It implies . . .

Pereira: Extremism to begin with.
Dove: Right.

Pereira: Well, you do fry Lee alive in the poem.
Dove: He and I are friends, too, you know.

Pereira: Have you come to a broader perspective now?
Dove: I think of it more as a generational poem, as opposed to one that deals with aesthetics: as a young girl, insecure as a writer, I was doing that killing the father thing. I remember having someone ask me, "Why do you say 'in a dream'? Why don't you just say it directly?" I answered, "No, I want it to be dreaming because it is a psychological poem, a poem that works on that kind of psychic landscape." It wasn't an excuse for the surrealism in the poem but a way to say not to take it at face value. I do think that when I was beginning to write, or beginning to contemplate putting the writing out into the world (which is a different thing altogether) when I was in college, I was terrified that I would be suffocated before I began, that I would be pulled into the whole net of whether this was Black enough, or whether I was denigrating my own people. There is a pressure, not just from the Black Arts movement, but from one's whole life, to be a credit to the race.

When I was in my twenties, I think I knew instinctively that I was not strong enough to be able to take that, that I would probably just stop writing, and I didn't want to stop writing. Which meant that I didn't publish for a while and really kept back and didn't want to get out into the fray, so to speak. I didn't want to get into the political stuff because I felt like I had to figure out what I was doing artistically, and if I didn't write my particular take on the world, if I could not find that conduit before I got out into the fray, then I was lost. So that poem, which is a very early poem, in fact I wrote it in college, was kind of clearing the way. It was this feeling of "I'm gonna be strong enough to stand up to you, at least in a dream. I don't know if I'm gonna be able to do it later." I think I was really lucky that I wasn't born a few years earlier, because when I began to develop, I had to publish, I had to see if it mattered to anyone else. Luckily for me, by that time there was more leeway being allowed. I have nothing against anyone in the Black Arts Movement.

Pereira: Not personally.
Dove: Not even artistically. I see how it was absolutely necessary, and I think a lot of it is really wonderful work, too.

Pereira: Perhaps it was the hegemony of some of their prescriptions that was upsetting to you.

Dove: Yes, that's what it was. It was a "Don't fence me in." And yet part of me could also see that given the stereotypical ways in which mainstream America looked at Blacks, it was necessary to build the base first, before you started admitting more complexity into that and perhaps even some negative things and negative characters. I feel that it is anathema to an artist to tamp down the truth for any kind of poetical goal. I don't see how you can be an artist at that point; I think you compromise yourself very severely. I think of Seamus Heaney's essay about the Eastern European writers, the poets, and how Heaney felt that the pressure of the political situation forced them to find a way to say the truth. And there is something to be said for that. There are ways, if you are dealing with any kind of constricting or restrictive artistic system, to pull through, but it takes an enormous character. It takes a very strong character, and I believe there are writers who have been lost because they simply could not take that. I don't think that it is anything to be ashamed of, either. Some people are stronger than others in that sense. So that poem was really when I first put my foot outside of the door. I was tempted to take it out of *Selected Poems* and thought, No, that's not fair.

Pereira: It's a good poem, too.

Dove: It is a part of how I developed, and so I thought I had to be honest.

Pereira: There is another place in your work where you seem to be answering back to something that could be read as a Black Arts Movement prescription. The opening sequence of the novel *Through the Ivory Gate*—the Penelope doll scene—is answering back to Toni Morrison's *The Bluest Eye* and the whole obsession with the doll that goes on there. But in your novel, Penelope, the white doll, is kept, and the other doll, the Black doll that the parents are so eager to give Virginia, is thrown out the window. What issues were you thinking about in that scene?

Dove: It's true that I had read *The Bluest Eye*, and that book struck me very deeply for several reasons. I stumbled across it in a stack in the library when I was in graduate school. I didn't know who the author was; I didn't even know that the author was Black. I just saw the title, picked up the book, and started to read it, and I thought, Oh my God, she's telling my life. It was the first time that I had ever read anything that dealt with Blacks in the Midwest. At that point I had felt very alone because I had had so many instances where people assumed that I came either from Harlem or from the South. You wonder, Do I have to go to the burden of explanation, or can I just start where I am and write this story? Here was someone who was doing that. So I felt suddenly not alone.

Pereira: It was a bridge.

Dove: Yes, it really was a bridge. The story of the doll was a bridge, too, because that's an autobiographical moment in the novel, although many are not. It was a moment in my life I had always felt ashamed of, that I had thrown the doll out the window. Why did I do it? It's not a justification for why I threw the one doll out, but what does this show us about how society's expectations and judgments impinge upon a small child? In a way it was, for me, a confession. And it was an answer to Toni Morrison, but it was more like an "Amen," like saying, "I know where people are coming from; this has happened to a lot of us."

Pereira: What's implied in Toni Morrison's novel is that the doll represents the white aesthetic of beauty which can be so destructive for young Black girls growing up. Are you agreeing with Morrison, then, in your sequence?

Dove: Yes, I am agreeing with her. I'm agreeing with her at that level. There is another part of it, too, and that is that with those two dolls, in my novel, the white doll had real hair that you could comb, and the Black doll had painted-on curls, and it was one of the first efforts at mass production of Black dolls and wasn't a very good likeness. It wasn't beautiful, not because it was Black, but because whoever had made it had decided that that's what a Black doll looks like. It didn't look like a person. When I went back and started to remember the scene and write it, I realized that that was what disturbed me about that moment. For years I had felt ashamed because I thought that I had rejected the Black doll. But it wasn't that at all. It just wasn't a good doll. They made an ugly little doll, and it wasn't useful: I couldn't comb its hair. That's essential! Obviously, there was not a big market for Black dolls, so they felt they didn't have to put in a lot of effort. At the end of that section of the novel, the protagonist, Virginia, has grown up and runs across the white doll again, which has gotten waterlogged and stinks now. She throws her away, and for me that was a moment when she got rid of the guilt and was feeling that she could move on as an individual, which was why it was important to have that at the beginning of the novel.

Pereira: I thought that it was a powerful scene for her. In relation to this, you might be familiar with Trey Ellis's essay in the Winter 1989 issue of

Callaloo where he talked about the new Black aesthetic, an aesthetic born of the Black middle class that he sees as combining all kinds of aesthetic influences—white and Black, counterculture and high art, and so on. He argued that the central feature of this was the artist, the Black artist, as a cultural mulatto. What do you think of his idea that now we are in the midst of this new Black aesthetic? Do you think that's true of your work, or of a lot of what's happening now?

Dove: My first reaction to Ellis's essay was that it was all manifesto: it gives people something to bounce off of. I didn't pay much attention. I read it, and I thought it was interesting, but it didn't help me. I don't feel the need artistically to have to take a stand all the time. I think that taking such a stance can be important in the whole critical history because it gives people points around which to swirl and to fight and . . .

Pereira: Publish.

Dove: And publish and burst out again. But I do think that my artistic temperament is to be a moving X-marks-the-spot, to keep going. I try not to think about the cultural history of literature right now. That doesn't help me as an artist. I would much rather be in the middle of it, totally confused.

Pereira: I found interesting Ellis's reinvention of the term "mulatto." It has had such a history, from the turn-of-the-century and Harlem Renaissance "tragic mulatto," who was often depicted as a pathetic soul who self-destructed, to the pejorative use of "mulatto" by Black Arts Movement writers such as Amiri Baraka in the 1960s. Ellis reclaims "mulatto" as a positive term for contemporary Black writers from middle-class backgrounds. It seems an attempt to give voice to something that I think was a closet issue for some Black writers, that "Yes, I can freely draw on iambic pentameter," as you were saying earlier. I think it does link back to Derek Walcott.

Dove: Yes, it does. I think that is what he is saying, and you are absolutely right. It does pull it out into the open, and it needs to be talked about. I had difficulty with the "mulatto" aspect only because, and this is a poet being obsessed with detail, "mulatto" implies that this only happens to one segment of humanity. When we say "mulatto," we only think of a Black who has white blood, but never the other way around—I mean, never that there are whites who have all sorts of ethnic blood mixed in. It's the way that it marginalizes again that makes me uneasy with the term, that's all. Not with what he's saying.

Pereira: He's claiming this group as Black, and I see it as actually a kind of pulling toward Blackness. I saw Ellis as trying to keep Blackness a center in the artistic lives of these artists. But you are right, it leaves out a whole other range of possibility, doesn't it?

Dove: It does, but it is the nature of manifestos to claim a certain ground and then say, "OK, come what may," and that's fine too. Even the surrealist has to say, "This is what is claimed as the center." I recognize that, given our society, it is hopelessly naive to imagine that one's own heritage will not disappear entirely or be ignored if we are not constantly reminding people that it's important. I'm very grateful that there are people who are doing that work, and I'm glad I don't have to do it.

Pereira: This also reminds me of that short story of yours, "The Spray Paint King," in the collection *Fifth Sunday*. That is sort of your portrait of the artist as a cultural "mulatto." I know you've said elsewhere that the character was based on a Swiss guy who was going about doing this graffiti when you were in Germany, but is it possible that you had Jean-Michel Basquiat in mind, or was he not impinging on your world then?

Dove: He wasn't impinging on my consciousness then. When I was working on that story there were these graffiti going up all over Germany and Switzerland, and no one knew who was doing them then. I made up a mixed-race artist to do them. In that sense, I think certainly that this artist is my symbol of the artist as a cultural "mulatto." I used the word "mulatto" there because "mulatto" also implies an oppression. It implies a psychological oppression. That's one of the reasons why I have problems with Ellis's use of "mulatto," you see. But in "The Spray Paint King" he has that oppression that he keeps trying to fight and feel his defiance against.

Pereira: I would like to talk about one of the very first subjects we exchanged correspondence on: the incest motif in your work. It transcends your genres.

Dove: Yes, it does. I must say that I wasn't even aware that it was there, and it's very obvious, once you brought it up. I thought, Oh, my God! I was baffled about it: there is no incidence of incest in my family, there is no autobiographical or even close-friend incidence of it. So it is something that I can't explain. I have decided that eventually I'll figure it out.

Pereira: And it remains exclusive to your work before *Grace Notes* and *Mother Love*. I was very much looking for it there, and I can't find it. It's in the short story "Aunt Carrie" in *Fifth Sunday*; it's in the novel, *Through the Ivory Gate*. It's in the play *The Darker Face of the Earth*, which now when you tell me that that is an earlier piece, I see it fitting there. It's in Beulah's life in *Thomas and Beulah*. There, we really have to look for it, because it could just be physical child abuse but for the mother's righteous anger, "I will cut you down." With Beulah, I wonder how much you consciously thought of her as being a victim of incest with the father and then negotiating this marriage with Thomas, or did it just end up in there somehow?

Dove: I didn't think about it at all. In fact, I can't say that the poem "Taking in Wash" in *Thomas and Beulah* was even on a conscious level for me about incest. I knew that it was about that moment when the mother comes in between the father and daughter; whether the mother has always come in between or not was not, for me, the issue. I felt the mother always managed to come in between them.

Pereira: Except there is evidence to the contrary. I mean, I can't argue with the person who wrote the poems, but Beulah has nightmares where she goes and sees herself in the mirror as this monster figure of nighttime terrors. And "Promises" and "Anniversary" are two poems that have a lot to do with her marriage, but they also suggest that she's overly involved with her father.

Dove: The father is always there.

Pereira: What's the father doing in her marriage?

Dove: I think there is probably an element not of incest necessarily, but of that unhealthy attachment of fathers to daughters, or even mothers to sons, that starts surfacing at the time of marriage. It is almost built into the whole tradition of bridal showers and weddings in the fact that the father can give the daughter away. Part of me also feels—and I think that this is why the Aunt Carrie stories are in *Fifth Sunday* and *Through the Ivory Gate*—that our fear, as a society, of incest and of sex in general fuels excessive guilt when we feel our love toward our children. I'm not talking about sexual love toward children but just that feeling of clinging and then not wanting to show too much because that could be cloying and that could be interpreted some way. We are really messed up, actually. I know I've seen it in me in my feelings with our daughter. As kids grow up they don't want you to touch them, just because they are growing up, and we are almost ashamed that we want to touch them. It's very natural to want to stroke her hair again. But we've gotten to the point now where we can't do that, and maybe we really should be doing it. I remember I wanted to be on my own, but I wanted to be held too. It just was unseemly to be held. You are supposed to grow up. That's part of why the incest thing comes up all the time, though it is obviously a very extreme example. I just can't give you any more because I don't know if it's over yet.

Pereira: It's unconscious.

Dove: Yes, unconscious, and I don't know if it's over. I don't think it is going to come up in a poem anytime soon.

Pereira: Another writer who appears on several occasions in your writing is H. D. It's interesting to me that every time you've cited her, you haven't cited her poetry, but her prose. When did you become familiar with her work, and what about her work interests you?

Dove: I became familiar with her work in graduate school at Iowa.

Pereira: Via Louise Glück?

Dove: I'm trying to think if it was Louise or not. I don't know who mentioned her, but I did study with Louise and that would make a lot of sense. Well, I'll tell you the first thing that fascinated me about H. D., though I can't remember who said it, or who mentioned the book. Someone mentioned Hermetic Definition, and I thought, H. D./hermetic definition—just that tension between her initials and the title made me think, I've got to read this person; she must be very strange and wonderful. I do only quote her prose, but I love her poetic work. It's so much itself, if that makes any sense, and it's so very musical in its own insistent phrasing that I take her in very small dosages; otherwise I'd start sounding like her.

Pereira: Do you read her poetry?

Dove: I do read her poetry. I haven't read it for a long time now. When I was working on the *Mother Love* poems I did not want to reread her because I did not want to approach myth in any way like the way that she approached it, so I wanted to forget. I haven't gotten back to her yet. I will.

Pereira: She is very intense.

Dove: Yes. What I admire about her is the way she could take the outrageous circumstances of her life sometimes and write a poem or sequence which was absolutely beautiful; I thought she could do that and it was not self-indulgent, it was not really confessional in any sense, and I'm glad I don't have that situation in my life.

Pereira: You've produced a pretty large body of work now, especially in poetry. Do you see any kind of development or phases? Do you feel that things got to a certain point and now you've turned somewhere?

Dove: I try not to look to see if there is any kind of development, because that'll stop me doing the next thing, but the other kind of language you were using about turning corners makes sense, and I do see those kinds of directions—like feeling that it is time to turn a corner to stop going down this road. Then there are certain things that I'll do sometimes very deliberately, technically to try to pull me down a different road.

When I finished *The Yellow House on the Corner*, the next book, *Museum*, was, on the one hand, inspired by my living in Europe at that time, living in Germany mostly, and what that did to my perspective of a history of the world. But the technical thing that happened was that almost every poem had its title first. In *The Yellow House* it was always the other way around. I had great difficulty with titles, and I despaired of ever being easy about titles. For some reason, in *Museum*, the titles were almost there first. It was very strange.

When *Museum* was finished and I was already working on *Thomas and Beulah*, but I didn't know it was *Thomas and Beulah*, the technical task that I gave myself was not to write an "I," because everyone was writing an "I" at that time, and not to write in "you," because everyone was doing that too and it seemed so weird. What's left is only "he" and "she," and so I thought I should try to write poems in which there were characters. It wasn't that I would throw something away if it had an "I" or a "you" in it, but I just did that, and it happened to come together with these poems.

After *Thomas and Beulah*, this expanded narrative, this poetic sequence, I had a great desire to write songs, something that was a lyric, which is what *Grace Notes* came out of. I enjoyed it. The mother-daughter poems in *Mother Love* were a product of my life, obviously, with a daughter growing up, but also of the fact that I had been reading Rilke's *Sonnets of Orpheus*: I suddenly started writing sonnets. There have been other things I've tried. This way of assigning myself little technical things is just a means to push me somewhere else in terms of the emotional or the artistic. But I don't want to define the emotional, artistic push; I'd rather just define the technical and let it fall where it may.

Pereira: What are you working on now?

Dove: It's a book of poems. I'm still at the point where I can't give you an idea of it, though it's almost finished. In fact, it has only one or two poems that need to go in it. But I don't know what it is, exactly, because the poems have occurred over a great period of time, as opposed to the other books, where they were much more concentrated. There's a point in *Mother Love* where I was only writing those poems and I had the sense of the book. This book is different. There is a very early poem in it, a long poem, that I've always tried to put in books, and it never fit, and now it's found its way. Then there are some very recent poems. And because I haven't been publishing a lot of these poems in my books, I didn't publish them in periodicals: I didn't want someone to start commenting on them before I could figure out where I was going with all of this stuff. A lot of them are short—lyrics, really, but they aren't private lyrics. It's like Wittgenstein's "To take yourself as the case"—to take it so the personal is more like the existential eye in the universe.

Pereira: Getting to the universal through the particular.

Dove: Getting to the universe through the particular but also assuming that the universe is a particular as well. Sounds kind of big and grand. Some of them I feel are kind of lonely poems. No, not lonely. Alone poems. At the risk of overinterpreting myself, I think that some of my experience of the schizophrenia of being a private person and a public person has informed these poems. Not in any autobiographical way, but in the sense that I think every one of us is alive in our skin, and at the same time we feel completely insubstantial. I want to get at that.

Pereira: I'd like to focus on two poems we had very interesting debates about in my class last semester. One of them is "Shakespeare Say" in *Museum*. What I read this poem as being about is that Champion Jack is creating art out of his sometimes brutal experience, in the blues tradition. A couple of my graduate students launched a very interesting counterargument claiming his art was false and failed, and they hung their argument on, particularly, the stanza that reads, "going down slow crooning," and then the Shakespearean paraphrase, "man must be careful what he kiss when he drunk," and then the repetition of going down and how nobody's listening to him. I wonder how you see Champion Jack and his art.

Dove: I never thought about it that way. At the beginning of the poem, we see the facade of Champion Jack, and his myth, in a sense, in debt and in his walking suit and all of that stuff, them leading him around. This is the public Champion Jack. Yet the public doesn't understand him at all: the essential Jack Dupree is not there and is never there for his audience, because they don't have any reference points. At the moment when he's going down, and he's not in good shape physically (the man is a drunk, and he's not at the height of his powers), you could say he's at his worst. But the mistakes sound like jazz. I think at that very moment, he comes back to what makes him an artist in the beginning, the blues. He comes back to, "My mother told me there would be days like this." At this moment he feels, again, the blues. Before that he's got his act, he's got his little rap, everything is fine, and he can say all this stuff about Shakespeare. I don't think it's great, but at that moment, when he's drunk, he can't hold his piss. "My mother told me there would be days like this"—that's where the art and the life come together. The blues lyric fits, and he feels it. He does the whole trajectory, but in the end, the moment when, to the outside world, he's washed up is really a moment when he found it again.

Pereira: Which is the blues tradition. It can't be an external thing—it can't be a facade, a show.

Dove: Right. On the physical level he's going down into the cellar, to do this stuff, and it's scary, but to "go down" means to get deeper, get deeper into something. With Persephone and Demeter in *Mother Love*, I always thought that going down meant, If this hurts a lot and it doesn't feel good, then most people don't want to be there, but you've got to get there in order to be able to know what you are walking on when you're above ground, not to just assume that that's all of reality. In contrast, going up for me is often a place of great loneliness. You know, the only dark spot in the sky.

Pereira: The other poem is "Roast Possum" from *Thomas and Beulah*. When I taught the poem last semester, I talked about how Thomas is in an honored role as the storyteller who's giving the tale to the grandchildren and using the animal tale as a mechanism to talk about race and survival and racism. Two students in the class wanted the whole issue about Strolling Jim to be brought into the reading of the poem a lot more than I had been doing. At the end, where Malcolm interrupts, which is an important word, "interrupts," asking "Who owns Strolling Jim and who paid for the tombstone?" and then Thomas corrects him, firmly recenters him on the main topic, which is the possum—"We ate that possum real slow"—I had always read it as being that Malcolm had gotten distracted by the story that was supposed to be for embellishment. These students pointed out that Strolling Jim brings issues of enslavement and ownership into the poem, and that maybe Malcolm is not so wrong to be paying attention to Strolling Jim. So I'm wondering how you read this showdown, man-to-man, between Malcolm and Thomas. What's going on?

Dove: It's a complex showdown because it is a generational showdown, too. Neither one of them is necessarily right, but they are right for their time, which is why I chose the name Malcolm. What Thomas is doing is telling a story the way I'd heard it as a child: you are given all these elements, and you have to decide what is important in the story. All of the tangents are important, too. But it's really up to you, as the listener, to decide which one of the tangents you are going to be frustrated by, or if you are going to listen to them, and the tellers change the tale as the years go by. One tangent becomes more important or one not. Thomas brings in Strolling Jim, and he tells his story against that possum. It is about a horse who did unique stuff, and remember that horseback riding is an elite sport for the rich and for the white. Then the horse gets buried under the ground like a man, and, of course, "man" is a charged word for African Americans. So when Malcolm interrupts Thomas, it is very important to ask who owned the horse. It is about ownership, and it's also about who qualifies as a man. Is a horse a man? Is a Black man a man? It's a little bit of all that, too. Are you a boy chasing a possum? Thomas doesn't contradict him, necessarily; but he tells him, "Don't forget the possum, that's all. It's not like you shouldn't remember the horse. I'm not going to answer this question because if I answer this question, to tell you who owned him and paid for the tombstone, you're going to get wrapped up in the details of that, or you are going to get so angry about the fact that this horse got a grave as a man that you are going to forget how to catch the possum, and you've got to know that, too." Now Malcolm is ready to go and demand stuff, and the grandfather is saying, "Sometimes, if you just look really closely you can see that someone is playing the possum, and that's how you catch him." SO both of them are right. It's a moment that, hopefully, Malcolm will remember later on in his life. It's probably too early right now for him to like that answer.

Pereira: Because he wants to be a hothead.

Dove: Yes, he wants to put the count on a man, you know, like Strolling Jim did. And he wants to be outraged, and he should be outraged because what Thomas has in his head, too, is the fact that in the encyclopedia this is what they are saying about Black people, and even though he's an old man, at that point, he's seen the changes that are happening in the country with the civil rights movement starting up. SO things have obviously changed from the encyclopedia saying that Black children are intelligent until puberty, then they are lazy. But he's got to let Malcolm figure it out on his own. Malcolm has a different history: Thomas's history goes back; Malcolm's is going forward.

Pereira: Yes, looking at it from different directions.

Dove: And then meeting at this moment. It's so interesting, because so many of the stories that should have had morals in my childhood didn't. They never told us the moral. They just told us a story. You wanted to try to get to the moral, so you'd ask, "What happened to them?" They would say, "I don't know." I can't tell you how many times I asked this. There are a lot of things that could have happened to them, but you go through the story to figure out what paths they would have taken.

Pereira: You've been living in the South now for over a decade. How has being in the South affected you or your writing?

Dove: Well, Virginia, particularly Charlottesville, is very strange South. This is the land of contradictions and nexuses, I think, and that's one of the things that I love about this place. You have Thomas Jefferson with all of his contradictions. You've got the cradle of democracy and the Constitution, you've got the cradle of the Confederacy . . .

Pereira: Your assistant told me about Lee-Jackson-King Day, how Martin Luther King Day is used to also honor white Confederate heroes Robert E. Lee and Stonewall Jackson.

Dove: It's astonishing, but that's really who we are as Americans: we contain all these contradictions, and our concept of what this country is and our great myths about America are riddled with contradictions. So I like being at this kind of place. I can't tell you what it's doing to my writing yet. It generally takes me a good many years before I start writing about wherever I'm at. I think it will do something to my writing; I just don't know if it's there yet.

Pereira: The South is a point of origin for so much. Understanding the South helps me understand how everything else got to be the way it is.

Dove: That's right, because the really bizarre thing is that we are more racially divided now in this country than we've been in I don't know how long, all because we've never dealt with the Civil War. I really think it's because we haven't done our work. When I was a kid, the South was this land of terror. I had relatives in the South, and we went down to visit them when I was ten and again when I was fourteen. I was absolutely convinced that I was going to be lynched and terrible things were going to happen. What I didn't understand, but really impressed me, was that Blacks and whites interacted, though there was great caution on both sides. They knew each other better than Blacks and whites in the North.

Pereira: They lived in proximity.

Dove: I realized that we didn't live in proximity in the North, where I had assumed that we would be this great integrated dream. That was amazing. I'd say Charlottesville is an academic community, mostly. It's a very strange place. It's really almost Washington, and so it's an odd place to be, in that sense. I taught at Tuskegee for a semester, in 1982, and that was much more like being in the South. That was real South.

I think that one of the ways being here will influence my writing is the interest in exploring our myth of ourselves as Americans, because I do feel that all the time here. I feel we're constantly rubbing up against what we've always, in our hearts, thought America was and how we contribute to this or fight against it, and what things aren't resolved. Here Jefferson's everywhere, and the vehemence of the arguments about Jefferson here is just absurd. When I first came here and went to dinner at the president's house, someone stood up to toast Mr. Jefferson. I was about to make a joke, but I realized they were serious and that every official academic function begins with a toast to Mr. Jefferson. That's bizarre. And yet you've got a whole influx of young professors and students who are coming in from all over the place who are amused by all of this. Jefferson was a wonderful man, don't get me wrong; he had talents, but he was also a man. He was a complicated and fallible human being. What startles me constantly is how it becomes a matter of life and death for people to have the Jefferson they want. Again we're getting back to the public person or the idea of a myth, whether you believe it or not. That's why I like being close to all this. I don't know where it will go. I've often joked with my husband that some day I'm going to write a play called "Jefferson" that will get me banned from Charlottesville, and then I'll have to go someplace else.

Pereira: People are making a big deal out of the end of the millennium, as you know. We're using it to structure our systems of meaning about all kinds of things. But it's the close to the twentieth century in American poetry. How do you see your work as coming at the end of the century in American poetry? Are there lineages you feel it fits into?

Dove: First of all, let me say that I'm fascinated by the millennium because it's a boundary that's totally constructed. When I lived in Arizona, my husband and I would often have a ball at New Year's because we would celebrate the new year every hour. Though there is no such thing as a new millennium, the fact that we believe that there is a new millennium means that there is a new millennium, that people are working toward it. I haven't thought of it in terms of a new millennium artistically because I don't believe in those kinds of boundaries, but somewhere it's going to, of course, pull it together; I think in my own life of where I'm at because I'm forty-five. At forty-five you still feel like you have a foot in youth, but it's getting there. At fifty, you can't do it anymore, or maybe I don't know, I'm working toward that. So it is true that there is something that I feel is starting, not closing down. What I really find exciting is to be a bridge. I have had the fleeting thought, Gosh, I'm glad that I'm not seventy-five at the end of the millennium. I mean, I'm glad that I'm this age so that I can actually say, "Yes, I've got a role." I like to be going through it, and I'm excited to see how people are going to react.

Pereira: If one goes back to DuBois opening the twentieth century with "The problem of the twentieth century is the problem of the color line" and uses that as an arc to construct it on, I think some of your work is a very interesting segue into the twenty-first century, because you're not interested in the line. Maybe you make it more of a dot-dot-dot, or a blur.

Dove: A demilitarized zone. I make it permeable. And yet the problem is still the problem, the gray zone.

Pereira: I don't think that people generally know what to do with gray areas.

Dove: No, they don't. Unfortunately, DuBois's wonderful statement (and because it's so beautifully put) still pertains. It is not a line anymore, but it's something else. I think that he was also dealing with the concept that people had to make a boundary between them. The fact is that we still think in terms of boundaries between peoples and groups and sexes. It's so depressing sometimes.

Pereira: Have the twentieth-century boundaries broken down?

Dove: I don't think that the boundaries can be broken down until people go deeper into themselves and admit that there are no unique compartments in themselves. I think that as human beings we have had such incredible denial in terms of how much we're certain of. Why can't we admit uncertainty into our lives? I really feel that we don't admit it into our lives, and when someone does, it's something very daring, when it should just be the way life is. I think that admitting uncertainty into one's life also allows you not to be afraid of anything that feels mysterious, something that is unknown, which then translates into the Other. What is this Other? We have others inside of us.

Language Is Not Enough

Robert McDowell / 2000

The following interview was conducted by Robert McDowell, publisher of Story Line Press, in April 2000. Interview reprinted from *The Darker Face of the Earth*, revised edition, published in 2001 by Story Line Press (www.storylinepress.com). Reprinted here by permission of Story Line Press.

McDowell: What are the differences between writing poetry and writing for the stage?

Dove: In an interesting way, poetry and drama are not that far apart. They seem much closer to me than poetry and novels, for instance, or even short stories. It's because of all the things you cannot say both in poetry and in drama—the fact that you know language is not enough, that it will never be enough. You go in there knowing that; you're armed with language, and it's all you have. So when I was writing this play, I almost never felt that I was in a strange country where I didn't know the landmarks. It wasn't quite a familiar landscape, but it wasn't really frightening. I could find my way. In poetry, there's so much you can't say because part of the task is to let the silence reverberate, to let each word mean everything that it can mean. In drama, you can't know what's running around in someone's head unless you write a soliloquy or an aside. So language-wise, the concerns and limitations are often very similar. While writing drama, I learned how to write a monologue, how much of the pacing of the words and silence can be controlled at the script level. How many stage directions are enough, how much of the time and pacing I can orchestrate in a particular scene on the page, so that when I leave the play to a cast and director, it doesn't turn into something totally different.

The most challenging aspect of writing this drama for me, oddly enough, was the soliloquy. Poetry is all about interior thought; the theater tends to be about action. And yet the most critical dramatic passages are often those in which one character shares her thoughts with the audience. In my earliest versions of the play, no one had any monologues. It seemed unnatural to have a character simply talk to the audience. Even though poetry can be one long soliloquy, the tone of voice is often a whisper, a voice overheard rather than heard. That leap was a difficult one for me.

When writing plays, you have to keep asking yourself, How do I get this into the most streamlined form without being histrionic? How do I pull the theatergoers into this world I am creating? As a poet, I tend toward understatement and subtlety. As a playwright, I must find other modes of expression. When working on the play, I found it liberating to use utterance and movement in order to introduce subtlety into the play. There were things I could do that would not work in a poem because it would seem too—I don't want to say bombastic—but flamboyant. Like shouting.

The play came out of love of the theatrical space, where some human beings are illuminated on the stage, and others are in darkness, watching. You have an interplay of breaths; you have tension between moving bodies and those stilled bodies attending. I have always found the theater to be a magical space, and I have always longed to enter it in some way.

In the end, I discovered that poetry and drama have more in common than Aristotle, with his "classic dramatic unities," may have cared to admit. Alfred Hitchcock once said that drama was "life the with the dull bits cut out," and Gwendolyn Brooks defines poetry as "life distilled"—where's the big difference? For if a poet planes away unnecessary matter so that we can see clearly to the very core of the soul, a playwright commits the same sacred enterprise by training her spotlight on some select souls and then summoning the audience to listen, to bear witness in the dark.

McDowell: How did your musical training influence you?

Dove: I grew up with all kinds of music—blues and jazz and popular R & B. I have been actively involved in music since the age of ten, when I began playing the cello. Playing chamber music taught me the cadences of fugues and the power of harmony. I believe my poetry reflects an intense relationship to the music of the spoken word. Writing plays involves not only language, but the interplay of various languages—different characters' varying speech patterns and inflections, personalities—as well as the visible rhythms of bodies relating to each other. A domestic scene in a play is like a string quartet.

McDowell: What difficulties can you share with readers regarding your adaptation of a classic?

Dove: Using the ancient Greek dramatic form, with its infamously difficult-to-handle master chorus, proved less problematic than I anticipated. I'd grown up in the Black church, where call-and-response was part of the ritual. The Black community extends beyond immediate family and even the neighborhood; it's a community that holds itself responsible for each member's actions. Running commentary provided by the Greek chorus sounds "down home" to me.

McDowell: When did the inspiration for *The Darker Face of Earth* come to you?

Dove: My husband and I spent five months in Jerusalem in 1979. I had recently finished the manuscript for my first book of poems, *The Yellow House on the Corner*, which contained a selection of poems based on slave narrative, and I suppose that was on my mind one late afternoon that summer, as I stood looking out over the walled city of Jerusalem with its turrets and citadels. I had just reread Sophocles's *Oedipus Rex*; and perhaps it was the natural amphitheater of the Kidron Valley, where King David cried out at the loss of his rebellious son Absalom, perhaps it was the slanted sunbeams striking the pale stones of the Old City like a spotlight dressed with the palest of ping gels—but I found myself musing on kings and all-too-human heartbreaks, looking for similarities between the classical sense of destiny and our contemporary attitudes toward history and its heroes. What is it, I wondered, that makes Oedipus interesting as a hero when his course has been set at birth? Why do we watch, enthralled, if we already know his fate? I searched for modern analogy, a set of circumstances where the social structure was rigid and all-powerful as the Greek universe, one against which even the noblest of characters would be powerless. And as the sun began to set behind the Mount of Olives, a Jimmy Cliff song floated from my husband's study:

> *Oh de wicked carry us away,*
> *Captivity require of us a song;*
> *How can we sing King Alpha's song*
> *In a strange land?*

The lines are adapted from Psalm 137, the cries of the Israelites in bondage—but sung, in Cliff's version, by the slaves in the Americas.

And there I had my analogy. Rarely has history seen a system which fostered such a sense of futility as slavery. For the Africans taken forcibly from their homes and their roots—language, family, tribal memory—systematically decimated, the white power structure must have seemed as all-encompassing as the implacable will of Zeus. In a flash, I had the basic constructs: A child born of a white plantation mistress and her African lover is sold off but returns twenty years later, unaware of his origins. The open secret of miscegenation would be the key that turns the lock of Fate, instead of Tiresias, a conjure woman would prophesy the curse. Pride and rebellious spirit have little chance in the systemic violence of slavery, which brutalizes both slave and master. In a different world, Amalia might have been a woman of independent means and Augustus a poet; instead, both are doomed to be crushed when their emotions run counter to the ruling status quo. The slaves know this function as a Greek chorus, commenting and warning, all to no avail.

McDowell: This was in 1979—but the play wouldn't see the light of day until 1994. What happened?

Dove: I wrote the first draft of the play in less than a month, but it would take a dozen or so years before I arrived at a version that I felt was ready to be shown to the world. I dutifully sent a few copies of that first draft to New York agents, knowing that it was everything a play couldn't be to succeed in the commercial theater world: a historical drama, an adaptation of a classic with too many non-mainstream characters. When the copies came back (some accompanied by encouraging but no-thanks notes), I put them in a drawer and went on with my life of poetry. Every five years or so my husband would drag out the manuscript and ask, "What are you planning to do with this?" I'd look at it, try to take out a few characters, maybe shuffle them around a bit, and put it away again. The next time I'd rewrite it as prose, then put it back in the drawer. Finally in 1989, I took a long, hard look at the play, said, "What the hell," and put it back into verse. Who cared if it never got published? At least when I was dead and gone, the version scholars would find among my papers would be the one I wanted them to see.

Story Line Press published that version of *The Darker Face of Earth* in early 1994. I still held no hopes for a production, but I thought it would be nice for literature studies—and maybe it would even get some exposure in staged readings like the one the Washington, D.C. director Jennifer Nelson— who had read the play in script—was able to arrange at the Roundhouse Theater in Silver Springs, Maryland, shortly after publication. But as it turned out, a board member of the Oregon Shakespeare Festival had gotten a copy of the galleys in her hands and recommended it to the Festival dramaturg, and before I knew it, OSF offered to workshop it with a first-production option. They hired Jennifer Nelson to direct the workshop, and so I spent three weeks in Ashland, Oregon, that summer watching my scenes come to life—some more, some less—in a rehearsal room, discussing, rewriting, making notes for possible changes to mull over later. At about that time the dramaturg of Crossroads Theater in New Brunswick, New Jersey, came across the play in a bookstore, and Crossroads approached the Oregon Shakespeare Festival to offer a pooling of resources. The play was first produced in Oregon in the summer of 1996, directed by Crossroads artistic director Ricardo Khan. By that time I had rewritten it, mostly on the basis of my experiences during the OSF workshop but also in response to several stages readings—among them the wonderful one that Derek Walcott directed in November 1995 at the 92nd Street "Y" in New York City, where Walcott and his talented cast brought out the full potential of what I was trying to say. Crossroads then staged *The Darker Face of Earth* in the fall of 1997; they had submitted it to the Fund for New American Plays at the Kennedy Center and had been granted major financial support from the Fund, which in turn led to a month-long run in Washington, D.C., right after the New Brunswick shows.

McDowell: Please tell us more about the productions the play has had so far. Your favorite?

Dove: The play has seen four professional productions to date (as of spring 2000), all at major not-for-profit theaters, and several college productions, with at least two more professional and maybe half a dozen colleges stagings under contract. The world premiere, August to October 1996 at the Oregon Shakespeare Festival, remains my favorite. The 600-seat Angus Bowmer Theater in Ashland, Oregon, is a semi-thrust stage built so ingeniously that every seat affords an unobstructed view; as an audience member one feels quite intimately involved with the action on stage even while being treated to a vision of a stage "set." And the set design by Richard Hay (who, incidentally, is also the architect of the Bowmer Theater) was stupendous. It was the production I felt kept the balance when exploring dramatic "effects" while remaining faithful to the spirit of the text and even the integrity of the lines. The actors were superbly cast, the artistic staff dedicated and fearless, the technical people topnotch. Every performance was met with a standing ovation, sometimes foot-stomping cheers. Some people were weeping so hard at the end that they actually had to be helped out of their seats by the ushers. Nothing can equal that experience!

Crossroads Theatre put up the next production a year later in their space in New Brunswick, New Jersey, again directed by Ricardo Khan. Crossroads has a three-quarter thrust stage in a very small space—approximately 260 seats—which made for very intimate theater indeed. The play was very accessible in that space, and the audience was so actively engaging that some people actually blurted out advice to characters onstage! That same production—set, cast and all—was then transferred in less than three days to the Kennedy Center, where it played for a month on the huge proscenium stage of the 1200-seat Eisenhower Theater. Talk about rapid adjustment! And needless to say, this transfer to a vastly different space caused some problems of its own.

I was less than pleased with the production at the Royal National Theatre in London, England, in the summer of 1999. It was staged "in the round," with the audience looking down on the set from all four sides, which is not only obscured sight lines for chunks of the audience but actually worked against the narrative thrust. The director disregarded my input while I was present during the last three weeks of rehearsals; he even tried to manipulate my text! By opening night we were no longer on speaking terms; the actors were primed to stage a little insurrection of their own.

The most recent production (in March 2000) occurred at the Guthrie Theatre in Minneapolis. It offered a good cast and a talented director, but it could have been longer had the Guthrie allotted more rehearsal time—four weeks, instead of the six to eight the play had for its other professional productions. The short rehearsal period made it hard for the director to adjust problems of blocking, timing, etc., in such a complex drama. Also, in my view the set design was unfortunate, with the most intimate scenes—in the bedroom and the parlor—situated the furthest away from the audience . . . and that in a 1300-seat house! Overbearing choreography contributed to the alienation and slowed the action instead of accelerating it.

A pleasant surprise was a college production in Oberlin, Ohio, in the spring of 1999. Caroline Jackson Smith, a professor of theater there, proved to be a congenial director, utilizing a well thought-out set design to direct a powerful interpretation that, cast with professional actors, I believe could have done Broadway proud.

McDowell: Are you working on another play?

Dove: Right now I'm working on several projects—poems, a memoir, a novel. I've started two theater projects: one full-length play, the other an evening of one-acts with interrelated characters. We'll have to wait and see which project will win out.

Not the Shouted Slogan but the Whisper for Help
Earl G. Ingersoll / 2002

The following interview took place 30 March 2002 in Rita Dove's home in Charlottesville, Virginia. © Earl G. Ingersoll.

Ingersoll: I'd like to begin by asking you some questions about being an interviewee, having people like me come into your home and take up your time, asking you questions some of which perhaps you would prefer not to answer. What are your reactions to being interviewed?

Dove: Number one, I don't mind being interviewed, and I mean that exactly—I don't mind. But I consent because I like reading interviews. I find it interesting to hear other writers or artists or even celebrities talk about their life—at least, as much as they want to tell you. I also enjoy the little details—I think every human being does—the description of the house, what the subject is wearing—because what the interviewer is trying to do for the person reading the interview is to give an insight into the way that person lives their life. You want to get to know them. And I think that's legitimate—as much as one can get to know someone through an interview.

What I do mind is editing interviews afterwards. That takes up so much more time. I realize how important it is to eliminate the "ahs" and "ums" of colloquial speech, but I never counted on the interrupted sentences, and I'm *terrible* at that. I always interrupt myself, thinking I'll complete the sentence later down the line. I speak in dashes. Editing my own interviews can become extremely time consuming.

I haven't given an interview in a while, for that very reason: I was beginning to resent the amount of time it took out of my life. I felt like saying, Why are you asking me these questions? I'd rather write a poem! So I decided that rather than be a snarling interviewee I'd better not interview. Now I'm cool about it again because I haven't done it in a while.

Ingersoll: I recall that in one of the early interviews you said that you'd been very moved with Toni Morrison interviews you read when you were starting to write. It was important to you to hear what she had to say about her craft.

180

Dove: Yes, it *mattered.* I think for a young writer it matters more to hear that voice directly than to read, say, an essay by the same author on craft, an essay which has been carefully considered and thought out. Sometimes the inspiration one garners as a young writer can be found in the pauses, the offhand remark. For instance, Toni Morrison mentioned that she likes to write in the morning, that she sits on her couch and waits with her paper and pen for the sunlight to reach her page. That's not a lot of information, but it told me something about the attentiveness she had, that you might have to wait for the idea to come to you: you don't go running after it. It made sense to me. That kind of a remark can make all the difference in the world.

Ingersoll: Are there questions that you feel you get asked again and again and you would prefer to avoid? Are there questions you don't ever get asked and you wish somebody would?

Dove: Yes, there are questions I get asked over and over again. For instance, What are the duties of the Poet Laureate? I could just print out a little sheet and hand it to them. But it's a necessary question. Or: How does it feel to be a role model? That one's difficult because I have to build in disclaimers about what people consider role models to be and how I define a role model. I don't get frustrated with being asked; I get frustrated with the way my answer's usually edited. I mean, someone decides a certain part isn't important—especially in newspaper interviews. They say, "Oh, let's just get to the nitty-gritty," and often it's exactly that nuance in my explanation of what a role model *should* be that gets cut out. Newspapers don't want to hear it; but the fact is, I think one's role models should be everyday people, the people you see living life minute-by-minute, because that's how you live your life. You don't live your life in the limelight; you don't live your life in sound bites or a brief interview. But that's what's seen when you look at the role models kids have today. You see the rock stars singing their songs and you may watch them briefly in an interview, but you don't see them get up in the morning and figure out how they're going to get through the day because they only had four hours of sleep the night before and there are 500 items on the agenda. How do they find the strength for a day like that? *That*'s what a role model is really important for. So hopefully, one's role models are parents and friends and neighbors—people that you see with regularity.

Ingersoll: You've been asked questions a number of times, I notice, about "influence."

Dove: I hate that one. I think it's a silly question, frankly—I really do—

because the reasons for asking it are usually strange. Interviewers think they can chart the way you've led your life and the way you write. To be truthful, I think most people don't know *what* their influences are. More often than not, we're more strongly influenced by things that are not literary. And as far as literary influences go, it's a continuum thing, one's constantly being influenced and is usually unaware of the influence until it's served its purpose. If at any given point you ask me what my influences are, they're already a done deal.

Ingersoll: More than once you've been asked to interpret your own works—somebody taking you back to a poem which you may not have read in years and years, expecting it to be right on the tip of your memory.

Dove: I guess I'm more New Criticism on that than some people. If I let go of a poem, it has to live on its own. If it dies out there . . . well I'm sad, but I can't do a thing about it. I believe a poem has to stand on its own. There are passages in many poems that I know are private, but I also know—or hope—there's a level in these poems that's accessible to everyone. In other words, there are things that I don't expect people to "get" unless they're researching my life. Writers tend to do that: You leave things you know are hermetic, just because they matter to you. We leave clues. And just like people who do crossword puzzles or love sleuthing, if someone's really interested it's possible to figure it out.

Ingersoll: I'm interested in what you say about being in sympathy with New Criticism because it's my sense that a lot of "theory" has been going on in the last thirty years or so but writers themselves are still "New Critical" in the sense that for them the "text itself" matters, the "poem itself" has to stand on its own.

Dove: Yes, the poem itself matters, and it has to stand on its own. Most poets are particular about this, I think. "Language Poets" might have a different idea, though, and there are perhaps some metafictionists interested in the more theoretical play with surfaces. But for the most part, yes, writers are still moving along the old-fashioned way.

Ingersoll: What about academics approaching you with "agendas," i.e. wanting you to answer questions to fit in with their interpretations.

Dove: Yes, obviously I dislike that—not so much because they're trying to make me fit into their agendas—but because it takes so much time and energy to answer people like that. What happens is a curious thing: if, as the interviewee, you simply cut off the question, you become known as a "difficult writer," even though what you've done is perfectly reasonable, and the interviewer is the one who's being rude by presuming to impose upon you his idea of who you should be. So you find yourself being polite so they won't think you're a "difficult writer," which causes a lot of negative energy churning around in you. It also requires answering the questions extremely carefully, weighing every single word so that it cannot be twisted in any way. That's *exhausting*.

Ingersoll: What about questions you *don't* get asked, things you'd like to talk about.

Dove: That's a hard one. Maybe it's the chameleon in me; I will adjust myself to a situation. I usually enter an interview open-minded to whatever kind of session the interviewer wants it to be; if the interviewer doesn't venture into certain areas, I think, OK, fine. Unless it's something I think that needs to be explained. That usually happens when the interviewer's got an agenda—then I'll have to say, "Wait a minute, there's this aspect of my personality to consider, another facet to my life." I rarely get asked personal questions—not that I long to answer really personal questions . . . but I rarely get asked, for instance, if I have hobbies that might influence my writing. Frankly, I think the way one leads one's everyday life is crucial to how the writing fits in. For instance, I like to solve crossword puzzles, or—a maybe more significant example—my husband and I took up ballroom dancing a few years ago. That does matter. It makes sense I would go from classical music—playing the cello and viola da gamba and singing *lieder* and opera—to ballroom dancing. That makes sense somewhere along the aesthetic line. But no one asks.

Ingersoll: Is it our preconceptions of the writer—that the writer is the person in the room? Margaret Atwood has said she couldn't imagine anybody wanting to do a biography of her because all she did was sit in front of a piece of paper with a pen and write. Perhaps we aren't used to thinking of the writer as a whole person.

Dove: Yes, a whole person with a life besides writing. And I don't quite believe Peggy [Atwood], because the few times I've met her she's been lots of fun, cracking jokes and all. I don't think you can be a fun person if you're sitting at your desk all the time just writing. Still, there are preconceptions of what a writer is, and therefore that question is rarely raised. The writer's image is very strange. Sometimes when I meet people, I notice they're sur-

prised when they find out I'm a poet; I don't fit into their template for
"poets." I can see it in their reaction. There's even pressure among writers
to project a certain "look"—particularly women writers. We joke about it—
what you're supposed to be like as a woman writer: You're supposed to have
glasses and tie your hair back; you're supposed to wear long, flowing skirts.
Or jeans. But you're certainly not supposed to care about fashion; you're not
supposed to paint your nails; you shouldn't like "good" jewelry or care about
anything frivolous—Heaven forbid you should look at a magazine like *Glamour* or *Vogue*, because that's not feminist. Other women poets and I used to
discuss what we should wear to give a poetry reading: We couldn't wear
anything that really *looked good* because everyone would think, What kind
of poet is *that*?! Of course, the men have their little uniforms, too: It used to
be jeans with a vest, and now it's the jeans with the sport coat. It used to be
cowboy boots; now it's loafers. No one talks about those things, which actually do bear upon the image—even among intellectuals—of what an artist is
in our society and how he or she fits in, how she lives her life. We think
writers sit in front of their desks all day long and write, and come out of their
drafty garrets a little dazed, you know, and bumble around with technical
equipment. And we might be capable of having funny little esoteric discussions among ourselves, but we're duds in social situations—especially poets.
Fiction writers fare a bit better, imagewise. People tend to think fiction writers are either quietly debonair or blatantly obnoxious, talking incessantly
about their new novel, but at least they can make simple conversation. Poets
can't even do that; we live in a dream world! And sometimes, sometimes, we
believe that image. Stanley Fish's essay "The Incredible Ugliness of Volvos"
is right on target—the idea that academics buy Volvos because they have
such a poor opinion of themselves and believe that this is all the car they're
supposed to have.

Ingersoll: Now that I've got you on the personal, I'd like to ask you about
your use of family and how you feel about autobiographical or biographical
readings of your work.

Dove: If people need to read that way, let them go ahead and do an autobiographical reading. I must say that sometimes I don't know which details
have been taken from my life and which have been taken, say, from a sister's
or a friend's life. Fact can blur very quickly because if I'm going to imagine
a moment thoroughly and vividly enough to convey it to a reader, then even
if I haven't experienced it, that moment—deeply imagined—becomes my

experience. To the writer in me, the question—whether it's autobiographical or not—is moot. If, conversely, the passage is autobiographical, then I have to distance myself enough to be able to find the technical means by which to render that moment to someone else completely as an experience—it's the same problem with trying to tell somebody about a wonderful dream; you can't do it because you're still in the thrall of the dream. Actually, for me it is much harder to render the autobiographical into poetry or fiction than imagining it. Yes, there are definitely autobiographical elements in my poems, especially the ones based on my grandparents; obviously those are based on facts, but some of those facts came from my grandparents' lives, some came from my mother's life or my father's life; some came emotionally from my own experience—everything having to do with pregnancy and motherhood in the Beulah section, for instance. I mixed and matched things up and that's why, in my mother's copy of *Thomas and Beulah* I wrote the dedication, "To Mom, the only one who knows which stories are true." Sure enough, I didn't know anymore! But she could sort them out.

I've had people try to figure out the autobiographical elements, especially with my novel. No doubt, there are key autobiographical elements: I lived in Arizona; I play the cello; I studied the Bach suites just like Virginia, and the revelation Virginia has about musical phrasing in the Bach suites is my own revelation. That's all true. But I never did any mime, for heaven's sake! And though I spent time in Oberlin, and I've been in many Home Depots and Lowes, I never went shopping for lumber with a guy named Terry or anybody like him—I went with my husband. Virginia's love interest, Terry, is a composite of all the sly-but-deep-inside-sincere guys one meets in life. And although I did live in Arizona, it was not at the time that Virginia was there—hers was an Arizona of the '60s, while I was there in the '80s. In fact, for those scenes I interviewed Black artists who had lived in Arizona at that time. And yet some critics and scholars rave about the Arizona connection and how it's so "autobiographical"!

Ingersoll: You seem a very private person. Do you feel sometimes that people are poking around in your life or in your family's life in ways that you find offensive.

Dove: *Offensive* is too strong a word.

Ingersoll: One interviewer asked you about the presence of incest in your work.

Dove: The incest is completely imagined. In fact, I was surprised myself

to see that there were—I don't know how many—three or so instances of
incest in my work, and I thought, Oh, my God, what are they going to think!
I actually approached that from a literary point of view: I'd always been
fascinated by *Oedipus Rex*. Finally I wrote *The Darker Face of the
Earth*—my *Oedipus Rex* play— but it was the incest in Sophocles' drama
that inspired mine. Also, I was riveted by Toni Morrison's *The Bluest Eye*,
which I discovered at a critical point in my life. One thing that struck me as
I read *The Bluest Eye:* We're always hearing horrible stories of incest, yet I
couldn't help but believe that it could be benign sometimes, particularly in
the case of siblings who are close in age, so that when adolescence strikes,
the most compatible person to experiment with is your sister or brother. This
notion of consensual incest led me to write the Aunt Carrie passage in
Through the Ivory Gate. So no, I don't get insulted by such questions; they're
legitimate. But I do get frustrated at the assumption that my life is always
present in my work, and sometimes I'm frustrated by the fact that my life is
not my own, that there's this "Rita Dove" whose life is a playing field for
people. But it's just the way things happened to turn out—I mean, that my
life has become interesting to others—and though I am by nature a private
person, I can't stop that inquiry. On the other hand, I recognize in myself
that prurient interest in other people's affairs—say, celebrities' lives—so I
understand the impulse.

There's a scene in Toni Morrison's *Song of Solomon* in which the character
Pilate is described as having a face that can shut up like a mask; the observa-
tion is then made that certain Africans developed this trick as a way of making their faces absolutely impassive, simply sealing the other person out. The
mask may still be talking, but the real person is not exposed. I used to see
my father do that, and I grew up watching that. It was an amazing act; it
usually didn't happen with family but in social situations or with people who
annoyed him. He could even have a smile on his face; my father is a great
teaser, and when I was a kid he would invite door-to-door salesmen in just to
lead them by the nose. He was smiling; but he had the mask on and I would
think, Uh-oh, they're in trouble. And I have that talent, too, sometimes: I can
be smiling, but I've shut myself off; I've closed the drapes. It's my kind of
defense, I suppose.

When critics speculate about the life appearing in the work, and then they
come up with some cockamamie idea based on that assumption, I just laugh
and think: OK, whatever.

Ingersoll: In the revelation scene in *The Darker Face of the Earth* I was impressed that you didn't seem to be interested in this "Oh, horrors, horrors, we've committed incest," but in other issues, offering the scene a deep sense of humanity. It's elsewhere in your work, your continual interest in working outside the box.

Dove: When we come to a piece of literature, if we come to it honestly, we should leave off that social wrap. This is a moment when you can truly be yourself. Which means that certain reactions defined by social conventions just don't make a lot of sense. When the revelation comes in my play, Augustus and Amalia—even Phebe—would have to be very shallow people to have reacted just with horror at that moment. For not only was there no time for it to sink in, but also in such a moment, with everything stripped away from the mortal coil, only the most immediate concerns would prevail. And, yes, even though they recognize that this is an awful state of affairs they've gotten themselves into, the most pressing need for Amalia is to protect Augustus from being executed by the conspirators—to keep her beloved and her child out of harm's way—while his foremost thought is that his entire survival system is crumbling around him; rather than gasp, "Oh, I slept with my mother!" he's thinking: My mother is also my love and my master. What do I do with my love and my hate and my anger now? And his belief system crashes.

Ingersoll: I noticed in *On the Bus with Rosa Parks* a number of poems in which it would have been safer to go with the conventional. Some of your characterizations of African Americans are not as positive as they might be. I'm impressed with the sense of integrity in your work: you do what you think you have to do.

Dove: I couldn't live with myself otherwise—that's number one. Number two, I haven't experienced life as a parade of perfect people. It would have been pretty boring, actually, if I had. And number three, no one is really interested in perfect people. I don't know what a perfect person would look like, anyway.

The Germans have a word for it: *Nestbeschmutzung*, to dirty the nest. It was originally directed toward those who spoke badly of or betrayed Nazi sympathizers. The accusation was that you're dirtying your own nest, airing dirty laundry, bring the skeletons out of the family closet—the German accusation is so powerful because you are actually befouling the very place you were born and must live, eat and sleep in. But basically the censure is the same: If you present a character in all of the complexity and ambivalence that each human being possesses, but this particular human being happens to be black, or gay, or a woman, or poor—then you're betraying the entire race, subculture, gender, class. I think we've gotten away from that fear a little bit. But it's a tendency that emerges almost necessarily in any group that is just beginning to establish its identity in the eyes of the mainstream. To make a grab for some kind of validation, it's important to prove that one is worthy of that approval. Knowing that any failing of an individual in that group might be used against the entire group makes it tempting to advocate presenting a united front. That's what happened in the '60s, when most every poem or story was about positive Blackness. It was very difficult to publish anything that wasn't about Good Blacks. Now we've advanced to where we can actually present fully realized human beings who are Black.

Ingersoll: I sense it was a rite of passage when you had difficulties with the Black Arts Movement, and, was it Alice Walker? who objected to your use of the n-word and you said essentially, "I'm my own person."

Dove: That was a very strange case. And no one has ever asked me about it! First of all, I think I was lucky to have been born too late to have come of age artistically during the Black Arts Movement. I was around thirteen in 1965, a little too young. By the time I began to write seriously and began to consider publishing, I was in graduate school in the mid-'70s, and I thought I had escaped the restrictions. This is why Toni Morrison was so important to me at the time: Here was a woman unafraid of presenting Black characters who did not fit into a stereotypical notion of what a Black person was or should be. Her characters lived in the Midwest, instead of in Harlem or in the South. And instead of everything being just hunky-dory, she wrote about incest! So when I wrote a poem called "Nigger-Song. An Odyssey," I didn't think anything of it. It was a way of reclaiming the word, because I grew up with people using it in a positive way—strictly among ourselves, of course, but it was such a part of the ethnic background and had been there for so long that it was time to recognize it. There were also those crazy movies in the '70s like "Superfly" and "Shaft," where the word was bandied about quite a bit. I was very surprised when Alice Walker refused to appear at a reading celebrating the anthology in which the poem appeared, citing racism. I've never met her—she's very reclusive—so I've never had the chance to talk with her about it. Obviously I disagreed with her reaction, and I wasn't going to be cowed. She knew good and well that there were circumstances where this word would be liberally sprinkled about, usually situations when the parties involved knew each other so well that all the ironic implications of saying "nigger" would be understood—like good friends driving home after a party. I guess Alice Walker just didn't want me to air the dirty laundry—laundry I didn't think was particularly "dirty." I thought, OK, this is it; I'm going to have to fight this one.

Ingersoll: I'd like to draw together a number of comments you've made in your interviews. You talk about your attraction to crossword puzzles because of that stage toward the end when the solution is in sight, and you've likened that to the late stages of writing some of your poems, a feeling that the poem begins to coalesce. You speak also of German syntax postponing the meaning of a sentence by positioning the verb at the end. And frequently you use the term "epiphany" in talking about your poems as well as your fiction. I'm seeing a pattern of concern with closure, "climax," if you will, and epiphany—that moment of coming together in intensity and awareness. I'm thinking of your father in the poem "Flash Cards" and that focus on an "answer." Some feminist theorists would gender these concerns as "masculine" in a context of gender separated from biological difference. I've spoken with a mutual friend about her "masculine" characteristics and my own "feminine" ones. I apologize for this long question with its intimations of a critical "agenda."

Dove: Well, it's a "feminine" question.

Ingersoll: You got me!

Dove: OK, where do we start? I suppose my first response is to ask you a question: If the epiphany is a "masculine" way of proceeding, what is a "feminine" way?

Ingersoll: A multiplicity of revelations or endings. Not simply an open ending, but a lack of concern with ending-ness, if you will. Or an undermining of ending.

Dove: It's a fascinating question. What these theorists might be writing against is the clicking shut of the box, the satisfaction which comes from hearing that click. You use the word "climax" as a synonym for "epiphany," but for me they're actually opposites. In sexual climax the senses are overloaded and you blank out, whereas in an epiphany the window opens, you say, "Ah," and you can see clearly. Although the sensation of pleasure may be analogous, what they do in terms of apprehension is different. For me an epiphany is always a door opening, not shutting. Others may disagree: some writers work towards tying up all the ends so that what you get is the satisfaction of seeing everything fit together, like a crossword puzzle.

I love crossword puzzles, but what's interesting to me is the moment before I fill in the last grid. Actually I'm not much interested at all in the last few boxes; it's trying to figure out what exactly *is* the thread of the puzzle, what's its trick, that enthralls me. I'll find one word, then the next, which opens up the possibility that this other five-letter word block that I hadn't been able to fill in could be this word or that word, but I'm not sure until I solve the intersecting word. . . ah, I *love* that opening up before the puzzle clicks into place.

Two things are at work in a poem which has that thrilling syntactical shutting of the box—the click, which is a very German syntax—and the "Ah!" that follows, opening into revelation. For a poem to be successful for me, I want the reader to feel things fitting together but not know quite how. There's the Ah, and still the syntactic click underneath. I've compared the poems in *Thomas and Beulah* to "beads in a necklace," or a series of epiphanies. In that book there were many clicks: The poem snapped shut at the end and the revelation left you satisfied, but there was still a sense that the story wasn't over yet. After that book, however, I knew I could not do another series because I was dissatisfied with that shutting down each time. I was much more interested in exploring what each poem does as it ends, how to keep the possibilities opening even after that particular moment has gone by. It's what makes every lyric poem an elegy, too—the moment has been captured, the moment's gone. This may have to do with growing older, because now I am much more interested in probing the moment, in extending the epiphany.

Ingersoll: I'd like you to talk about your relationship with your father. You say, "I *am* my father's daughter." He seems to have had a tremendous effect upon your life in a number of ways.

Dove: My father is a very orderly man; in fact, whenever he reads a book he writes a brief synopsis on the inside cover. I was *astonished* the first time I noticed it. I was home from college one summer and opened up one of his books and there was this little book review in there! My father is also an *intensely* private person. When we were kids we spent most of our childhood watching him closely, reading his moods: How's he today? And as I've said elsewhere, I didn't know about his experiences with discrimination in the army until I was much older—out of graduate school, in fact. In a certain way my father's secretiveness and silence was a cautionary tale; being so private in order to protect himself from the sting of injustice, and to protect his children from the same kind of hurt, has resulted in his not being able to open up to others. In many ways he's had a wildly successful life, but the heartbreak is there, and he's locked his emotions inside. Oh, he can relax in family situations; he can laugh, and he's a big joker. And he can open up in social situations where it's not required that anybody know who he is. I can do that, too: Set me in front of a thousand people and I can put on my mask, and go on. But he's almost awkward when trying to have a personal conversation with his kids. It's the result of having to "suck it in" just once too often. So, yes, he's had a great influence on me, both positive and negative— positive in terms of education and also just learning how his mind works. He has a fascinating mind. It's not *my* mind, though there are similar quirks— such as looking up a word and spending hours browsing, getting blissfully lost in the dictionary. Or working hard so that I know that I've done my best—so even if I don't come in first, I know I've done my best. He taught us to be comfortable with our best, too. I'm sure that's been a tremendous help in my life. It's helped me to be more serene, though I don't think of my father as a serene person. What I've learned is not to keep my anger and resentment bottled up to such an extent that it's damaging; if something bothers me, it's not so bad to admit it to somebody. It's a lesson I'm still learning.

Ingersoll: In one poem, "Against Self-Pity," I thought of your Dad's influence, that sense of self-discipline, of not giving in to self-pity.

Dove: Oh yes, definitely. It's something familial, but also racial—*ethnic*, excuse me, not racial. There's this current that runs through the generations: don't show them what you're thinking, don't expose a weak spot. Be 150% better than them and don't get angry if they think you're only doing 85% when you know you're doing 150, because *you* know how well you're doing. Don't stoop to their level.

Ingersoll: One of the things I'm noticing, too, in these poems in *Rosa Parks* is—I don't know how to say this politely—

Dove: Then just say it!

Ingersoll: that they're poems of middle age.

Dove: Yes.

Ingersoll: Like "Götterdämmerung." I love the last lines: "but I've never / stopped wanting to cross the equator, or touch an elk's / horns, or sing *Tosca* or screw / James Dean in a field of wheat. / To hell with wisdom. They're all

wrong: / I'll never be through with my life." It's an earthy exuberance remi-
niscent of the later Yeats. There's just so much life left to live. Let's go for
it.

Dove: That's how I want to be. Yeah, they're poems of middle age—some
of them. I didn't even think of it until a reviewer brought up middle age, and
I thought, Oh, really? That's what they're about? I was thinking more along
the lines of wisdom! Just this week I got a call from *Modern Maturity*. They
wanted to print my picture. *Modern Maturity*—great! Fred was afraid to tell
me they had called. And I said, Well, I am *mature*; maybe not the way they
think of it, but I am mature.

Ingersoll: One last question. I noticed in one of your interviews you men-
tioned D. H. Lawrence's phrase "the courage of [our] own tenderness" from
Lady Chatterley's Lover. That's surprising because so many people consider
Lawrence so out of fashion and politically incorrect.

Dove: Yes, yes, yes.

Ingersoll: And I know you have a high regard for Derek Walcott's work.
Am I correct in remembering that some people said he didn't deserve the
Nobel Prize for Literature because of his relationships with women?

Dove: I don't know the facts. But he's an astonishing writer. You know,
we still want our writers—if they move us deeply—to be as wise and kind
and sweet in real life as they are in their work. I've met some perfectly
horrible people whose work I admire. I don't include Derek in that category;
he's a marvelous human being, with a kind, witty, deeply generous soul. His
getting the Nobel Prize should have nothing to do with his private life. In that
sense, I'll defend Ezra Pound—although I don't like Pound's poetry. But one
should always—New Criticism again—go to the work. And Pound swerves
in the *Cantos*; he lets his prejudices enter the writing and skew the work—so
that the results are disappointing, shrill. I've heard demagogues that were
absolutely mesmerizing; that doesn't mean I have to follow them, or even
applaud. I may acknowledge that the speech they gave was brilliant, and it's
probably wise to acknowledge that brilliance in order to be able to work
toward countering it. Pooh-poohing demagoguery doesn't make it go away;
it just becomes more dangerous. I believe it's crucial to separate the artistic
excellence of the work from both its content and the author's character.

There were lots of questionable aspects about Lawrence which even creep
into his work. But he was also a product of his times, and you've got to factor
that in. (I feel this way about Thomas Jefferson, too.) *Lady Chatterley's Lover*

is an illuminating book. Sure, it spouts preconceived notions of what a woman is, but it also offers some pretty bold notions of what a woman can be. Which no one else was doing at that time; imagine—a woman who actually takes her life into her own hands! I think his phrase "the courage of our own tenderness" is a very important one, for it takes more courage to be tender, to expose oneself to the possibility of hurt or damage, than it does to gird one's loins and go into battle. It takes more courage to let down your shield than to put it up. And that's something that *everyone* has got to remember—men and women, feminists and male chauvinists. What moves us most, I am convinced, is not the shouted slogan but the whisper for help. I mean, we yearn for heart-to-heart talks. We may deny such desires afterwards, but oh, how we hunger! I guess I get rather impatient with political correctness of all kinds, because it can deaden you. It shuts off avenues. I understand the desire to make sure that all people are good and kind and respectful towards others, but trying to legislate sensitivity is dangerous, because it puts blinders on the way you look at the world.

Index

Ai, 116, 117
Alexander, Elizabeth, 85
Amichai, Yehuda, 107
Angus Bowmer Theater, 178
Aristotle, 175
Arizona State University, 30, 86
Atwood, Margaret, 183

Bach, Johann Sebastian, 185
Bachelard, Gaston, 43; *Poetics of Space*, 43
Bakunin, Michael, 26
Baldwin, James, 64, 125; *The Evidence of Things Not Seen*, 78
Banneker, Benjamin, 7, 53
Basquiat, Jean-Michel, 163
Beats, 36
Bennett, William, 75, 79
Bishop, Elizabeth, 125
Black Power Movement, 78–79, 158, 159, 188
Bloom, Harold, 125, 133; *The Anxiety of Influence*, 125
Blue Angel, The (*Der Blaue Engel*), 25
Boccaccio, Giovanni, 6, 7
Bread and Puppet Theater, 89, 90
Brecht, Bertolt, 24
Breytenbach, Breyten, 156–57; *Confessions of an Albino Terrorist*, 157
Brooks, Gwendolyn, 62, 64, 175
Bukowski, Charles, 35
Bush, George H. W., 75

Callaloo, 22, 143, 162
Carnegie-Mellon University Press, 29
Catherine of Alexandria (Saint), 7, 143–44
Catherine of Siena (Saint), 7, 143–44
Chopin, Frédéric, 26
Ciardi, John, 40, 122
Civil War, 170
Cliff, Jimmy, 176
Confederacy, 170
Constitution, 170
Costanzo, Gerald, 29
Crossroads Theater, 178
Cullen, Countee, 80; "What Africa Is to Me," 80

Dante, Alighieri, 122; *Inferno*, 122
Delius, Friedrich Christian, 25
Demeter, 128, 168
Derricote, Toi, 85
Dickinson, Emily, 125
Doolittle, Hilda (H. D.), 165
Dove, Aviva, 28, 31, 41, 48, 81, 118, 129, 131–32, 142
Dove, Elvira Hord (mother), 33, 34, 93–94, 108, 139, 144, 151, 185
Dove, Ray, 8–9, 15, 23, 33, 34, 53, 74–75, 107, 108–09, 111, 121, 136, 144, 151, 190–91
Dove, Rita: on the academy, 34; on Africa, 80; on the American Southwest, 29–30; on anger, 20, 70–71, 116; on archaeology, 9; on artifacts, 6, 7, 9; on artistic integrity, 81–83, 160; on the arts, 112–13; on attending church, 13, 175; on audience, 12, 21–22, 49–50, 58–59, 93, 119–20; on the autobiographical, 19, 33, 82, 105, 136, 150, 161, 184–85, 186; on ballroom dancing, 183; on being African American, 6, 20–21, 22, 97, 98–99, 105–06, 151, 159, 160–61, 162–63, 169–71, 186, 188, 190–91; on being interviewed, 180–81, 182–83, 185; on being Poet Laureate, 124, 136, 153, 181; on being a role model, 181; on the body, 117, 118; on book publishing, 36; on children, 5, 112, 164–65; on choosing to become a poet, 9, 34, 109; on the coalescing of poems, 10, 47–48, 61, 72–73, 76, 92, 93, 99; on composing, 40–41, 54–55; on crossword puzzles, 92, 182, 183, 190; on cruelty, 5, 8, 53; on deadlines, 49; on the environment for writing, 31, 40–41, 47–48, 59, 76, 92; on epiphany, 10, 61, 106, 113, 123, 130, 189–90; on evil, 5, 45; on "failed poems," 45; on feminism, 81, 82; on film, 25–26; on form in poetry, 4–5, 32–33, 46, 50, 56–58; on gender in composing, 55, 58; on gendered writing, 118; on the German language, 15, 18, 48, 60, 61, 76–77, 96, 130, 190; on German poetry, 26–27; on "getting stuck" in composing, 47, 55; on history, 3, 4, 6, 7, 10, 26, 65, 67, 68, 81, 96, 103–04, 126–27, 143, 151, 152–53; on the incest motif, 163–64, 185–86, 187; on influences, 24–25, 84–85, 125, 156, 158,

195